Canonic Texts in
Media Research

CANONIC TEXTS IN MEDIA RESEARCH

Are There Any?
Should There Be?
How About These?

Edited by
ELIHU KATZ
JOHN DURHAM PETERS
TAMAR LIEBES
AVRIL ORLOFF

polity

First published in 2003 by Polity Press in association with
Blackwell Publishing Ltd

Editorial office:
Polity Press
65 Bridge Street
Cambridge CB2 1UR, UK

Marketing and production:
Blackwell Publishing Ltd
108 Cowley Road
Oxford OX4 1JF, UK

Distributed in the USA by
Blackwell Publishers Inc.
350 Main Street
Malden, MA 02148, USA

A catalogue record for this book is available from the British Library.

Library of Congress Cataloging-in-Publication Data
Canonic texts in media research : are there any? should there be?
  how about these? / edited by Elihu Katz . . . [et al.].
    p. cm.
  Includes bibliographical references and index.
  ISBN 0-7456-2933-4 (hard :alk. paper) — ISBN 0-7456-2934-2 (pbk. :
alk. paper)
  1. Mass media—Research—Methodology. 2. Mass media—Philosophy.
I. Katz, Elihu, 1926–
P91.3 .C36 2002
302.23′07′2—dc21   2002006727

Typeset in 10 on 12 pt Sabon
by Graphicraft Limited, Hong Kong
Printed in Great Britain by
TJ International Ltd, Padstow, Cornwall

Contents

Contents

Contributors

Menahem Blondheim is Senior Lecturer, Departments of Communication and American Studies, at The Hebrew University of Jerusalem.

Daniel Dayan is Professor of Media Sociology at the Centre national de la recherche scientifique and Institut d'études politiques de Paris.

Michael Gurevitch is Professor at the College of Journalism, University of Maryland, College Park, MD.

Don Handelman is Shaine Professor of Anthropology, Department of Sociology and Anthropology, at The Hebrew University of Jerusalem.

Eva Illouz is Senior Lecturer, Department of Sociology and Anthropology, at The Hebrew University of Jerusalem.

Elihu Katz is Professor at the Annenberg School for Communication, University of Pennsylvania, and Professor Emeritus, Departments of Sociology and Communication, at The Hebrew University of Jerusalem.

Tamar Liebes is Professor, Department of Communication, at The Hebrew University of Jerusalem.

Yosefa Loshitzky is Associate Professor, Department of Communication, at The Hebrew University of Jerusalem.

Joshua Meyrowitz is Professor, Department of Communication, at the University of New Hampshire.

Avril Orloff obtained her MA at the Annenberg School for Communication, University of Pennsylvania, and is a writer/researcher in Toronto.

John Durham Peters is Professor, Communication Studies, at the University of Iowa.

Eric W. Rothenbuhler is Director of Graduate Media Studies at The New School, New York.

Paddy Scannell is Professor and Head of Research, School of Communication and Creative Industries, at the University of Westminster, Harrow Campus.

Peter Simonson is Assistant Professor, Department of Communication, at the University of Pittsburgh.

Gabriel Weimann is Professor and Chair, Department of Communication, at the University of Haifa.

Introduction:
Shoulders to Stand On

Even without the double "n," canons are explosive. Try announcing that you're editing a book called "Canonic Texts," and you'll find yourself at war. That has been our experience since concocting this idea at a conference in Jerusalem and, later, at an International Communication Association session in Acapulco. In Acapulco, an irate colleague shouted, "You can't do that!" Our friends said, "If you have to do it, change the name. Call the texts 'foundational,' or 'generative,' or 'classical,' but don't call them canonic." "Why not?" we asked, and the firing resumed.

"Because canonic connotes authoritative," somebody said, "and that means choosing some and marginalizing others." "And who gets to do the choosing?" asked another. "Old-timers and elitists, as usual," came the answer. "Required readings stultify creativity," we were told. "Give us inventions, not monuments." "We're a field, not a discipline, and it's better to wander, even to get lost, than to follow a hewn path," said someone. And another said, "We're not even a field. Media studies is barely fifty years old; it's too soon to look for ancestors. Moreover," he added, "our job is to cope with the changing reality of the present, not to dig up some irrelevant past." In short, these objections centered on the dangers of constraint and the need for freedom – from authority, from discipline, from method, from tradition.

We aren't about to surrender – or even to retreat from the idea of canon. That doesn't mean we have no sympathy with some of the arguments. But on the big point we are adamant. We wish to contribute to the community of scholars who are interested in the interdisciplinary field – yes, the field – of communications research. It is simply romantic to deny that such a field exists, even if it is still struggling to define itself. We leave it to cultural studies to resist becoming a field. As far as media studies is concerned, the evidence from a dozen or more journals suggests that disciplinary processes are at work – not in any monolithic sense, but in a useful dialogue among theories, methods, and "boundaries." A field is a process of constant sifting (McPhee, 1963) of what deserves to be dropped and what deserves to be continued. The test of time, however, is based not on reverence – though honor may attach itself to long-lasting texts – but on continued relevance. Nor is it based on dogmatic or over-powering assertiveness; it is just as likely to be based on spokesmanship for different sides of lively controversies. Ironically, therefore, canonic texts may cross the generation gap as sparring partners – like Karl Marx and Max Weber, for example – so long as their argument seems relevant. This comes close to what we are trying to do in this book.

When we speak of canons – texts, works, artifacts that are set aside as relatively durable objects by members of a community of inquiry – we are talking about appropriations and staking claims, not about unthinking inheritance. Two related metaphors have been applied to this process. One is "standing on the shoulders of giants"; the other is "giving birth to one's parents."

Robert K. Merton (1985) has written a whimsical guide to the origin and history of the "shoulders" metaphor. He wants us to understand that science does not monumentalize its giants or memorize their writings; rather, it climbs upon their shoulders in order to see further than they did. But the giants are not givens; they do not appear ready-made. We choose them, and that's where the second metaphor comes in. It is in the workaday world of reading and writing and researching – inspired by predecessors and contemporaries – that we look over our own shoulders, sensing the presence of an ancestor, dimly discerned at first, who is cheering us on in the direction that we ourselves (so we think) have chosen. That is how we give birth to those whom we recognize as intellectual parents. And, often, we find it worthwhile to get to know these parents better.[1]

Both metaphors are about interactions between us and our predecessors. For the process to work, the storing of prior knowledge is required. Education is what it's sometimes called – and it may be summoned at some later time. Sometimes it is for the sake of continuity, as in Kuhn's (1970) normal science; sometimes, as a target to rebel against. Science works both within and against tradition, which has an element of election and affinity to it. In history, all of the features of the past are more or less equally interesting. In tradition, however, some features assume enormous salience, while others recede into nothingness. So when Stuart Hall, for example, discovers an account of media power in Gramsci, that's tradition – a willed ancestry.

Canons are produced and reproduced. One of the most interesting things about them is their retroactive effects. They reorganize the past. They discover (or invent) origins. Once a canon has been made – in the sense of a group of texts or works of art or saints – it enables certain routes and passageways to time past and, yes, bars others. The canon is always a genealogical errand, a turning of the hearts of the fathers to the children and of the children to the fathers (to use the biblical phrase), in the name of a charter, a legacy, a lost deed to vast properties.

The two views of canon presented so far imply active participation on our part: whether we stand on someone's shoulders or look over our own, it is we who are perceiving the giant. This freedom to canonize is at odds with two other views of canon. One is the hegemonic view that sees canonization as manipulation; the other is the classic view that has no trouble telling a Real Giant from a PR-inflated balloon.

It is clear from Foucault-inspired work on disciplinary formations, as well as older work in the sociology of knowledge and more general wranglings about who's included and who's excluded in the process of canon formation, that canons are institutional constructions of the first importance. Some studies of literary canons, for instance, quickly disillusion the notion that the inherent merit of a work accounts for its place in the canon any more than it determines people's place in society. Canons can be seen as fashion systems, as means for the reproduction of elite taste, or as microcosms of social hierarchy. In this view, canonized texts are regarded as something like an elected assembly of interest groups (the parliament of immortals), so that a literary canon consisting of all men, or all Europeans, or all whites, mirrors the distribution of extant social power. The story of the status of Homer, for instance, is a record of white male elite taste (Herrnstein-Smith, 1988, ch. 3).

Objects also end up in canons for a variety of institutional reasons that, again, have little to do with their intrinsic sanctity or excellence. Alice Walker's *The Color Purple* was canonized in the 1980s because it fit a crucial niche in undergraduate English courses: a novel by an African-American woman chronicling the sexual abuses of slavery. Similarly, Albert Camus's *L'Étranger* (*The Stranger*) was central to the postwar canon simply because it was short and readable, with contemporary relevance for advanced undergraduates studying French. Much sociological work aims to demystify the idea that something nominated for inclusion in a canon must be without blemish.

The beatific sense of canon is indeed something to suspect, as our critics claim. Still, there is another position worth considering. For literary critic Harold Bloom, canons are made not by class conspiracies, but by thinkers and artists who choose their ancestors. Here canons are less institutional operations than artistic resources for inspiration. For Bloom, it is the sheer imaginative audacity or superiority of a work – such as Plato's, or Shakespeare's, or Beethoven's, or the Beatles' – that exercises a claim on subsequent artists, not sociological networks of access, affiliation, and distribution. Bloom's critics see him as an arch-individualist blinded by elitist (and worse) visions of grandeur. Bloom, in turn, sees multiculturalists as a "pride of displaced social workers" who can no longer recognize excellence in literature.

Leaving the details of this debate to one side, it is clear that canons can be artifacts of social power as well as archives of artistic invention. This is an old point from the sociology of culture: cultural objects do not cease being cultural by being studied sociologically! One can study the production of films, newspapers, or popular music in the same way as the production of cars, textiles, and frozen peas without ignoring the important symbolic status of the former. You can explain canon formation sociologically, but such explanation does not exhaust the ways in which works in (and out of) canons can inspire or disgust readers. Some things that are canonized behave both institutionally *and* imaginatively. The choice of objects of emulation is certainly not sociologically neutral, but neither should it be reduced to demographic categories of affiliation or taste.

A canon is a device of intellectual organization. Hence, it is an error to reduce canons to institutional machinations that operate without reference to intellectual quality and interest. The canon is most manifest in course syllabi, which have a duty to select and cull rather than offer everything. Canons serve as efficiency mechanisms to protect students or scholars from wandering in the wilderness of the literature. They are nodal points for emulation, ways to cut through overwhelming amounts of material. In an age when relevant scholarship, like cultural production more generally, outstrips any mortal's capacity to follow it in its depth and breadth, the need for portals (to borrow the Internet term) to literatures is more crucial than ever. For pedagogical purposes, some principle of selection and organization among the vast amounts of print is indispensable. No such principle will ever be sociologically neutral, but no scholarly or artistic institution will be able to operate practically without one either. Canons are editing devices, search engines in a world in which intelligent editing is one of the most crucial needs and scarcest resources.

Canons entail labors of preservation and appreciation. They are conservative institutions, of course, since their aim is precisely to conserve heritages and establish lineages. But as such, they also provide the conditions of novelty. Originality, after all, is never a leap in the dark;

it is intelligible only as a move within (including away from) a tradition. Every great work of art, said Walter Benjamin, either founds or destroys a genre. He could have said the same of science.

Canons offer shortcuts. They establish standards and starting points which, if unknown, doom work to being not out of date, but simply out of kilter. Work in the humanities and social sciences is inevitably in dialogue with previous work (and though the hermeneutic element in natural science is often suppressed or irrelevant, it is still often surprisingly important). Canons are dynamic categories with porous edges. Authors or texts may come and go – today Ruskin is back after a long hibernation, Marx's stock has dropped, etc. – and new works may completely realign the order among old works.

Canons also run the risk of stultification, a danger found in all official culture. Yet we need them precisely to inspire the sense of naughtiness and defiance so important to much new work, since there is no originality without tradition. Canons may be necessary devices to produce the sense of rebellion and defiance at the heart of so much scholarly activity. Marx is perhaps best read by flashlight underneath the sheets with a sense of naughty excitement – the way scores of intellectuals have read and found nourishment in him (and myriads more who, finding him official doctrine, discovered boredom *and* discipline).

Scholarship, like most forms of creative work, involves long-distance correspondence with imaginary pen pals. Canons help us select our correspondents. The trouble with choosing your ancestors is that once you have adopted them (or they you), divorce or disinheritance is messy and expensive; plus you have to put up with the cousins and other pretenders who are closer in the line of succession. Lineage and affiliation are strategic questions in academic politics. Too ancient an origin can be bad for claims of disciplinary uniqueness; too recent, too thin for intellectual richness.

Even our harshest critics – those who decry this enterprise – hide canonic texts among their secrets. They may not like it, but chances are that they, like us, are haunted by certain essays and studies that accompany them into the classroom and into the field. These texts inspire, they argue, they may even annoy – but they don't go away. They reappear on our reading lists year after year, and figure prominently in our bibliographies – not out of inertia, but because they truly belong. Typically, though, we keep them to ourselves. That's the trouble. We each have our favorite texts, but they're somehow private, as though we're embarrassed that they're still around. So when it comes to the question, at the departmental meeting, of whether to compile a list of core readings for the exam that qualifies aspiring Ph.D.s, the majority votes no. Together, well yes, we are the field; but we each do different things, and there's no use jumbling it all together. In fact, each of us should be doing his or her own thing – with no special awareness of each other's private canons – and, with luck, the students will put it all together.

Maybe so, but this book is our offer of help. It proposes a selection of thirteen texts – papers, not books – as nominees for canonization, or, put less controversially, as foundational for media studies. The original essays collected here are critical appreciations of thirteen worthy texts; in fact, some of the essays are so critical that they raise second thoughts about whether their subjects – the original texts – will make it all the way to canonization. With only two exceptions, the papers selected were published some 40 to 60 years ago.

Since the book is intended for use by advanced students in communication, media studies, and – yes! – cultural studies, as well as by their mentors, we have not included the nominated texts themselves. Many will be familiar. They are all readily accessible in libraries. Not all of them are "famous" just now, however. Some, like Lazarsfeld's and Merton's "Mass Communication, Popular Taste and Organized Social Action" and Horkheimer and Adorno's "The Culture Industry," have never dropped out of sight; nobody can doubt their qualifications as both "revolutionary and relevant," to quote Blondheim's criteria. Others, like Marshall McLuhan's *Understanding Media*, have dropped in and out. Some were once very prominent, such as Lowenthal's "Biographies in Popular Magazines," Kurt and Gladys Lang's "Unique Perspective of Television," Horton's and Wohl's "Mass Communication and Para-Social Interaction," and Herta Herzog's paper on radio soaps. Still others, like Louis Wirth's "Consensus and Mass Communication," are long forgotten but worthy of resurrection.

The texts are associated with five "schools" of communications research: Chicago, where it all began; Columbia, known for persuasion and gratification studies; Frankfurt, proverbial home of the critical school of media studies; Toronto, famous for technological determinism; and British cultural studies, which might better be named Birmingham if it weren't for the pervasiveness of its influence throughout Britain – and the rest of the world. Each school is represented by at least one "foundational" text and one or more satellite texts that give expression to the work of the school. Readers will note the absence of other centers, such as Paris, famous for its semiotic studies of cinema and culture, and Yale, which tried to study mass persuasion experimentally. For these and other omissions, we offer editorial apologies.

The essays can also be divided along thematic lines, not just according to schools. Obviously, the debate between critical and administrative approaches is represented here, in the ideological debate between Frankfurt and Columbia. There is also a methodological debate between Chicago and Columbia over ethnography versus survey research. The debate over the "active" audience is also represented here, with Stuart Hall and Horton and Wohl on one side and, say, the Langs (in their MacArthur essay) on the other. The influence of technology versus the influence of text is evident in the juxtaposition of Innis and McLuhan with, say, Lazarsfeld and Merton or Lowenthal. The relevance of feminism to studies of the media and cinema is represented by Laura Mulvey, and also – in a muted anticipation – by Herzog. In other words – to say it one last time – our canonic texts contain a lot of *differences* of opinion. There is no reason to believe that these debates will subside. But, paradoxically, the boundaries of a field emerge from such debates.

Within-school differences are such that it might have served equally well (or better) to group the papers thematically. Indeed, an underlying theme of the essays in the book – one that the editors had not anticipated at the outset – is that collective memory in the field may have mistakenly catalogued these canonic texts by provenance rather than by theme. Thus, our authors argue that Herzog, even Lazarsfeld and Merton, and certainly Lang and Lang, deserve an honored place among critical theorists, while Benjamin may be placed just as well among technological theorists, despite his membership in the Frankfurt School.

The Smart Institute of Communication at the Hebrew University initiated this project with a conference, organized by Tamar Liebes, in May 1996. John Peters and Elihu Katz climbed aboard, and Avril Orloff offered so much assistance that she was promoted to co-editor as the project progressed. Editorial work was facilitated by grants-in-aid from the Annenberg School at the University of Pennsylvania, for which we thank Dean Kathleen Jamieson. We also owe thanks to the Annenberg Public Policy Center in Washington, and to its director, Lorie Slass, for hosting a working session of the editorial team. For advice and encouragement, and for the pleasure of corresponding with a kindred soul, we are indebted to John Thompson, editor of Polity Press.

Note

1 "The Sayings of the Fathers" in the Mishna includes the injunction to "appoint a rabbi/teacher for yourself," and the interpreters insist on the function of shared learning and of deference to the judgments of the appointee even if the person chosen should prove less worthy or less learned than oneself.

References

Herrnstein-Smith, B. (1988) *Contingencies of Value: Alternative Perspectives for Critical Theory*. Cambridge, MA: Harvard University Press.

Kuhn, T. (1970) *The Structure of Scientific Revolutions*, 2nd edn. Chicago: University of Chicago Press.

McPhee, W. N. (1963) *Formal Theories of Mass Behavior*. New York: Free Press.

Merton, R. K. (1985) *On the Shoulders of Giants: A Shandean Postscript*. New York: Harcourt Brace Jovanovich.

PART I
The Columbia School

———

Introduction

That canonic texts refuse to stand still applies, *a fortiori*, to the classics of the Columbia "school." The pioneering work of Paul Lazarsfeld and associates in the 1940s and 1950s gave communications research its very name and yet, at the same time, evoked devastating criticism. The Chicago school decried Columbia's psychologistic and positivistic bias and denounced its pronouncement of "limited effects"; the Frankfurt school refused to accept that audience likes and dislikes had any bearing on understanding the culture industry; and British cultural studies threw darts at the idea of defining media functions by asking audiences how they "use" them. Todd Gitlin went so far as to accuse Lazarsfeld's "dominant paradigm" of willfully understating the persuasive powers of the media, thereby relieving their owners and managers of the guilt they ought to feel.

It is true that the Columbia school – not satisfied to infer effects from content – developed methodologies for studying audience attitudes and behavior; it is true that sample surveys were preferred to ethnographic study or other forms of qualitative analysis; it is true that many studies were commercially sponsored, even if their products were academic; and it is true that media campaigns, like it or not, have only limited effects on the opinions, attitudes, and actions of the mass audience. But it is also true that, in the meantime, some of Columbia's harshest critics have themselves turned (perhaps too much so) to "reception" studies – that is to say, toward Columbia-like observations of the relative autonomy of audience decodings.

Columbia's map of media effects runs the gamut from a series of anti-hate advertisements to the effect of the introduction of television in the Middle East. Its work and thinking go far beyond immediate effects. Its view of the audience is not at all limited to reporting on what people do "with" the media, but also, in the spirit of critical theory, on what the media do "to" them. Indeed, émigré critical theorists Adorno, Lowenthal, and Kracauer were all welcomed at Columbia. Tamar Liebes sees this interaction in her rereading of Herzog's famous study of soap opera listeners; so do Simonson and Weimann in their review of Lazarsfeld's and Merton's foundational paper on how the media induce "conformity," "confer status," and instigate the dialectical process of withdrawal from politics through ostensible immersion in it (the "narcotizing dysfunction").

The whole of the Columbia oeuvre – from its earliest observations on the introduction of radio to the study, 20 years later, of how doctors adopt new drugs – would have been impossible without an organizational framework for the conduct and continuity of such large-scale empirical research. Lazarsfeld's biographers think that his most important innovation may have been the design of laboratories for social research of the kind he began in Vienna, imported to the United States, and exported to Europe and elsewhere. His wide-ranging Bureau of Applied Social Research (1937–77) demonstrates clearly how "the discipline of communication research" and the sophisticated study of opinions and attitudes grew up together at Columbia.

1

Critical Research at Columbia: Lazarsfeld's and Merton's "Mass Communication, Popular Taste, and Organized Social Action"

Peter Simonson and Gabriel Weimann

To see "Mass Communication, Popular Taste, and Organized Social Action" (Lazarsfeld and Merton, 1948) for what it is, we need to be clear about what it is not. It is not an expression of "the dominant paradigm" in media sociology, not an example of "administrative research," and most certainly not an argument that media are weak or insignificant social forces. It is sometimes viewed as a classic essay in the limited effects tradition of media research, but that is at most a partial truth. Key sections of the piece are not about "effects" at all, much less "limited effects," as that model has been interpreted by its critics.

Over fifty years have passed since Paul Lazarsfeld and Robert K. Merton published their classic piece, one of the most frequently cited and anthologized in communication studies, but the full qualities and contributions of the essay are revealed only when we clear away the underbrush of received wisdom about Lazarsfeld, Columbia's Bureau of Applied Social Research, and mid-century communication studies in the USA. Contrary to the popular impression of the Bureau's work, "Mass Communication, Popular Taste, and Organized Social Action" (hereafter referred to as "Mass Communication"[1]) is in fundamental ways a historically informed, critical account of mass communication. It is a nuanced overview of the socio-political functions of mass media in modern society that highlights the role of commercial media in maintaining capitalist hegemony. This was a minor theme of Lazarsfeld's work throughout the 1940s, but it was amplified by Merton, whose strong editorial hand was decisive in creating *the* classic essay of US media studies.

Their essay is significant, both historically and theoretically. Historically, it offers a window into the varied and relatively unsettled world of media studies in the 1940s, when the idea of communication enticed intellectual imaginations across many fields of study. If there was a dominant paradigm of US communication research centered on the social-scientific study of media effects, it was not established before the 1950s, and in 1948 the field was still rich with intellectual possibility. Even at Columbia there was important diversity, something both critics and defenders of that tradition have often overlooked. Lazarsfeld has become a synecdoche for the Bureau, coming to stand in for all Bureau research, but Merton was a key player as well. The two men had important intellectual differences, which are evident in "Mass Communication." As we show, the essay moves between conceptual vocabularies of social roles and media effects, blends positivistic caution with grander historical and conceptual sweep, and gives lie to many of the generalizations that have been made about mid-century media studies in the USA.

Rereading "Mass Communication" does more than shake loose the calcified histories of media studies. It also pays handsome theoretical dividends that can be tendered in a variety of contemporary currencies. The essay contains an abundance of insights that remain stunningly alive today: from the hegemonic and narcotizing power of media to their ability to maintain social norms and shape popular taste; from media's role in conferring status and orienting public attention to the idea that mass communication is most effective when it supplements other modes of communication and channels existing beliefs and values. These are themes pursued and hypotheses confirmed by media scholars of many theoretical stripes working in dramatically different technological and social environments than Lazarsfeld's and Merton's. With great subtlety and insight, these two authors carefully identified the specific conditions under which media might have strong effects, drew attention to the ideological force of commercial media systems, conceptualized cultural and political roles of everyday news and investigative reporting, and discussed the drive to maximize audience size and its relation to forms of media entertainment. And they did these things with style and grace of prose. The article is a classic because it is still good to think with, and still a pleasure to read.

The history of an error: the received wisdom

After his death in August 1976, Paul Lazarsfeld became a symbolic light-ning rod in media studies. He was seen as the founding father who needed to be either symbolically killed or canonized for siring the "domin-ant paradigm" of limited media effects. Critics and celebrants both con-tributed to a collective sense that the limited effects paradigm enjoyed a long and steady reign from the 1940s through at least the 1960s. This was a misleading narrative, and one that needs to be corrected to get a clearer bead on Lazarsfeld's and Merton's piece.

Beginning with Todd Gitlin's influential 1978 essay, Lazarsfeld, "admin-istrative research," and objectivist social science became favored tar-gets for defenders of critical and cultural studies seeking to stake out firmer ground for themselves in the field of media studies. Gitlin asserted that "The dominant paradigm in the field since World War II has been, clearly, the cluster of ideas, methods, and findings associated with Paul F. Lazarsfeld and his school: the search for specific, measurable, short-term, individual, attitudinal and behavioral 'effects' of media content, and the conclusion that media are not very important in the formation of public opinion" (p. 207). The dominant paradigm purportedly "drained the power of the media to define normal and abnormal social and polit-ical activity, to say what is politically real and legitimate and what is not" (p. 205) and ignored "the corporate structure of ownership and control . . . [and] the corporate criteria for media content that follow from it" (p. 225). Gitlin concluded that Lazarsfeld and "the mainstream of Amer-ican media sociology [have] done [their] share to consolidate and legitim-ize the cornucopian regime of mid-century capitalism" (p. 245).

In the early 1980s, others also weighed in on the "dominant para-digms" which the field had inherited, typically with some reference to Lazarsfeld. Stuart Hall (1982), for instance, offered sweeping statements (with few citations) about "mainstream" and "critical paradigms" and asserted that "issues of social and political power, of social structure and economic relations, were simply absent" from the mainstream tradition of mid-century US social science (p. 59).[2] Daniel Czitrom, a cultural and intellectual historian influenced by James Carey, also identified a "domin-ant paradigm" that focused on persuasion and short-term behavioral effects and ignored "issues concerning which social groups controlled the messages communicated through the media" (p. 132), as well as ques-tions about "the relationship between communication and the broader social order" (p. 146). Lazarsfeld was the main culprit. Carey (1982) recast the terms and players of team center and team periphery,[3] but he too contributed to the narrative of objectivist social science long and unfortunately triumphant in US media studies. Elihu Katz (1987) eventually heard enough and came to his teacher Lazarsfeld's defense. He agreed that Lazarsfeld represented the "dominant paradigm" and center of the field, but insisted that the media effects tradition was far broader, richer, and of more ongoing vitality than the critics' caricatured portraits suggested.

There was a strange convergence in the dominant paradigm talk of both the critics and the defenders. Though Katz resisted the idea that media effects was a monolithic tradition and rightly pointed out that Lazarsfeld had a spacious understanding of media effects that extended far beyond short-term behavioral changes (see Lazarsfeld, 1942, 1948a), like Gitlin, he saw Lazarsfeld as the father, read "effects" as the master frame of media studies, and put persuasion studies and limited effects at the center of Columbia research from 1940 to 1960 (Katz, 1987, pp. S34, S25–6, S37ff; see also Katz 1980, 1989, 1996). This was a variation on the influential but misleading narrative found in the first chapter of Katz's and Lazarsfeld's *Personal Influence* (1955), which asserted that "fundamentally, all of communications research aims at the study of effect." Surveying the field, they wrote, "There are a variety of mass media consequences which surely merit research attention but have not received it." Instead, "the overriding interest of mass media research is in the study of the effectiveness of mass media attempts to influence – usually, to change – opinions and attitudes in the very short run" (pp. 18–19). This was exactly what Gitlin was saying 30 years later about postwar research, and he drew primarily upon *Personal Influence* to illustrate a paradigm he claimed was dominant since Lazarsfeld's et al.'s 1944 election study, *The People's Choice*. This was simply inaccurate.

If there was a dominant paradigm for the field, it was not established before the 1950s. In the 1940s, even within the relatively localized institutional world of Columbia, "effects" was one conceptual vocabulary among several. Short-term persuasion studies were important at the bureau, but there was a variety of other kinds of research, from content and institutional analysis to broader comparative studies of radio and print, to functional analyses of media within larger social systems. If there was an "overriding interest of mass media research" at the Bureau in the 1940s, it was not effects or persuasion studies, but audience analysis – survey research and focused interviews that ascertained audience size and demographics, personality traits of listeners and readers, and the needs they fulfilled by using mass media (see J. S. Barton, 1984, pp. 7–20, 155–64; Lazarsfeld, 1948a, pp. 218–48). It is misleadingly reductive to say that all this research aimed at the study of effect, as both Katz and Gitlin suggested, and historically inaccurate to reify the administrative–critical divide, as Gitlin and Hall did. To claim that Lazarsfeld and company taught "that media are not very important in the formation of public opinion" (Gitlin, 1978, p. 207), or that "issues ... of social structure and economic relations were simply absent" from Columbia research (Hall, 1982, p. 59) is to ignore some of the most important Bureau publications of the 1940s, most particularly "Mass Communication."[4]

Communication research in the 1940s

The 1940s deserve to be set off as a distinct era in media studies. Communication was a concept that resonated with a huge array of intellectuals, from the literary critic and linguist I. A. Richards to Continental philosophers such as Hannah Arendt and Emmanuel Levinas and anthropologists like Margaret Mead and Edward Sapir (on the variety, see Cmiel, 1996; Peters, 1993; 1999, pp. 22–9). The USA did not settle into the Cold War until the late 1940s, so communication research in American universities did not yet fully feel its ideological and financial weight, as it would in the next decade (see Simpson, 1994). Even within the institutional center for the social scientific study of media, the Bureau of Applied Social Research, there was not yet a clear paradigm, and the limited effects perspective had not become dominant.

"Mass Communication" was first published in Lyman Bryson's edited collection, *The Communication of Ideas*, a volume that reveals some of the theoretical and methodological diversity of 1940s communication research. Bryson had been a member of the important Rockefeller Communications Group of 1939–40, which gave institutional and intellectual force to the emerging academic field of media study. Part of the Rockefeller Foundation's broader backing of media and communication research in the 1930s and 1940s, the Communications Group composed several documents that influenced academic study in the USA, including one coining the idea that "the job of research in mass communication is to determine who, and with what intentions, said what, to whom, and with what effects" (quoted in Gary, 1996, p. 138). The group came to be dominated by quantitative social scientists, especially Lazarsfeld and Harold Lasswell, but it also included humanists and qualitative researchers such as I. A. Richards, Robert Lynd, and Bryson, who was a specialist in adult education and professor at Columbia's Teacher's College. (On the Rockefeller seminar, see Gary, 1996; Glander, 2000, pp. 41–7; Converse, 1987; Morrison, 1978, 1988, 1998; and Rogers, 1994, pp. 142–5.)

In the winter of 1946–7, Bryson moderated a course on "The Problems of the Communication of Ideas" at the Jewish Theological Seminary in New York, a series of lectures by a wide range of scholars that issued in the 1948 volume. It was a spiritually and intellectually ecumenical undertaking by the Institute for Religious and Social Studies, a graduate school "conducted with the cooperation of Catholic, Jewish, and Protestant scholars" (Bryson, 1948, p. xii), and it reflected the hold that "communication" was taking across academic fields. The symposium included scholars from anthropology (Margaret Mead contributed two essays on cross-cultural communication), classics, psychology, literature, political science, sociology, education, and law. As Bryson observed in his introduction to the book, "nearly every thoughtful student of human behavior today, no matter what he calls his field, is likely to find something which he will have to call 'communication'" (pp. 1–2).

The Communication of Ideas was one of several important collections that vied to shape the emerging field of communication research. With far less intellectual ecumenism, Wilbur Schramm's *Communications in Modern Society* (1948) staked out a place for his new Institute for Communication Research at the University of Illinois and attempted to create a canon for the new field with an appendix of "one hundred titles for further reading on communication in modern society."[5] The next year Schramm published the first volume of his more spacious collection, *Mass Communications*, which reprinted Lazarsfeld's and Merton's "Mass Communication" and helped disseminate the essay to a generation of students.[6] Lazarsfeld and Stanton also resumed their Radio Research series of the early 1940s, now under the title *Communications Research*, and announced confidently, "it is no longer necessary to justify communications research as a special discipline or to outline its general scope" (1949, p. xiii). The field was settling in.

"Mass Communication" was originally Lazarsfeld's lecture to the Bryson seminar. As Lazarsfeld later recalled, the lecture "was, as usual, unprintable," perhaps because it was pieced together from at least two previous speeches.

> I asked Merton to make it suitable for publication. When I got the text back from him, my own ideas were put into fluent English and occasionally enriched by references to classical writers I probably had never heard of. But he had included a four-page section called "Some Social Functions of the Mass Media." It contained Merton's own analytical reflections, and therefore I felt the paper should be published jointly. . . . Each idea in this section was new at the time. (Lazarsfeld, 1975, pp. 52–3)

Merton's contributions were new and distinctive, but the collaboration was characteristic of a long and rich working relationship between the two men.

Merton and Lazarsfeld at Columbia

Merton and Lazarsfeld came to Columbia in the same year, 1941, and over the next three decades became what one student called the "giant double star" around which its department of sociology orbited (Selvin, 1975, p. 339). The story of their joint hiring has become a minor classic of academic history: a deeply divided department could not agree on a senior appointment and instead made two at lower levels, Merton the theorist and Lazarsfeld the methodologist.[7] Lazarsfeld's importance to media studies is well known, and he has become almost synonymous with mass communication research at Columbia; but this is unfortunate, for it occludes Merton's central role there and the deep and wide influence the two men had on each other.

Rarely at a loss for the right turn of phrase, Merton once confessed, "I have failed miserably in every attempt at even a meager digest of the influence Paul Lazarsfeld and I may have had on each other" (1996, p. 355). Over the years, the two co-authored five articles and edited a book together, but their collaboration ran far deeper. By Merton's estimation, they averaged ten to fifteen hours of conversation a week between 1942 and 1965 (Converse, 1987, p. 503). In the preface to *Social Theory and Social Structure*, Merton made extended acknowledgment of the importance of working "in double harness" at Columbia and being treated to Lazarsfeld's "skeptical curiosity" about functional analysis (1949, p. xiv). Assistance ran both ways. Merton was a virtuoso editor who made copious suggestions on other people's work, and he edited virtually every one of Lazarsfeld's monographs over the three decades of their friendship (Merton, 1998, p. 163; see also Caplovitz, 1977). His editorial contributions to "Mass Communication" were part of a larger scholarly pattern for Merton.

For both men, the 1940s marked their main period of interest in mass communication. When they came to Columbia in 1941, Lazarsfeld was four years into his most productive period in the field, which was largely over by 1950. He had begun the Office of Radio Research at Princeton in 1937, and between then and 1949 published more than 35 articles and books on broadcast and print media. After 1950, his energies were increasingly diverted elsewhere, though he continued to publish scattered monographs and co-authored *Personal Influence* with Katz (see

Neurath, 1979; A. H. Barton, 1982; J. S. Barton, 1984). Merton had not heard of communication research as a field before 1941, though his pioneering work in the historical sociology of science was clearly relevant to the study of communication, and, as an undergraduate at Temple, he had engaged in a content analysis of newspapers without conceptualizing it as such (Merton, 1994). Lazarsfeld was always a collaborator, though, and quickly brought Merton into mass communication research as well. In 1942, Merton became associate director of the Bureau (a post he held until 1971), and though his main interests lay elsewhere, he authored two of the most important mass communication studies of the 1940s: *Mass Persuasion* (1946), his study of Kate Smith's war bond drive, and "Patterns of Influence," his examination of local and cosmopolitan influential persons in Rovere, New Jersey (derived from a 1943 Bureau report and published in 1949). Merton also co-authored three media pieces with Lazarsfeld during the decade, including their classic essay. Like Lazarsfeld, he also turned away from mass communication after 1950.

They were in some ways an unlikely pair, "the original odd couple in the domain of social science," in Merton's words. Though both were (ethnic, agnostic) Jews within the largely Protestant establishment of US higher education, they came from very different cultural milieus: Lazarsfeld from bourgeois Vienna, Merton from the slums of south Philadelphia. Observers saw the two of them as "incorrigibly opposed," but they were also deep friends who sent lines from Rilke's poetry to each other (Merton, 1998, pp. 171, 200–1).[8] As Merton described them, they were "the inveterate creator of research institutes" and "the inveterate loner working chiefly in libraries and [his] study at home"; "the matter-of-fact but methodologically demanding positivist" and the "doubting Thomas . . . [who] had dared satirize the 'enlightened Boojum of Positivism'" in his first published paper in 1934; "the mathematically-minded methodologist" indebted to the Belgian statistician and astronomer Adolphe Quetelet and "the confirmed social theorist" who drew his bearings from Durkheim (Merton, 1996 [1994], p. 494; 1998, pp. 169–78; see also Hunt, 1961, pp. 56–7). In Lazarsfeld's words, Merton was "never an 'organization man'" and had initial misgivings about the rather new idea of an "organized research project" like the Bureau conducted. Quickly, though, the two developed a "simple division of labor." "I abstracted a series of methodological publications, and he derived from each empirical report some new theoretical idea," Lazarsfeld wrote (1975, p. 38). The two men worked closely, but Merton also retained a certain distance from the Bureau's more positivist side. He once described mass communication researchers as scholars who rallied around the motto,

"We don't know that what we say is particularly significant, but it is at least true" (Merton, 1968 [1949], p. 200).

The two men brought productive intellectual differences as well as elective affinities to their joint study of communication. Lazarsfeld had been overseeing empirical investigations of mass communication for nearly a decade and brought a positivist's caution against making grand and unsupported knowledge claims. Merton was "an excellent specimen of a concept maker" (Hunt, 1961, p. 60) who "had an alliance with empiricists that tended to give them concepts to label their findings" (Collins, 1977, p. 152). Throughout his career he showed a knack for coining concepts: unanticipated consequence, self-fulfilling prophecy, role model, manifest and latent functions all originated with Merton or gained new force from his pen. Lazarsfeld was disposed to use survey methods to determine the effects of media and other inputs on aggregated individual actions (see Coleman, 1980, pp. 163–5; Merton, 1998, pp. 173–5). Merton meanwhile drew upon social and intellectual history to develop functionalist and structural "theories of the middle range" informed by a Durkheimian sense of collective life. As a result, he was more likely than Lazarsfeld to situate media within broader social systems and historical contexts, and to do so with fluid, graceful prose and crisp analytic concepts.

Contrary to one-dimensional portraits of Columbia, both Lazarsfeld and Merton had sympathies for critical-Marxian research and social theory. Far from drawing a line in the sand, Lazarsfeld's "Administrative and Critical Communications Research" attempted to present German critical sociology sympathetically to an English-speaking audience and argued that empirically oriented US research would be vitalized by attending to "problems of control" and other questions of critical research (1941a, pp. 165–7; see also 1969, p. 325; and Morrison, 1988). Critical themes were evident in an important 1942 piece, where Lazarsfeld wrote that "by and large, radio has so far been a conservative force in American life." He also noted, in an analysis that Adorno or Lowenthal could have written, that on soap operas "All problems are of an individualistic nature. It is not social forces but the virtues and vices of the central characters that move the events along. People lose their jobs not for economic reasons but because their fellow men lie or are envious" (Lazarsfeld, 1942, p. 66; see also 1948b, 1948c). This was a minor but persistent thread in Lazarsfeld's work in the 1940s. Merton, meanwhile, was in the 1940s one of the world's experts on Marx. In 1942 the Frankfurt school's Franz Neumann recommended him to Oxford University Press "as the best possible person to review a manuscript on the economics of Karl Marx." This turned out to be Paul M. Sweezy's classic, *The Theory of Capitalist Development*, which Merton called "a painstaking, brilliant, exposition of Marxian economics unequalled by anything else in the literature, so far as I know." He also offered nine single-spaced pages of comments on the book (Caplovitz, 1977, pp. 146–7).

It was Merton the reviewer-editor who made "Mass Communication" a minor masterpiece. As an editor, he "has a knack for sharpening or highlighting the prose by finding a more expressive word or phrase than the word you chose" (Caplovitz, 1977, p. 145), and he did this for Lazarsfeld, putting his "unprintable" lecture "into fluent English" enriched by broadening references and resonant new concepts. As Merton reads manuscripts, "the author's arguments or problems trigger his own thought processes, and he offers to his client, free of charge, brilliant reformulations of and additions to the arguments that reflect falsely on the brilliance of the author" (Caplovitz, 1977, p. 145). When he read Lazarsfeld's lecture, the "excellent specimen of a concept maker" created a wholly new section that turned out to be the essay's richest theoretically. Finally, Merton, the leading expert on Marx, sharpened and amplified critical-historical themes that had long been minor chords in Lazarsfeld's scholarship. In collaboration, the two men created a beautifully written, conceptually elegant, and historically informed overview of the mass media's roles and social effects in the mid-twentieth century.

The article's themes

Like the Bryson volume as a whole, Lazarsfeld's and Merton's essay displayed significant breadth of vision and was no singular argument about limited media effects. To read the essay freshly today is to find a far richer view of mass media in society than has often been associated with Bureau work. The essay begins by summarizing public concerns about mass media in modern society, then goes on to address three areas: the social functions of mass communication, especially in a commercial media system like that of the USA; the impact of mass media upon popular taste; and the conditions under which "propaganda for social objectives" can be effective. Only the last of these three areas, roughly a quarter of the manuscript, is devoted to the sorts of explicit persuasion campaigns that became associated with the limited effects understanding of media. The essay centrally addresses critical institutional questions about commercial mass media and their hegemonic force, as well as broad-angle sociological questions about popular taste in historical perspective. In addition, it offers a far more nuanced position regarding the conditions for limited media effects than critics have typically acknowledged.

Lazarsfeld and Merton begin their essay by acknowledging the historicity of the study of communication. In an opening line that any historical materialist would be happy to have written, they proclaim: "Problems engaging the attention of men change, and they change not at random but largely in accord with the altering demands of society and economy." A generation ago, a group like that assembled for the Bryson symposium would have been discussing child labor, women's suffrage, or old age pensions, but now public interest had shifted to "problems of the media of mass communication" (p. 95). They go on to identify "three organically related elements" of contemporary concern with mass media, which roughly line up with the three terms in the title of the essay: (i) fear of "the ubiquity and potential power" of mass communication as such, which they call "an almost magical belief"; (ii) "a more realistic" fear about "changing types of social control exercised by powerful interest groups in society" through advertising and public relations, and the possibility that they might lead to "the unconditional surrender of critical faculties and an unthinking conformism"; and (iii) the fear that "these technically advanced instruments of mass communication constitute a major avenue for the deterioration of esthetic tastes and popular cultural standards" (pp. 96, 97). The remainder of the essay is "a review of the current state of actual knowledge concerning the social role of the mass media of communication and their effects upon the contemporary American community" – an "ungrateful task," they observe, "for certified knowledge of this kind is impressively slight." This positivist caution yields to acute, far-reaching critical insights, however, which make the essay the living theoretical resource it is today.

The introductory section actually frames the issues three times and in two distinct ways, an index of conceptual differences at Columbia as well as a reflection on the essay's composite quality (Merton's contributions added to two speeches by Lazarsfeld). The first (pp. 95–6) frames the "three great concerns" about mass media through a vocabulary of social control, social role, and social structure, while the second (p. 97) and third (p. 98) conceptualize them as worries about "'the effects' of mass media upon society." "Social roles" was characteristic of Merton, on the verge of publishing the first edition of his *Social Theory and Social Structure* (1949), while "effects" was Lazarsfeld's preferred language. Though "effects" appeared in places, Merton's social structure/social function idiom dominated the ensuing arguments in the essay. The slippage between the two vocabularies should be read as an index of both the intellectual differences between Merton and Lazarsfeld and the conceptually unsettled quality of 1940s communication research.[9]

Their succeeding discussion of mass media as such moves in two different directions. On the one hand, they are dismissive of "grossly speculative" claims equating the power of radio to that of the atomic bomb or concluding that media have an enormous impact simply because they are distributed to millions of people. "We cannot resort to experiment by comparing contemporary American society with and without mass media," they caution, so one needs to tread carefully when drawing conclusions about media's impact. "To know the number of hours people keep the radio turned on gives no indication of the effect upon them of what they hear" (pp. 98, 99). This was a position that Lazarsfeld had maintained for some time, and it was one that Merton had sympathy for as well. It was a rejection of technological determinism and ungrounded speculation, and it was part of what would later become the limited effects paradigm.

But then comes the section that Merton added, "Some Social Functions of the Mass Media," which "temporarily abstract[s] from the social structure in which the media find their place." Here Merton discards the "effects" vocabulary and argues instead that "mass media undoubtedly serve many social functions which might become the object of sustained research" (p. 101). He names and discusses three: the status conferral function, the enforcement of social norms, and the narcotizing dysfunction. Status conferral names the fact that media enhance the social standing of the policies, persons, and groups they cover – regardless of whether this coverage is favorable or not. Enforcement of social norms refers to media's ability to close "the gap between 'private attitudes' and 'public morality,'" to reaffirm mainstream moral standards by calling attention to deviations from the norm, and thus, through publicity, to exert pressure toward social conformism (p. 103). The narcotizing dysfunction then labels the way in which media keep "large masses of the population politically apathetic and inert" by supplying them with vast quantities of a product that elicits "only a superficial concern with the problems of society" (p. 105). The reader or listener "comes to mistake knowing about problems of the day for doing something about them." In another line that would make a Marxist mother proud, Merton writes: "In this peculiar respect, mass communications may be included among the most respectable and efficient of social narcotics. They may be so fully effective as to keep the addict from recognizing his own malady" (p. 106).

From this point, the essay turns to a consideration of the commercial ownership of US media and its role in what today we would call capitalist hegemony and the structured silencing of system-challenging critique. As we noted earlier, Lazarsfeld had touched on these themes in his important but overlooked 1942 article, "The Effects of Radio on Public Opinion." That article cites Adorno and Herta Herzog, argues that American commercial media maintain the status quo instead of contributing to positive social change, and makes moderate criticism of a commercial model of broadcasting from a liberal/social democratic perspective.[10] The point gains sharper critical edges, though, in the Lazarsfeld and Merton essay. These themes are foreign to the collective portrait of Bureau research, so we quote at some length:

> Since the mass media are supported by great business concerns geared into the current social and economic system, the media contribute to the maintenance of that system. . . . To the extent that the media of mass communication have had an influence upon their audiences, it has stemmed not only from what is said, but more significantly from what is not said. For these media not only continue to affirm the status quo but, in the same measure, they fail to raise essential questions about the structure of society. . . . This is not to ignore the occasionally critical journal article or radio program. But these exceptions are so few that they are lost in the overwhelming flood of conformist materials. . . . Since our commercially sponsored mass media promote a largely unthinking allegiance to our social structure, they cannot be relied upon to work for changes, even minor changes, in that structure. (Lazarsfeld 1942, pp. 107–8)

Here were the essential components of a critical theory of mass communication and socio-political hegemony, and it should caution us about reifying the "critical" versus "administrative" dichotomy.

After these broad-angle considerations of media within capitalist and other social systems, Lazarsfeld and Merton move to a briefer discussion of media and popular taste. This was a rarer theme for Bureau researchers, though it did attract the attention of Lazarsfeld and others in the immediate postwar period.[11] This is the most dated part of the essay, a mildly elitist and sexist consideration of the "seeming decline of popular taste" instantiated by mass-communicated entertainment, and the possibilities for improving aesthetic standards. "There can be no doubt that the women who are daily entranced for three or four hours by some twelve consecutive 'soap operas,' all cut to the same dismal pattern, exhibit an appalling lack of esthetic judgment," they write. "Nor is this impression altered by the contents of pulp and slick magazines, or by the depressing abundance of formula motion pictures" (pp. 108–9). These were sentiments shared by Adorno and other mid-century theorists as well, but Lazarsfeld and Merton reject any facile version of mass culture criticism. They reject a narrative of historical decline, refuse to conclude that tastes have deteriorated, and insist that the issue is more complex. "If esthetic tastes are to be considered in their social setting, we must recognize that the effective audience for the arts has become historically transformed," they argue. "Mass audiences probably include a larger number of persons with cultivated esthetic standards, but these are swallowed up by the large masses who constitute the new and untutored audience for the arts" (pp. 109, 110). They suggest that mass media may have had an impact on the standards of artistic production, but here too they are cautious. "Literary hacks have existed in every age," they point out, "but it would be important to learn if the electrification of the arts supplies power for a significantly greater proportion of dim literary lights" (pp. 110–11).

Only in the final section of the essay do Lazarsfeld and Merton address persuasion campaigns, or what they call "propaganda for social objectives." The study of such campaigns is often linked to Lazarsfeld's interests in marketing, but it was long a Bureau focus disconnected from commercialized activity and applied to processes of audience building in educational broadcasting (Lazarsfeld 1941b), wartime propaganda (Lazarsfeld and Merton, 1943; Merton, 1946, esp. pp. 171–2), election campaigns (Lazarsfeld et al., 1944), and racial tolerance efforts (Lazarsfeld, 1947). This section of the essay draws upon all these studies, but in particular reworks three "conditions of effect" that Lazarsfeld identified in "Effects of Radio on Public Opinion" (1942, pp. 70–5). Perhaps owing to the "concept maker" Merton, these conditions in 1948 gain crisp new theoretical labels: *monopolization, canalization,* and *supplementation.*

Far from arguing that the media have little or no effect on the formation of public opinion, as critics of the limited effects paradigm sometimes assert, Lazarsfeld and Merton identify the specific conditions under which media could have powerful effects. *Monopolization* refers to situations in which "there is little or no opposition in the mass media to the diffusion of values, policies, or public images" – in other words, "in the absence of counterpropaganda" (p. 113; see also Lazarsfeld, 1942, pp. 74–6; Merton, 1946, pp. 171–2). *Canalization* means that propaganda is most successful when it channels pre-existing attitudes and values, and is far less likely to create "significantly new behavior patterns" or bring about radical conversions (p. 114; cf. Lazarsfeld, 1942, pp. 70–3; 1947, pp. 18ff). *Supplementation* is shorthand for the notion that media are most effective "when they operate in conjunction with face-to-face contacts" (p. 117; cf. Lazarsfeld, 1942, pp. 73–4; 1947, pp. 21–3).[12]

The essay then ends in a way that critics of limited effects might find surprising. On the one hand, because "these three conditions are rarely satisfied conjointly in propaganda for social objectives," Lazarsfeld and Merton conclude that "media do not exhibit the degree of social power commonly attributed to them." This is where the critics stop reading. But the last two paragraphs of the article are worth quoting from in detail:

> By the same token, and in view of the present organization of business ownership and control of the mass media, they have served to cement the structure of our society. Organized business does approach a virtual "psychological monopoly" of the mass media. . . . Moreover, the world of commerce is primarily concerned with canalizing rather than radically changing basic attitudes; it seeks only to create preferences for one rather than another brand of product. Face to face contacts with those who have been socialized in our culture serve primarily to reinforce the prevailing culture patterns. Thus, the very conditions which make for the maximum effectiveness of the mass media of communication operate toward the maintenance of the going social and cultural structure rather than toward its change. (pp. 117–18)

Commercial forces hold a virtual monopoly of mass media and uphold consumerist practices of brand selection. These forces are supplemented and reinforced in face-to-face life, where there is little organized opposition to them. Media maintain the status quo and uphold the dominant structures of capitalism and consumerism. And this is how the essay ends.[13]

The continuing relevance of Lazarsfeld and Merton

The power of a theoretical essay can be measured by the ongoing vitality of its ideas, and Merton's and Lazarsfeld's is exemplary. The essay can be read as a conceptual font for a range of contemporary media theories and schools of thought. The "three conditions" postulate – monopolization, canalization, and supplementation – is of continuing relevance to media effects studies operating in disparate social and technological contexts. Merton's social functions of media can be read as precursors to agenda-setting theory, the third-person effect, the ritual view of communication, and theories of media and hegemony.

The three conditions

The continuing relevance of the three conditions postulate is well illustrated by looking at modern election campaigns. Monopolization continues to occur in a variety of ways, arising not just from a concentration of ownership, but also from a strongly socialized and tightly knit journalistic elite (Hart, 1994) that lacks any fundamental variety of opinion or attitude. Politicians often argue that the news media form a solid front against them, following unknowingly the monopolization idea. Politicians themselves can contribute to this process by effectively monopolizing rhetorical appeals that make it difficult for their opponents even to weigh in on particular issues. Ronald Reagan's war on crime, for instance, largely eliminated crime from his opponents' public agendas. In Israel, the political right has long mobilized the rhetoric of nationalism, while the left has monopolized the rhetoric of peace. Noelle-Neumann's (1984) spiral of silence theory likewise offers a sophisticated present-day account of monopolization in which media end up contributing to the convergence of public opinion and the absence of counter-propaganda.

Lazarsfeld's and Merton's third condition for successful propaganda addresses the combined impact of personal and mass communication. As they noted of radio broadcasts followed by face-to-face discussions, "this complex of reciprocal reinforcement by mass media and personal relations proved spectacularly successful" (p. 115). Fifty years later, in a media environment enriched by computer-mediated communication, television, satellites, and cables, the validity of the supplementation hypothesis is still being demonstrated. The active role played by face-to-face interactions is evident in many modern election campaigns. This can take the form of small-scale social gatherings such as "meet-the-candidate" evenings held in the homes of party activists and supporters, petition signings, or group letter-writing campaigns. Many modern parties also employ hegemonic institutions described by Lazarsfeld and Merton as "organized centers of local indoctrination" – religious and community centers and universities, for instance. The tactics may be new, but the motivating insight is old.

Social functions of media

In 1948 Merton could write that the narcotizing dysfunction – media's way of keeping "large masses of the population politically apathetic and inert" – was "a social consequence of the mass media [that] has gone largely unnoticed" (Lazarsfeld and Merton, 1948, p. 105). Few today would say that the mass media's apparently detrimental effects on political life have gone unnoticed. Many scholars, most notably Robert Putnam (1995a, 1995b, 2000), have attempted to show that the US electorate has, in fact, been narcotized – or at least discouraged from getting actively involved in politics – by the mass media, especially television. But for Putnam, it is television entertainment that is the problem. "Watching the news is not harmful to your civic health," he confidently asserts (2000, p. 221). Merton, on the other hand, is suggesting something different: that conscientious use of news media may ironically be part of the problem, for citizens can come to equate being informed with being active. By saturating people with information, news media can help render the public politically inert. The concept of the narcotizing dysfunction is subtler than most recent worries about civic engagement: Merton has a sense for the ironic.

Merton's notions of status conferral and the enforcement of social norms are two of the more suggestive ideas to come out of the essay. In those two concepts, as well as his other contributions to Lazarsfeld's original manuscript, Merton put forth core notions for a socio-cultural theory of media that he never fully worked out, pointing to media's contributions to the moral-political life of a society, their role in maintaining and altering norms, practices, and socio-political institutions, or what Hegel termed *Sittlichkeit* (see Simonson, 1996, pp. 325ff). His comments anticipate many theoretical arguments that have been made since. From a theoretical perspective, "agenda-setting" is an extended footnote on status conferral. McCombs's and Shaw's (1972) metaphor gave Merton's concept a quasi-deliberative ring that has captured the imagination of social scientists (see McCombs and Shaw, 1993); but, as an idea, it offers little that Merton had not recognized in 1948. Status conferral also offers a way to think about media and public confidence (Simonson, 1999). Contrary to the belief that the media are most likely to promote cynicism, status conferral can also be understood as a process of charismatic transfer of positive social value.

Merton's discussion of the enforcement of social norms, meanwhile, should be placed in intellectual genealogies of studies of investigative journalism, the third-person effect, pluralistic ignorance, and ritual views of communication. It offers a nuanced account of the various mechanisms through which media "crusades" and publicized wrongdoing might prove efficacious (by alarming the culprits, by affecting the public directly, by strengthening the hand of reformers within the targeted organization, or by enhancing the prestige of the mass medium itself), a central concern of recent studies by Protess et al. (1991) and by Ettema and Glasser (1998). One of these mechanisms – "the directors of corruption may fear the crusade only because of the effect they anticipate it will have upon the electorate" (p. 104) – is essentially the third-person effect hypothesis (see Davison, 1983). As Katz (1981) has argued, Merton's enforcement of social norms also helps to explain both pluralistic ignorance and

Noelle-Neumann's spiral of silence. Finally, when Merton writes that media can "call forth public reaffirmation" and application of social norms (p. 103), we might hear aspects of Carey's ritual view of communication (1988, pp. 18ff). In fact, we could add Merton to Carey's genealogy of North American intellectual resources for a cultural approach to communication, putting him alongside better-incorporated figures like John Dewey, George Herbert Mead, and Kenneth Burke (Carey, 1988, pp. 23, 96–7; see also Simonson, 2000). More broadly, we could place Merton's brief original section of the article in a longer line of thought that runs from Durkheim and Charles Horton Cooley to Carey and Dayan and Katz (1992) and explores the role of communication in constituting and maintaining the moral-political life of groups.

Conclusion

It is a challenge to read old texts with fresh eyes. As Walter Lippmann observed many years ago, "for the most part we do not first see, and then define, we define first and then see" (1922, p. 54). Before we sat down to write this article, we were guided by discourse about Lazarsfeld and media effects circulated by critics and defenders since the 1970s. Though we had read and taught "Mass Communication, Popular Taste, and Organized Social Action" a number of times, we still tended to group it with the limited effects model that has come to be associated with Lazarsfeld, Katz, Joseph Klapper, and mid-century communication research at Columbia. We believed that critiques of that model often misinterpreted or caricatured what "limited effects" actually meant, but we still tended to think about "Mass Communication" as one of the classic statements of the position. Given the received wisdom about Lazarsfeld and his research, this was, as they say, the preferred reading of the text. We were only partly right.

The last six pages of their essay are in fact a classic statement of the limited effects paradigm, but one must be precise about what that means. Limited effects does not mean "no effects." It does not mean "weak effects." As a careful reading of the final pages reveals, limited effects means that there are limited conditions under which "propaganda for social objectives" might actually have quite powerful persuasive effects. In most cases, there are social and psychological mechanisms that defend audiences from being automatically influenced by mass media, thus minimizing the possibility of direct, immediate, and uniform effects. As Lazarsfeld and Merton argued, media are most influential when their messages are supplemented by other modes of communicative contact, when they are not significantly challenged by other broad-circulation media, and when they draw upon and channel existing values, beliefs, and structures of feeling. These conditions are sometimes met: in some authoritarian regimes, in some media events (Dayan and Katz, 1992), and, as Lazarsfeld and Merton very clearly point out, in a commercially oriented media system where mass-communicated capitalism goes relatively unchallenged in mediated or face-to-face life.

Much of the article, though, is about the social functions and dysfunctions of mass communication and the differential consequences for those variously located in the social structure. It is not about "media effects," and it is here that the essay most strongly departs from the qualities typically associated with the limited effects model – an "administrative" focus on explicit media campaigns and the short-run, behavioral changes they might bring about. In point of fact, throughout the 1940s Lazarsfeld had a spacious understanding of media effects – they could be either short- or long-term, caused by messages as well as institutional structures, result in ways of thinking as well as ways of acting, and issue in preserving the status quo as much as changing it (see Lazarsfeld, 1942, 1948a; and Katz, 1987, pp. S35–7). He was sympathetic to critical issues of media control, and could write broadly about media in "the total environment of a country" (Lazarsfeld, 1949, p. 3). At the same time, Lazarsfeld was always drawn to the positivistic analysis of aggregated decision making and to questions of measurable change brought about by identifiable causes, topics he pursued in election and marketing research. Lazarsfeld was both hedgehog and fox (Merton, 1998, pp. 173ff); he had wide-ranging interdisciplinary interests and often conceptualized media effects in broad terms, but the study of short-term behavioral changes lay at the core of his own research.

This is where Merton came in: elegant writer, virtuoso editor of other people's work, and "excellent specimen of a concept maker." He created a widely anthologized, classic essay from Lazarsfeld's original, composite speech, an essay that in the end was more "critical" than "administrative," more about media's socio-historical roles, functions, and dysfunctions than its effects. While Lazarsfeld was drawn to the study of aggregated individual actions, Merton approached the social order in less atomistic ways, and consequently had a different lens through which to view mass media in society. Lazarsfeld was a polymath, but he didn't have the broad theoretical and historical range of Merton, who combined pioneering work in the historical sociology of science with social theory that drew richly upon Durkheim, Weber, and Marx, among many others. Though Merton was in many ways a liberal, he was also in the 1940s an expert on Marx, and he brought critical-theoretical insights to bear in "Mass Communication." As detailed above, if we can get past the stereotyped wisdom about Bureau research, we can read the essay for what it is: a nuanced account of the socio-political roles of mass media in modern society and the part played by commercial media in maintaining capitalist hegemony.

As we also argued, Lazarsfeld's and Merton's essay is a window into the ecumenical and relatively open-ended world of media studies in the immediate postwar period. Neither a dominant conceptual paradigm nor a dominant method of study had yet established itself, and the field was rich in intellectual possibility. "Mass Communication" offered a number of starting points for research, which have borne considerable fruit over a wide variety of media and social environments in the past five decades. From their three conditions for powerful media effects to their three social roles played by the media in modern societies, Lazarsfeld's and Merton's ideas have been successfully applied and tested in conditions far different from those in the USA in 1948. Moreover, their ideas have found unanticipated resonances in quite distinct modes of present-day research, from media effects to critical and cultural studies of communication.

But if there is a richness suggested by this classic essay, there is also a sense of loss tied to it. For the most part, the intellectual breadth of the Bryson volume was not realized in US media studies after 1948. Some of that has changed in the last two decades, but it is balanced by the subdisciplinary parochialism that characterizes the professionalized field of study. There are also questions about what Lazarsfeld and Merton might have done after the 1940s. In the 1950s and 1960s, Lazarsfeld wrote sparingly about media, though Elihu Katz and others extended his trajectory and maintained his legacy. Merton, on the other hand, was effectively out of the business of media study after 1949. To be sure, he had never been as deeply involved as Lazarsfeld, but Merton's publications were some of the very best things written on media in the 1940s. Given the richness and clarity of "Mass Communication, Popular Taste, and Organized Social Action," one is left to wonder what the two might have produced had they continued to collaborate in media theory and research. The field would surely have been richer intellectually.

Notes

1 Not to be confused with Wilbur Schramm's *Mass Communications* (1949).
2 As we show below, this characterization is dead wrong if applied to Lazarsfeld's and Merton's classic piece. The administrative/mainstream

versus critical/Marxian dichotomy that both Gitlin and Hall used is a distinction that Lazarsfeld himself made (drawing upon Horkheimer's idea of traditional and critical theory), but Gitlin and Hall essentialize a distinction that Lazarsfeld imagined more fluidly; his 1941 essay, "Administrative and Critical Communications Research," argues that each type would benefit by borrowing from the other. This clearly happened in the 1940s; "Mass Communication" is one good example, Leo Lowenthal's "Biographies in Popular Magazines" (1944) another.

3   The teams shifted from administrative versus critical research to objectivist versus expressivist, and their captains became Walter Lippmann and John Dewey, not Lazarsfeld and Adorno, but the structure of the argument remained the same: social-scientific insiders against critical-cultural outsiders.

4   Gitlin makes just one reference to Lazarsfeld's and Merton's article, an unrepresentative quote from the introductory section of the essay (Gitlin, 1978, p. 222).

5   For another example of an early suggested reading list in media studies, see Waples, 1942, pp. 185–9.

6   Lazarsfeld's and Merton's essay also appeared in the widely circulated collection by Rosenberg and White, *Mass Culture: The Popular Arts in America* (1957). Through the 1960s, new editions of both books included the article.

7   The story began with a *New Yorker* profile (Hunt, 1961, esp. pp. 59–61) and has been reproduced many times (e.g. Rogers, 1994, pp. 244ff). For useful accounts of Merton and Lazarsfeld at Columbia, see Merton, 1994, 1998; Lazarsfeld, 1975, pp. 35–7; Sills, 1996, pp. 111–14; Bierstedt, 1980, pp. 88ff; Coleman, 1972, pp. 400–1; and Converse, 1987, pp. 267ff). At the time of their hiring, Robert S. Lynd supported Lazarsfeld, while Robert M. MacIver championed Merton.

8   The Rilke-quoting Lazarsfeld doesn't appear in the collective portrait painted by Gitlin and others, which emphasizes the methodologist, mathematician, "institution man," "abstract empiricist," and fallen socialist turned administrative researcher intent on marketing questions. For a far different picture of Lazarsfeld – as charming conversationalist with wide-ranging curiosity who read esoteric history journals and detective novels and loved Paris more than any other city – see the recollections of his son-in-law, the historian Bernard Bailyn (1979). Far from being a single-minded methodologist, Lazarsfeld had complex intellectual interests that gave him something of an academic identity crisis. In 1939 Robert Lynd wrote of him, "Every researcher has an Achilles' heel. His is his intellectual curiosity about everything interesting" (quoted in Morrison, 1978, p. 356; see also Jahoda, 1979; Merton, 1979; and DiRenzo, 1981).

9   One might object to our contrast between social roles and effects. Following Lazarsfeld's own spacious understanding of the term (1948a), Katz (1987, 1989) has attempted to conceptualize all of media studies via the "effects"

vocabulary. If one follows this strategy, then the social roles of media identified in Lazarsfeld's and Merton's essay are simply another way of talking about what are at base media's effects. We would answer that vocabularies make a difference in constituting fields of study. Historically, to avoid anachronism, we must remain attentive to idioms in use. Theoretically, to maintain intellectual richness, we must preserve distinct languages of inquiry instead of collapsing them into one master idiom. "Effects" differs from "roles" insofar as "effects" foregrounds questions of causality instantiated by media, while "roles" conceptualizes media as players within a broader totality of social processes. These are not mutually exclusive perspectives, but there is a difference of emphasis.

10   Lazarsfeld argued that American commercial media "accentuate . . . [and] bring into sharp relief certain tendencies in our industrial society" (1942, p. 71). Rather cautiously, he wrote that the commercial model was "useful for entertainment programs only" and could limit "opening up radio more widely to public discussion and . . . using it more systematically to communicate the new social ideas which the immediate public interest so evidently requires" (pp. 77, 76). Lazarsfeld rarely made explicit political pronouncements in his scholarship, but here was a halting expression of his positive political vision in the 1940s.

11   In 1946, Joseph Klapper was working on an unusual project for the Bureau entitled "Literary Criticism Analysis," which issued in an unpublished 1947 report, "Aesthetic Standards and the Criticism of Mass Media" (J. S. Barton, 1984, pp. 16, 160). Lazarsfeld also addressed the question of criticism and taste in two other 1947 speeches that incorporated excerpts from Lazarsfeld and Merton (Lazarsfeld 1948b, 1948c), and returned to the subject in one of his later pieces (Lazarsfeld, 1961). Some of the Bureau's mid-1940s work on media and public taste appears, as well, in the memorandum composed in response to a request by the Public Library Inquiry of the Social Science Research Council in 1948, distributed in mimeograph form as *The Effects of Mass Media* (Klapper, 1949, esp. memorandum 1, "The Impact of Mass Media upon Public Taste," and Introduction, pp. 8–9).

12   Merton was applying the idea of supplementation in a different way during this period. In a study of a biracial Pittsburgh community that Lazarsfeld (1947) quoted from, Merton wrote that "single institutions, such as community housing, have only a limited effectiveness in producing tolerance. Only when it is further supported by other institutions does it achieve its full potential for tolerance" (Lazarsfeld, 1947, p. 21). This commitment to tolerance and the social institutions that foster it is another reminder of the liberal/social democratic politics of Lazarsfeld and Merton, and the critical component of it.

13   Compare Katz (1981), who wrote that "Lazarsfeld and Merton noted that monopolization of the media does, indeed, produce more powerful effects, but they do not associate media monopolization with Western democracy" (p. 30).

References

Bailyn, B. (1979) Recollections of PFL. In R. K. Merton, J. S. Coleman, and
P. H. Rossi (eds), *Qualitative and Quantitative Research: Papers in Honor of Paul F. Lazarsfeld*, New York: Free Press, 16–18.

Barton, A. H. (1982) Paul Lazarsfeld and the Invention of the University Institute for Applied Social Research. In B. Holzner and J. Nehnevajsa (eds), *Organizing for Social Research*, Cambridge, MA: Schenkman Publishing, 17–83.

Barton, J. S. (ed.) (1984) *Guide to the Bureau of Applied Social Research*. New York: Clearwater Publishing.

Bierstedt, R. (1980) *Robert M. MacIver: Political Philosopher and Sociologist*. In R. K. Merton and M. W. Riley (eds), *Sociological Traditions from Generation to Generation: Glimpses of the American Experience*, Norwood, NJ: Ablex, 81–92.

Bryson, L. (ed.) (1948) *The Communication of Ideas: A Series of Addresses*. New York: Harper & Brothers.

Caplovitz, D. (1977) Review of "The Idea of Social Structure." *Contemporary Sociology*, 6 (2), 142–50.

Carey, J. W. (1982) Mass Media: The Critical View. In *Communications Yearbook V*, Beverly Hills, CA: Sage. Repr. as "Reconceiving 'Mass' and 'Media'," in Carey, 1988, 69–88.

Carey, J. W. (1988) *Communication as Culture*. Boston: Unwin Hyman.

Cmiel, K. (1996) On Cynicism, Evil, and the Discovery of Communication in the 1940s. *Journal of Communication*, 46 (3), 88–107.

Coleman, J. (1972) Paul Lazarsfeld's Work in Survey Research and Mathematical Sociology. In P. F. Lazarsfeld, *Qualitative Analysis: Historical and Critical Essays*, Boston: Allyn and Bacon, 395–409.

Coleman, J. (1980) Paul F. Lazarsfeld: The Substance and Style of his Work. In R. K. Merton and M. W. Riley (eds), *Sociological Traditions from Generation to Generation: Glimpses of the American Experience*, Norwood, NJ: Ablex, 153–74.

Collins, R. (1977) Review of "The Idea of Social Structure." *Contemporary Sociology*, 6 (2), 150–4.

Converse, J. (1987) *Survey Research in the United States: Roots and Emergence 1890–1960*. Berkeley: University of California Press.

Czitrom, D. (1982) *Media and the American Mind*. Chapel Hill: University of North Carolina Press.

Davison, W. P. (1983) The Third-Person Effect in Communication. *Public Opinion Quarterly*, 47 (1), 1–15.

Dayan, D. and Katz, E. (1992) *Media Events: The Live Broadcasting of History*. Cambridge, MA: Harvard University Press.

DiRenzo, G. (1981) Meta-Sociology and Academic Identities. *Contemporary Sociology*, 10 (3), 355–7.

Ettema, J. S. and Glasser, T. L. (1998) *Custodians of Conscience: Investigative Journalism and Public Virtue*. New York: Columbia University Press.

Gary, B. (1996) Communications Research, the Rockefeller Foundation, and Mobilization for the War on Words, 1938–1944. *Journal of Communication*, 46 (3), 124–48.

Gitlin, T. (1978) Media Sociology: The Dominant Paradigm. *Theory and Society*, 6, 205–53.

Glander, T. (2000) *Origins of Mass Communications Research during the American Cold War*. Mahwah, NJ: Lawrence Erlbaum.

Hall, S. (1982) The Rediscovery of "Ideology": Return of the Repressed in Media Studies. In M. Gurevitch et al. (eds), *Culture, Society, and the Media*, London: Methuen, 56–90.

Hart, R. P. (1994) *Seducing America: How Television Charms the Modern Voter*. New York: Oxford University Press.

Hunt, M. (1961) How Does it Come to Be So? *New Yorker*, Jan. 28, 39–63.

Jahoda, M. (1979) PFL: Hedgehog or Fox? In R. K. Merton, J. S. Coleman, and P. H. Rossi (eds), *Qualitative and Quantitative Research: Papers in Honor of Paul F. Lazarsfeld*, New York: Free Press, 3–9.

Katz, E. (1980) On Conceptualizing Media Effects. *Studies in Communication*, 1, 119–41.

Katz, E. (1981) Publicity and Pluralistic Ignorance: Notes on "The Spiral of Silence." In H. Baier, H. M. Kepplinger, and K. Reumann (eds), *Public Opinion and Social Change: For Elisabeth Noelle-Neumann*, Wiesbaden: Westdeutscher Verlag, 28–38.

Katz, E. (1987) Communications Research Since Lazarsfeld. *Public Opinion Quarterly*, 51, S25–45.

Katz, E. (1989) Mass Media Effects. In E. Barnouw (ed.), *The International Encylopedia of Communications*, vol. 2, New York: Oxford University Press, 492–7.

Katz, E. (1996) Diffusion Research at Columbia. In E. Dennis and E. Wartella (eds), *American Communication Research: The Remembered History*, Mahwah, NJ: Lawrence Erlbaum, 61–70.

Katz, E. and Lazarsfeld, P. F. (1955) *Personal Influence: The Part Played by People in the Flow of Mass Communications*. New York: Free Press.

Klapper, J. (1949) *The Effects of Mass Media*. New York: Bureau of Applied Social Research.

Lazarsfeld, P. F. (1941a) Administrative and Critical Communications Research. Repr. in Lazarsfeld, 1972, pp. 155–67.

Lazarsfeld, P. F. (1941b) Audience Building in Educational Broadcasting. *Journal of Educational Sociology*, 14 (9), 533–41.

Lazarsfeld, P. F. (1942) The Effects of Radio on Public Opinion. In D. Waples (ed.), *Print, Radio, and Film in a Democracy*, Chicago: University of Chicago Press, 66–78.

Lazarsfeld, P. F. (1947) Some Remarks on the Role of Mass Media in So-called Tolerance Propaganda. *Journal of Social Issues*, 3 (3), 17–25.

Lazarsfeld, P. F. (1948a) Communication Research and the Social Psychologist. In W. Dennis (ed.), *Current Trends in Social Psychology*, Pittsburgh: University of Pittsburgh Press, 218–73.

Lazarsfeld, P. F. (1948b) Role of Criticism in the Management of Mass Communications. In W. Schramm (ed.), *Communications in Modern Society*, Urbana: University of Illinois Press, 186–203.

Lazarsfeld, P. F. (1948c) The Role of Criticism in the Management of Mass Media. *Journalism Quarterly*, 25, 115–26.

Lazarsfeld, P. F. (1949) Foreword to Joseph T. Klapper, *The Effects of Mass Media*, New York: Bureau of Applied Social Research, 1–9.

Lazarsfeld, P. F. (1961) Mass Culture Today. In N. Jacobs (ed.), *Culture for the Millions?*, Princeton: Van Nostrand, pp. ix–xxiii. Repr. in Lazarsfeld, 1972, pp. 139–54.

Lazarsfeld, P. F. (1969) An Episode in the History of Social Research: A Memoir. In D. Fleming and B. Bailyn (eds), *The Intellectual Migration: Europe and America, 1930–1960*, Cambridge, MA: Harvard University Press, 270–337.

Lazarsfeld, P. F. (1972) *Qualitative Analysis: Historical and Critical Essays*. Boston: Allyn and Bacon.

Lazarsfeld, P. F. (1975) Working with Merton. In L. A. Coser (ed.), *The Idea of Social Structure: Papers in Honor of Robert K. Merton*, New York: Harcourt Brace, 35–66.

Lazarsfeld, P. F. and Merton, R. K. (1943) Studies in Radio and Film Propaganda. *Transactions of the New York Academy of Sciences*, 6 (2), 58–79. Repr. in Merton, 1968, 563–82.

Lazarsfeld, P. F. and Merton, R. K. (1948) Mass Communication, Popular Taste, and Organized Social Action. In L. Bryson (ed.), *The Communication of Ideas*, New York: Harper, 95–118.

Lazarsfeld, P. F. and Stanton, F. N. (eds) (1949) *Communications Research, 1948–1949*. New York: Harper and Brothers.

Lazarsfeld, P. F., Berelson, B., and Gaudet, H. (1944) *The People's Choice: How the Voter Makes up his Mind in a Presidential Campaign*. New York: Columbia University Press.

Lippmann, W. (1922) *Public Opinion*. New York: Free Press.

Lowenthal, L. (1944) Biographies in Popular Magazines. In P. F. Lazarsfeld and F. N. Stanton (eds.), *Radio Research 1942–1943*, New York: Duell, Sloan, 507–48.

McCombs, M. and Shaw, D. (1972) The Agenda-Setting Function of Mass Media. *Public Opinion Quarterly*, 36, 176–85.

McCombs, M. and Shaw, D. (1993) The Evolution of Agenda-Setting Research: Twenty-Five Years in the Marketplace of Ideas. *Journal of Communication*, 43 (2), 58–67.

Merton, R. K. (1946) *Mass Persuasion: The Social Psychology of a War Bond Drive*. New York: Harper.

Merton, R. K. (1968 [1949]) *Social Theory and Social Structure*. Glencoe, IL: Free Press.

Merton, R. K. (1979) Remembering Paul Lazarsfeld. In R. K. Merton, J. S. Coleman, and P. H. Rossi (eds), *Qualitative and Quantitative Research: Papers in Honor of Paul F. Lazarsfeld*, New York: Free Press, 19–22.

Merton, R. K. (1996 [1994]) A Life of Learning. *American Council of Learned Societies Occasional Papers*, 25. Repr. in R. K. Merton, *On Social Structure and Science*, ed. P. Stompka, Chicago: University of Chicago Press, 1996, 339–59.

Merton, R. K. (1998) Working with Lazarsfeld: Notes and Contexts. In J. Lautman and B-P. Lecuyer (eds), *Paul Lazarsfeld (1901–1976): La sociologie de Vienne à New York*, Paris: L'Harmattan, 163–211.

Morrison, D. E. (1978) The Beginning of Modern Mass Communication Research. *European Journal of Sociology*, 29, 327–59.

Morrison, D. E. (1988) The Transference of Experience and the Impact of Ideas: Paul Lazarsfeld and Mass Communication Research. *Communication*, 10 (2), 185–210.

Morrison, D. E. (1998) *The Search for a Method: Focus Groups and the Development of Mass Communication Research*. Luton: University of Luton Press.

Neurath, P. M. (1979) The Writings of Paul F. Lazarsfeld: A Topical Bibliography. In R. K. Merton, J. S. Coleman, and P. H. Rossi (eds), *Qualitative and Quantitative Social Research: Papers in Honor of Paul F. Lazarsfeld*, New York: Free Press, 365–87.

Noelle-Neumann, E. (1984) *The Spiral of Silence: Public Opinion – Our Social Skin*. Chicago: University of Chicago Press.

Peters, J. D. (1993) Genealogical Notes on "the Field." *Journal of Communication*, 43 (4), 132–9.

Peters, J. D. (1999) *Speaking into the Air: A History of the Idea of Communication*. Chicago: University of Chicago Press.

Protess, D., et al. (1991) *The Journalism of Outrage: Investigative Reporting and Agenda Building in America*. New York: Guilford.

Putnam, R. D. (1995a) Bowling Alone: America's Declining Social Capital. *Journal of Democracy*, 6, 65–78.

Putnam, R. D. (1995b) Tuning In, Tuning Out: The Strange Disappearance of Social Capital in America. *PS: Political Science and Politics*, 28, 664–83.

Putnam, R. D. (2000) *Bowling Alone: The Collapse and Revival of American Community*. New York: Simon & Schuster.

Rogers, E. (1994) *A History of Communication Study: A Biographical Approach*. New York: Free Press.

Rosenberg, B. and White, D. M. (eds) (1957) *Mass Culture: The Popular Arts in America*. Glencoe, IL: Free Press.

Schramm, W. (ed.) (1948) *Communications in Modern Society*. Urbana: University of Illinois Press.

Schramm, W. (ed.) (1949) *Mass Communications*. Urbana: University of Illinois Press.

Selvin, H. (1975) On Formalising Theory. In L. Coser (ed.), *The Idea of Social Structure: Papers in Honor of Robert K. Merton*, New York: Harcourt Brace, 339–54.

Sills, D. (1996) Stanton, Lazarsfeld, and Merton – Pioneers in Communication Research. In E. Dennis and E. Wartella (eds), *American Communication Research: The Remembered History*, Mahwah, NJ: Lawrence Erlbaum, 105–16.

Simonson, P. (1996) Dreams of Democratic Togetherness: Communication Hope from Cooley to Katz. *Critical Studies in Mass Communication*, 13, 324–42.

Simonson, P. (1999) Mediated Sources of Public Confidence: Lazarsfeld and Merton Revisited. *Journal of Communication*, 49 (2), 109–22.

Simonson, P. (2000) Varieties of Pragmatism and Communication: Visions and Revisions from Peirce to Peters. In D. K. Perry (ed.), *Pragmatism and American Communication Research*, Mahwah, NJ: Lawrence Erlbaum, 1–26.

Simpson, C. (1994) *The Science of Coercion: Communication Research and Psychological Warfare, 1945–1960*. Oxford: Oxford University Press.

Waples, D. (ed.) (1942) *Print, Radio, and Film in a Democracy*. Chicago: University of Chicago Press.

2

Herzog's "On Borrowed Experience": Its Place in the Debate over the Active Audience

Tamar Liebes

Herzog misconceived?

In the tradition of uses and gratifications, Herta Herzog's study on listeners to daytime soaps on radio is regarded as a pioneer. "On Borrowed Experience" (1941) is an example of early research based on listening to listeners (that is, asking *them* to report on what they are getting out of media), one which attributes greater power to audiences than did earlier research. The question is whether Herzog's study is correctly remembered. Should it be considered a classic in the gratifications tradition? Does it contribute to the image of audiences as empowered consumers, aware of their needs, who make considered choices vis-à-vis both the media and their social environment (McQuail and Gurevitch, 1974)? I argue here that the story is more complex.

Gratifications research substitutes "active" receivers, who cannot be told by media what to think, what to believe, or how to behave (Katz, 1989), for the atomized, alienated audiences of mass society, easy prey for brainwashing by media campaigns. No longer victims of media, the receivers themselves are now at the wheel, making use of media as a social utility, a "tool kit from which to choose," and a resource to think with, according to their needs (Swidler, 1986). In this view, media audiences are self-aware consumers who use media in a goal-oriented manner and are selective "not only in defense of prior opinions and habits but also to satisfy needs, interests and strivings" (McQuail and Gurevitch, 1974).

Even today, Herzog's classic paper powerfully brings to life the authentic and vigorous voices of the soap fans she interviewed. Herzog does not adopt the perspective of her interviewees, however, but rather that of a distanced observer who psychoanalyzes their unconscious layers from a strictly predetermined Freudian perspective. Her analysis draws a picture of disempowered listeners driven by unconscious motives and "fulfilled" by false and harmful satisfactions. This image of the audience is a far cry from the gratificationists' active audiences, who supposedly control their radios, TV sets, and lives, and who are able to elaborate knowingly on what they are doing and why. Why, then, is Herzog typically viewed in the history of media research as a pioneer of the notion of "active audiences"? How is it that "On Borrowed Experience" has become classified as a gratifications study?

One reason for putting Herzog in with the gratificationists may be that her study is part of a shift away from mass communication studies that focused on the effects of short-run campaigns. The narrow focus on specific, directly "persuasive" messages of propaganda or advertising gave way to an interest in information, ideology, and entertainment. This move is exemplified by the Lazarsfeldian shift from the study of "hypodermic" effects to more subtle approaches to the relationship between media and audiences. Another possible reason is that, in focusing on soap operas, which are broadcast in daytime and addressed to women – mostly lower-middle and lower-class housewives – Herzog conferred status on what was then considered a marginal, lowly genre. This legitimized soap operas as worthy subjects of research, and they have since become the most studied genre after the news. The third, and perhaps most important, reason is Herzog's decision to conduct focus interviews with fans, rather than analyze the *content* of the serials. This is read as treating audiences with respect, analyzing the content from their own perspective, and thus seeing reception as "a free (and) meaningful act" (McQuail and Gurevitch, 1974).

This glorified image of "readers," however, does not emerge from Herzog's study. Far from being active audiences, Herzog's radio listeners come across as alienated, isolated, helpless victims of mass society, of the patriarchal system, and of the mass media, which operate as an effective tool in the service of both the society and the system. With the active assistance of their favorite soaps, Herzog's female audiences are enslaved in their kitchens, dependent on the texts as vicarious, self-repeating fantasies that serve as false, and ultimately harmful, substitutes for the misery of their real lives (Livingstone and Liebes, 1995). Thus, rather than serving as the foremother of gratifications research (McGuire, 1974; Katz et al., 1974; Elliot, 1974; Livingstone, 1998) – in particular that focusing on women's genres – Herzog's work may be better understood within the paradigm of the Frankfurt school, which condemns popular consumerist culture for providing false gratifications to disempowered individuals in mass society.

Some of the responsibility for the misreading of Herzog's essay as a gratifications study lies in the automatic identification of focus interviews with "active consumers" and of textual analysis with "powerful" effects. According to this logic, there is little point in interviewing audiences if they are simply victims of technological or ideological effects. Such audiences would, by definition, supply answers that reflect the manipulation of their very way of thinking or of perceiving reality. In other words, interviewing would produce only the false consciousness inflicted on them. But assigning content analysis to critical research and audiences to uses and gratifications is too simple. It is true that researchers who do in-depth or focus-group interviews with audiences are motivated by the belief that audiences are more critical, and less homogeneous, than hegemonists or pollsters make them out to be. They therefore aim to demonstrate the nuances and variety in people's talk, to bring out "authentic" voices enriched by genuine experience and folk wisdom – in short, to show that audiences are not just "dumb couch potatoes." Nevertheless, the researcher's approach (or hypothesis) still determines the choice of respondents, the degree of openness, the focus of questions, the method of interviewing, and the choice of examples to be highlighted.

Moreover, just as texts do not have to be treated as homogeneous and closed, but can be analyzed to show ambiguity and multiple voices, so talking to audiences does not necessarily mean regarding them as free agents, nor does it ensure an openness to, or sympathy for, their points of view. Receivers may also be addressed in ways that substantiate textual analysis. The question remains the theoretical perspective from which texts and receivers are selected and analyzed.

Why "On Borrowed Experience" may belong in the Frankfurt school

Reading Herzog's report makes it clear that her view of audiences is taken from the lofty perspective of the analyst's sofa, applying Frankfurt's macro-cultural analysis to the micro world of individuals. Although her (partly quantifiable) interviews with listeners technically go against

Adorno's lifelong opposition to the idea of empirical audience research, she manages to substantiate his critique of popular culture and its effects on consumers. The reason for Adorno's opposition to consumers as a primary source of sociological knowledge, as he argued in the case of popular music, was that their opinions could not be trusted (Morrison, 1998, p. 42). This, he claimed, was due to their incapacity to overcome conformity to cultural norms and, worse, to the psychological degeneration of their ability to judge. Consumerist culture had caused people to regress to an infantile state of passive dependency, making them docile and afraid of anything new. Thus, Adorno compares audiences to children who only like to eat what they have enjoyed in the past (Jay, 1973, p. 190). Social scientists should not expect such depoliticized and passive audiences, capable of responding only to repetitions of what they have heard before, to reflect freely on popular culture.

As consumers could not be reliable informants, Frankfurt scholars themselves analyzed various forms and contents of capitalist culture, to see how these worked to subvert individual psyches. Regarding popular culture as "psychoanalysis in reverse" (Lowenthal, in Jay, 1973, p. 173), they exposed the ways in which it unknowingly enslaved individuals by working on their subconscious. Expressions of popular culture – jazz, radio sketches, magazine biographies – were all analyzed in terms of the psychoanalytic mechanisms, such as fetishization and displaced wish fulfillment, that they implanted in the psyches of their consumers. Consumerist culture was condemned by showing how it played on human needs at unconscious levels, enslaving receivers to empty, repetitious pseudo-experience and robbing them of both their own folk culture and real art.

Herzog's analysis fits beautifully into the Frankfurt school tradition, complementing its picture of the ills that commodified culture inflicts on implied readers with examples of its effects on real readers. The return to the reader also closes the psychoanalytic circle by rediscovering the workings of the unconscious mechanisms in their original context of the individual psyche. Herzog's questions and her analysis of the answers are underpinned by strong hypotheses about human nature, consumerist culture, and the interaction between the two. Soap fans are treated on the couch, as it were, as subjects of psychoanalysis (which they unfortunately cannot profit from), a method she repeats in her 1980s study of *Dallas* and *Dynasty* viewers in Germany (Herzog-Massing, 1986). The texts produced by her interviewees are not regarded as expressions of rational, self-aware people. On the contrary, Herzog uses them to expose the interviewees as alienated women – lonely, self-pitying, subconsciously driven by emotional forces of which they are unaware. She sees their moral, often pious, presentation of self as a projection of various forms of pent-up aggression onto others to compensate for their own suffering. This aggression may be displaced onto characters in soaps, who become "scapegoats for aggressiveness," or onto people in the interviewees' environment, via the creation of "a union of sufferers" with the characters (sometimes demonstrating a deeply rooted racist bias). Either way, this is experienced by the interviewees as pleasure.

Formulaic texts – enslaving or liberating?

The major source of the pleasure of soaps is described in Herzog's main finding: "The listeners' reports on the content of their favorite stories boils down almost invariably to one stereotyped formula: 'getting into trouble and out again' " (p. 66). Three examples that will be discussed later – a town philosopher who "always is in trouble and out again," a newly married couple "who are going to have some kind of trouble . . . they will find a way out though," and a widowed mother who "will settle everything, [and] something will come up" – all underscore the common theme.

Its formulaic nature constitutes the core of the Frankfurt school's condemnation of mass culture, the key for explaining its hold on consumers' souls. According to Adorno, the formula operates as an end in itself, not as the means for intelligent appraisal. And "once [it is] successful, the industry reproduces it endlessly, making it operate like a social cement through distraction, displaced self-fulfillment, and intensification of passivity" (Jay, 1973). Herzog establishes at the outset of her essay that soap fans unknowingly supply clues for the notion that stereotypical formulae provide a safe anchor to hold on to. She then demonstrates how the narrative formula works on the unconscious of childishly dependent listeners, using the mechanisms prescribed by Adorno as guidelines for her analysis. Accordingly, she decides that formulae cultivate a fear of anything new, deaden listeners' ability to take risks, and reduce them to a docile state of regression that allows them to imagine they are living "exciting lives" while "relaxing" and "smoking a cigarette" (p. 76). (Erich Fromm's 1937 article, "The Feeling of Impotency," quoted in Jay, 1973, p. 190, describes a similar process.)

While the uses and gratifications paradigm provides an umbrella for various approaches that allocate more or less control, purpose, and activity to audiences, Herzog's view of her listeners is nevertheless a far cry from that of the type of research she is supposed to represent. A striking example is her placement, in McGuire's (1974) ambitious schema of the relationship between psychological motives and media gratifications, as a classic demonstration of utilitarian theories that regard people as cognitive beings – striving problem solvers who approach media texts as an opportunity to acquire useful information or new skills for coping with life's challenges.

Herzog, Radway, Ang: a matrilineal line?

Evaluating Herzog more than half a century later places her first in a line of women scholars who study feminine genres from a feminist perspective – that is, for their potential for social change. But evaluating the potential of consuming melodrama and romance to improve women's lives depends on the extent to which the researchers adopt the "reader's" perspective. In other words, where does the voice of the interviewee leave off and the voice of the researcher take over? Difficult to pinpoint, there is a hidden stage in any interpretive study based on readers' talk – the skipping of a step between the words that have been said and transcribed and the researcher's commentary. Should readers' words be taken at face value or decoded for their unconscious intentions? Is the speaker expected to be aware of all the meanings implied in what she is saying, or may the researcher unravel and elaborate on an intuition in order to bring out and explicate the full cognitive and/or emotional force behind it? In other words, how does the interaction between prior assumptions and audiences' talk play out in the evaluation of receivers as "active?"

The ways in which researchers make these decisions, whether or not they are aware of the problematics of what they have decided to do, make it possible to distinguish among different theoretical approaches. I propose to examine Herzog's interpretive strategy in hindsight by comparing it with those of two distinguished scholars, Janice Radway and Ien Ang, who followed in her steps a generation later. I have chosen these two for continuing her line of research into popular women's genres (thereby endowing these lowly genres with status), for their methodological choice of letting the readers speak for themselves, and for going beyond Herzog in showing how women's involvement in romance and soaps is potentially (Radway) or actually (Ang) empowering.

Formula as safe house: Janice Radway

As I have already argued, Herzog – at least in the piece under consideration – does not qualify as a gratificationist. I further contend that neither does Radway, though she too has been adopted into the gratifications canon. Herzog's choice to highlight the formula ("in and out of trouble") and ignore the variety of plotlines is based on the assumption that the formula leads to passivity and dependence, no matter what the content. In her study of romance readers 40 years later, Radway (1985) expresses a similar concern over their habit of ascertaining in advance that the book they buy has a happy ending. Radway sees this as suggesting an incapacity to bear "the threat of the unknown as it opens up before them," causing them to "demand continual reassurance that the events they suspect will happen" (Radway, 1985, p. 106).

Another theme that puzzles Radway is the claim of romance lovers that they cannot describe the "typical" characters of the romance because they are all different. Ironically, in expressing her disappointment over her readers' failure to recognize the common stereotypical element in all the stories, Radway herself acknowledges that from the reader's point of view it is the individual variations, not the formulas, that count. As an aside, it should be noted that the lack of consistency between listeners' acknowledgment and approval of a formula and their intense interest in different individual characters fits Susan Douglas's (2001) analysis of Herzog's interpretation of a quiz show, in which she argues that Herzog "revels in [bringing out the] contradictory relationships to radio" and finds Herzog "decades ahead of her time in anticipating how poststructuralism, feminism would inform media criticism."

Despite her acknowledgment of the potentially redeeming features of the romance, Radway, like Herzog, comes from a strong ideological position. When all is said and done, both Herzog's Frankfurt-style critique of mass society and Radway's feminism regard the formulae of feminine genres as instruments of women's enslavement. The pleasures they provide are seen as symptomatic of fundamental ills in the lives of consumers, pleasures that would not be needed if their (real) lives could be put on track.

Formula as liberation: Ien Ang

Not all literary analysts regard the formula as an evil source of audience pleasure. As Eco (1985) points out, formulaic plots are not exclusive to popular culture. Moreover, the audience's involvement in such plots does not necessarily signal inactivity, but may rather result from the relaxation that the formula provides, giving viewers the luxury of concentrating on how the story evolves (Thorburn, 1982). The knowledge that there are no surprises in the general story line and that there is no point in waiting for a happy ending frees fans to enjoy the nuances of the process. They can concentrate on the details of expression and look, indulge in the variations of expected behavior, and notice deviations from the idiosyncratic behavior of familiar characters (Eco, 1985).

Ien Ang (1985) offers a more positive interpretation than either Herzog or Radway of the pleasures of the "getting in and out of trouble" formula. Though Ang actually distances herself from gratificationism, she comes closer than either Herzog or Radway to accepting her viewers as partners in the analysis of popular fiction. She claims that Radway's disappointment in her readers misses the point that, for them, it is not the repetitive formula but the texture and context of a particular story that count. In her critique of Radway, Ang proposes that the readers' insistence on learning about a happy ending in advance may, in fact, be a clever reading strategy to ensure maximum pleasure from the *scenario* of romance – in particular, the *process* of seduction.

In another interpretation of the pleasure of "getting in and out of trouble," Ang analyzes a statement similar to the ones recorded by Herzog: "It's nice to get dizzy on their problems. And you know all along that everything will turn out all right in the end" (p. 67). For Ang, the words of this fan suggest that the formula plays a major role in escaping into a fantasy world, not as denial of reality, but as "a game that enables one to place the limits of the fictional and the real under discussion, to make them fluid. And in that game an imaginary participation in the fictional world is experienced as pleasurable" (Ang, 1985, p. 45). Thus, Ang attempts to understand the viewing (listening, reading) experience from the fan's point of view, rather than worrying about its effects on her "real" life.

In short, prioritizing the common formula over individual variations in readers' readings is an ideological choice on the part of the analyst. Each of the listeners' quotes presented by Herzog and Radway may also be seen as providing "thick descriptions" of a particular story, with its own texture, setup, and loved characters. The "town philosopher who solves everyone's problems, even his enemies'" is not to be confused with "the young man who marries the boss's daughter" and moves with her to "a beautiful estate house on Long Island." The human variations on "getting in and out of trouble" are endlessly rich, and involve numerous aspects of people's lives.

Vicarious pleasures: projecting aggression or escaping into "emotionally real" fantasy?

Since the choice of a psychoanalytic framework means that any answer is translated (decoded) according to the Freudian code, Herzog's listeners' enjoyment is read as compensation for their own misery through aggressiveness against others. As an example, one listener's answer to "Why watch?" is, "If I am gloomy it makes me feel better to know that other people have hardships too. They are so smart and still have to suffer." This example highlights a major problem in the interpretation of audience responses, however: the inevitable skipping of a step that occurs between the respondent's spoken or written words and the researcher's interpretation. Every interpretation assumes, more or less rigidly, a theory of reception – in the best cases modified and improved on by the encounter with "real" audiences – according to which readers' words can evoke but never "prove." For Herzog, this listener's statement demonstrates that "most frequently listeners enjoy the troubles of other people as a means to compensate for their own," all the more so when these people "are supposedly 'smarter' than they are" (p. 73). But "displaced aggression" is not the only way to interpret the listener's statement; nor is it necessarily an accurate reflection of what she is consciously saying.

Notwithstanding the similarity with Herzog's listeners (remarkably – "There is always a surprise coming up. Happy or sad – love it"), Ang has a different view of the pleasure derived from soaps. Starting with the identical formula, she argues that the serials are "true to life" in the sense that life is a "question of falling down and getting up again" (p. 72), that human life, anybody's, is always moving between success and tragedy and evokes a tragic structure of feeling which comes with the recognition of the precariousness and vulnerability which characterize the endless fluctuation between happiness and unhappiness, in which happiness cannot last forever. Note, for example, the central quote Ang uses, from letters of *Dallas*' fans, to support her theory about the source of pleasure supplied by soaps:

> Now I'll tell you why I like watching Dallas. Here goes! 1. There is suspense in it. 2. It can also be romantic. 3. There is sadness in it. 4. And fear. 5. And happiness. In short, there is simply everything in that film. (Letter 16, p. 16)

Ang's theory has a certain freshness over the (by now) clichéd Freudian idea of displacement. But is it really rooted in the viewers' words? In both Herzog's and Ang's cases it is clear that meaning must be extracted and made explicit from the soap fans' words. Ang's interpretation attempts to adopt the perspective of the viewer/writer by creating a "meta"-generalization that groups the various elements of the responses under a coherent umbrella of melodramatic emotional identification (Ang, 1996). Whereas Ang relates directly to the *surface* of her respondents' words and tries to formalize the "naïve" feelings expressed, however, Herzog *interprets* their words, turning their meaning upside-down (or, rather, inside-out) to show how humans are driven by unconscious motives. For Herzog, the pleasure of viewing soaps is a sickness that can be cured, once brought to consciousness; whereas for Ang the pleasure taken from fantasy is based on a true emotional insight, can never be fulfilled in real life, and should not be taken away from consumers. For Ang, the receivers derive their pleasure not as the result of a damaged psychological makeup but from a recognition that the densely packed web of never-ending plots expresses something emotionally real about life. Thus, Ang's interpretation is fundamentally different from Herzog's. She does not see her informants as unaware of the meaning of what they are saying, but simply as unable to put it into the appropriate (abstract?) words.

Strategies for interpreting viewers' motives: psychoanalytic, utilitarian, literary

In direct contradiction to gratifications theorists, who stress the idea of media use as a rational, goal-oriented activity, the psychoanalytic paradigm discards goal-directed explanations for listening and tries to prove them false. Listeners' answers to the general question, "Why do you listen to the sketches?" often show a desire for advice: "Because the people in them are so brave about their own troubles . . . they teach you to be good," or "to learn to be still more helpful." This type of answer is the stuff that gratifications research is looking for; in this case it shows how the genre is used to obtain advice for real life. But Herzog rejects this kind of answer, claiming that it is merely a normative response for the sake of social desirability. By juxtaposing it with an answer to a more specific question, "Which episode did you like best?," Herzog shows how a question not hampered by such desirability, and thus less guarded or self-conscious, reveals a truth: "I liked it best when they were so happy before the husband got murdered, and so sad afterwards" (p. 75). By demonstrating that the listener's aspiration to learn how to be good contradicts her preference for "the episode which dealt with a catastrophe suffered by the heroine," and by favoring the latter response, Herzog can discard the answer of "advice" for the one expressing joy over someone's downfall. But a less rigid framework could give equal status to both answers and/or interpret the second one differently.

Another example, taken from an interview with a widow who brings up her children alone, is analyzed as "compensating for her resented fate by wishing a slightly worse one upon her favorite radio character." The words that give her away are the following:

> I like *Hilltop*. The woman there is always doing things for children. . . . I wonder whether she will ever get married. Perhaps it isn't right for her to do it and give up the orphanage. She is doing such a wonderful thing. I really don't think she should get married. (p. 73)

"In return for the death of her own husband," explains Herzog, "she wants the heroine to have no husband at all" (p. 73). Alternative interpretations are plentiful, however. At the psychological level, by identifying with the heroine, the listener may be experiencing anxiety over the fate of her own children who would become orphans if anything happened to her, or reflecting on their lot if she married a man who rejected them. A more literary interpretation may find this kind of talk the type of pleasure derived from endless speculation about the future of characters, closely connected to the soap's narrative structure, based as it is on a never-ending middle, which cannot give the assurance of a happy ending but plays on the tragic knowledge of the holding-off of a satisfactory end (Ang, 1996).

Crying: is there a price to pay?

For Herzog, the emotional release provided by soaps is displaced pleasure, which is highly paid for later. For Radway, it is ideologically functional in the long run. For Ang, the pleasure of soaps lies in the realm of melodramatic fantasy, which is autonomous, separate from reality, and therefore never experienced in reality. (See also Liebes and Katz, 1992, which points to the pleasure of fantasy in interactive social games.) Thus, while both Herzog and Ang start from the easy crying evoked by soaps, they conceptualize it very differently. One Herzog fan says: "You can go crazy just sitting and thinking, thinking. Sometimes the stories get me and I cry. I think I am a fool but it makes me feel better" (p. 70).

For Herzog this emotional release is only a temporary cure for anxiety. It gives the listener "a right to cry" and does not demand a reason. But a vicarious experience is poor compensation for "real" experience. It does not answer real needs, and is a poor substitute for real experience. According to Herzog, the catharsis offered by soaps may exact a heavy price by intensifying the listeners' frustration in the long run and destroying their capacity to have real emotional experiences outside of the stories. By contrast, Ang sees their crying as one of two key aspects of melodramatic identification. For her, it expresses sentimental, melancholic feelings of masochism and powerlessness, which are aroused by the women's recognition of outside powers that prevent them from ever getting everything under control. It is the realization that identity is not a real and conscious choice, but rather acquires its shape under circumstances not of one's own making.

Reformulating the argument in this chapter, I now propose that my effort to place Herzog within the critical rather than the empirical, positivistic, or administrative research paradigms may miss the point. It may be more accurate to adopt Peters's (1993) perspective on Lazarsfeld's and Adorno's communication studies of the 1940s, which sees them as drawing on a common heritage that later gets developed in different ways.

In a similar vein, Simonson and Weimann's analysis of Lazarsfeld's and Merton's classic article, "Mass Communication, Popular Taste, and Organized Social Action" (chapter 1), concludes that reifying two-dimensional portraits of dominant paradigms blinds us to important dimensions in Lazarsfeld's research. Far from arguing for "limited effects," Lazarsfeld's and Merton's article ascribes major effects to media in maintaining and reinforcing social and cultural structures. It is worth noting, however, that neither Lazarsfeld nor Adorno viewed soap operas very favorably. Though Lazarsfeld and Merton are more cautious than Adorno about possible effects, they are nevertheless critical of the "seeming decline of popular taste" and point the finger directly at soap fans, declaring "there is no doubt that women who are daily entranced for three or four hours by some twelve consecutive soap operas, all cut to the same dismal pattern, exhibit an appalling lack of esthetic judgment" (Lazarsfeld and Merton, 1957, p. 27).

Soap fans: Herzog's second project

A close look at "On Borrowed Experience" cannot be complete without a mention of the much less noticed, surprisingly different, second stage of Herzog's research on soap listeners. Her essay entitled "What do we Really Know about Daytime Serial Listeners?" (1944) is based on a nationwide survey using closed questions formally designed to address five hypotheses. Analyzing her sample as a comparison between listeners and non-listeners, Herzog sets out to prove that soap fans are more isolated, less intellectual, more interested in personal problems, and more frustrated and anxious than the control group. It is curious, to put it mildly, that while Herzog's expectations are clearly derived from the insights gained from her earlier study, the first study is not even mentioned until the end of the later paper.

A possible explanation for this omission may have to do with the results of the second study, in which almost all the insights gained from the interviews that form the basis of "On Borrowed Experience" fail to be confirmed when applied to a nationwide sample. Soap opera listeners prove to be no more isolated socially or less sound psychologically (i.e. more anxious) than non-listeners. Though less educated formally, they do not differ from the latter in the amount of their reading, their interest in news, or their intention to vote – only in actually going out to vote. Finally, at the very end of the paper Herzog appends a short summary of her first paper, in a framework of bringing in other sources to gain a more "complex" understanding of "the gratifications that women derive from daytime series" (1944, p. 23). But she does not explicitly address the obvious contradictions between the conclusions of the first and second studies.

One way to explain the lack of explicit continuity between the two studies may be that the insights of the first were supposed to provide the basis for the second, but that they were not presented as such once the more positivistic quantitative method of the latter failed to deliver the goods. One wonders whether Herzog was aware of Katz's and Lazarsfeld's Decatur study several years later, which vindicated her original expectations. Dealing yet another blow to the stereotypical images of critical scholars versus gratificationists, Katz and Lazarsfeld (1955, pp. 377–80) found that women of lower socio-economic status, lower levels of gregariousness, and higher levels of anxiety were likely to have been more exposed to popular fiction, including daytime series.

It is ironic that Herzog's methods and her image of her respondents work against each other. Her qualitative interviews, which fit with later feminist approaches, conclude with "closed" deterministic interpretations, which rob her interviewees of the (false) status they were granted. In the later article, quantitative methods end up, at least by default, restoring to soap listeners their lost status. Their assumed inferiority could not be proved. But since the content of the hypotheses could not be convincingly supported, the findings were framed simply as "no findings," rather than as a basis for a potentially more "positive" findings about the listeners.

One conclusion from the comparison between Herzog's two articles relates to the question of the kind of text that stays in the collective memory. The answer is: the text which invokes some insights that resonate with readers. In Herzog's case, the voice that later readers of her essay heard was ultimately that of the subjects, not of the interpreter.

Given the chance to express themselves, Herzog's interviewees were heard louder by posterity than Herzog herself. In the long run, her choice of method proved to be more meaningful than her analysis. This may explain why the conclusions of the two articles have been reversed in the collective memory of the field, and why one sank into oblivion while the other achieved canonization. Whereas the later paper was merely a survey, "On Borrowed Experience" seemed to be an original privileging of ethnocriticism.

References

Adorno, T. W. (1941) On Popular Music. *Studies in Philosophy and Social Science*, 11 (1), 17–48.

Adorno, T. W. (1969) Scientific Experiences of a European Scholar in America. Quoted in D. Morrison (1998): *The Search for a Method: Focus Groups and the Development of Mass Communication Research*. Luton: University of Luton Press, 42.

Ang, I. (1985) *Watching Dallas*. London and New York: Methuen.

Ang, I. (1996) Melodramatic Identification: Television Fiction and Women's Fantasy. In *Livingroom Wars: Rethinking Media Audiences for a Postmodern World*, London: Routledge, 85–97.

Douglas, S. J. (2001) The Birth of Audience Research in the 1930s: A Reconsideration. Lecture given at the annual meeting of the International Communication Association, Washington, June.

Eco, U. (1985) Innovation and Repetition: Between Modern and Post Modern Aesthetics. *Daedalus*, 74 (4), 161–84.

Elliot, P. (1974) Uses and Gratifications Research: A Critique and a Sociological Alternative. In J. G. Blumler and E. Katz (eds), *The Uses of Mass Communication*, Beverley Hills and London: Sage, 249–68.

Fromm, E. (1937) Zum Gefuhl der Ohnmacht, *Z/S* VI. Quoted in M. Jay (1973): *The Dialectical Imagination*. London: Heinemann, 190.

Herzog, H. (1941) On Borrowed Experience. *Studies in Philosophy and Social Science*, 11 (1), 65–95.

Herzog, Herta (1944) What do we Really Know about Daytime Serial Listeners? In P. F. Lazarsfeld and F. N. Stanton (eds), *Radio Research 1942–43*, New York: Duell, Pearce and Sloan, 3–33.

Herzog-Massing, H. (1986) Decoding Dallas. *Society*, 24 (1), 74–7.

Jay, M. (1973) *The Dialectical Imagination: A History of the Frankfurt School and the Institute of Social Research 1923–1950*. London: Heinemann.

Katz, E. (1989) Mass Media Effects. In G. Gerbner (ed.), *International Encyclopedia of Communication*, vol. 2, New York: Oxford University Press, 492–7.

Katz, E. and Lazarsfeld, P. (1955) *Personal Influence: The Part Played by People in the Flow of Mass Communication*. Glencoe, IL: Free Press.

Katz, E., Blumler, J. G. and Gurevitch, M. (1974) Utilization of Mass Communication by the Individual. In J. G. Blumler and E. Katz (eds), *The Uses of Mass Communication*, Beverly Hills and London: Sage, 1–16.

Lazarsfeld, P. and Merton, R. K. (1957) Mass Communication, Popular Taste and Organized Social Action. In D. Rosenberg and D. M. White (eds), *Mass Culture: The Popular Art in America*, New York: Free Press, 24–42.

Liebes, T. and Katz, E. (1992) *The Export of Meaning: Cross-Cultural Reading of "Dallas."* Cambridge: Polity.

Livingstone, S. M. (1998) *Making Sense of Television: The Psychology of Audience Interpretation*. London: Routledge.

Livingstone, S. and Liebes, T. (1995) Where have all the Mothers Gone? Soap Opera's Replaying of the Oedipal Story. *Critical Studies in Mass Communication*, 12 (2), 155–75.

Lowenthal, L. Quoted in M. Jay (1973): *The Dialectical Imagination: A History of the Frankfurt School and the Institute of Social Research 1923–1950*. London: Heinemann.

McGuire, W. J. (1974) Psychological Motives and Communication Gratifications. In J. Blumler and E. Katz (eds), *The Uses of Mass Communications*, Beverly Hills, CA, and London: Sage, 167–98.

McQuail, D. and Gurevitch, M. (1974) Explaining Audience Behavior: Three Approaches Considered. In J. Blumler and E. Katz (eds), *The Uses of Mass Communication*, Beverly Hills, CA, and London: Sage, 287–302.

Morrison, D. E. (1998) *The Search for a Method: Focus Groups and the Development of Mass Communication Research*. Luton: University of Luton Press.

Peters, J. D. (1993) Genealogical Notes on "The Field." *Journal of Communication*, 43 (4), 132–9. Repr. in M. Levy and M. Gurevitch (eds), *Defining Media Studies*, New York: Oxford University Press, 1994, 374–81.

Radway, J. (1985) *Reading the Romance: Women, Patriarchy and Popular Culture*. Chapel Hill: University of North Carolina Press.

Swidler, A. (1986) Culture in Action: Symbols and Strategies. *American Sociological Review*, 51 (14), 273–86.

Thorburn, D. (1982) Television Melodrama. In H. Newcomb (ed.), *Television: The Critical View*, New York: Oxford University Press, 529–46.

PART II
The Frankfurt School

———

Introduction

In their writings on the mass media, the Frankfurt school – that famous group of philosophers, sociologists, psychoanalysts, and literary theorists who found refuge in the United States during World War II – turned Marxist theory on its head. Rejecting the idea of popular culture as a mere reflection of the economic base of society, they conceived of American culture as an industry with an assembly line for the manufacture of messages of false consciousness.

For Horkheimer and Adorno, the school's two leaders, the escapist elements of mass culture were designed to deflect criticism from hegemonic power by distributing small pleasures along with the assurance that ours is the best of all possible worlds. Their suspicion of the media was such that they branded programs that mixed popular with classical music ("Benny Goodman and the Budapest String Quartet") as conspiratorial efforts to tempt the working classes to abandon their own culture and identity – that is, their solidarity – on the altar of national togetherness.

Critical theorists of the Frankfurt school developed a program of scholarship aimed at removing the disguise from this exploitation. They attacked the Columbia School for its servility to the culture industry. Lazarsfeld replied that his group of "administrative researchers" was indeed helping the broadcasters to improve broadcasting for the public good. But he granted equal legitimacy to the "critical theorists" of the Frankfurt school, who preferred to theorize the broadcasters – owners and managers – as part of the problem, rather than allow the broadcasters themselves to pose the problem.

While all members of the school contrasted the truth of high art with the political abuse of popular culture, Walter Benjamin spelled out the functions, as well as the dysfunctions, of popularization. Mechanical reproduction, he agreed, undermined the "aura" of the original, and the pilgrimage to the Louvre, for example, was superseded by mass circulation of its art. But Benjamin saw equality emerging from the possibility of bringing the center to the periphery, and heralded the cinema as the art without an original, and hence the art without privilege.

Leo Lowenthal read the weekly biographies in *Colliers* and the *Saturday Evening Post* as traffic signals devised by the media to help regulate the manpower market. When the system wished to encourage upward mobility, the biographies provided recipes for moving in the footsteps of the "idols of production," and when the system wished to discourage mobility, the biographies featured stars of sports and entertainment. Horkheimer and Adorno also pointed to the element of luck implicit in the "idols of consumption" who, like lottery winners, serve as a sop that is thrown to the deprived. Eva Illouz regrets this seeming preference for the mobility ladder of production over the post-modern pleasures afforded by the changing rooms of consumption. Regardless of preferences, we would add that the point of Lowenthal's study is to show how the media serve as spokesmen for the system.

Over the four decades of their activity, the Frankfurt School imbued an impressive array of followers with their suspicious attitude towards the culture industry and their pessimism over the prospect of diffusing enlightenment. Only their third-generation scion, Jürgen Habermas, caught a glimpse of the functional, rather than dysfunctional, potential of the media as an agent of the "public sphere."

3

The Subtlety of Horkheimer and Adorno: Reading "The Culture Industry"

John Durham Peters

"The Culture Industry: Enlightenment as Mass Deception," a chapter in Max Horkheimer's and Theodor W. Adorno's *Dialectic of Enlightenment*, represents a position hailed, vilified, and misunderstood. To write a history of the reception of these 50-odd pages would be, in a sense, to write the history of critical media studies. The social fact of industrialized culture can be productively read as the core problem of the field in the last half-century, even among those who are removed from German critical theory, such as those in British cultural studies (Liu, 1999). The chapter's preoccupations remain very much alive today: What are the cultural and political consequences of concentrated corporate power in media and cultural production? What and how do media audiences read? What is the value of the canon of high art (Cook, 1995)? Few texts provoke such strong passions as this one. It raises hackles instantly. What righteous scholar wants to risk being considered a snob or an elitist? What left-leaning intellectual wants to doubt the wisdom of the people? This text, for many readers, seems to promote precisely those attitudes academics are most nervous about professing in public (although many, discussing their undergraduate students privately, can sound even bleaker than the Frankfurters).

Canonization does not always mean beatification; it can also mean demonization. Such is the case with this text, especially in the more populist circles of 1980s' cultural studies, which, finding its view of popular capacities unremittingly gloomy, consigned it to outer darkness.

"The Frankfurt School," says John Fiske, "have no room in their scenario for resistant or evasive practices." Marxist theory, he continues, neglects "the idea that popular pleasure must necessarily contain traces of resistance" (1989, p. 183). This claim, unfortunately, does not fit Marxist theory very well: certainly not Gramsci, even less the heretical strain of Marxism in Germany from Bertolt Brecht and Walter Benjamin through Enzensberger and Negt and Kluge, whose hallmark is an insistence on the emancipatory potentials of popular art, the value of feelings, and the call to turn audiences into authors. Even Horkheimer and Adorno do not fit. Fiske is right to note a certain puritanical strain in Marxism, but he overlooks the fact that the Frankfurt school was one of its sharpest critics. Populism, to be sure, is not even a trace element in the critical theory of the Frankfurt school (compared with the Brechtian tradition or British cultural studies). In terms of the fundamental triad of media studies – industry, text, audience – Horkheimer and Adorno make their greatest and most lasting contributions in industrial and textual analysis. Their understanding of economy and culture is subtler than that of society (audiences). Even so, some aspects of their argument complicate their reputation for misanthropy, and even anticipate current wisdom about audiences.

"The Culture Industry" is a remarkably subtle text within an even more subtle body of thought. It is curious that writing so dialectical and difficult should consistently be read as simple or totalizing. Experimental, elliptical, the chapter evokes for many a monochrome image of zombified masses presided over by an unholy alliance of Hitler and Hollywood. To be sure, this picture is not groundless, but the detailed arguments are far more nuanced and contradictory. The chapter offers both a critique of a dystopian world suffocatingly controlled by instrumental reason *and* a utopian gambit to redeem the promise of happiness teasingly and incessantly offered by mass culture. "The Culture Industry" offers a package deal: both a critique of domination and a quest, hoping against hope, for freedom.

It is this double project that is highly suggestive for media studies today. Horkheimer and Adorno do not countenance the false, and by now tired, dichotomy of either audience resistance or industrial manipulation. Before the fact, they blend the best of political economy (analytic tools for exposing concentrated power) and cultural studies (appreciation for the protest hidden in small gestures). "The Culture Industry" settles the debate between these wings of media analysis, decades before it happened, with a resounding: Both! Ironically, thinkers who reject the Frankfurt school for its dour view of human agency in order to celebrate the emancipatory potentials of popular culture unwittingly walk in paths they fancy they are rejecting, reinventing the utopian half of the Frankfurt analysis without its necessarily sober counterweight. The pleasure principle needs the reality principle; in contrast to many of their critics, Horkheimer and Adorno possess both.

Barriers to understanding

Two major barriers impede understanding of "The Culture Industry." The first is its odd composition. *Dialektik der Aufklärung* (hereinafter *DA*) was originally meant to be a full statement of the theoretical position shared by Horkheimer and Adorno, to be the *summa* of Frankfurt critical theory. Large portions seem to derive from notes taken by Gretel Karplus Adorno, Adorno's wife, during discussions in the early 1940s between the two men in their exile in Santa Monica, California (sometimes called "Weimar on the Pacific" because of its substantial German intellectual refugee population). As the definitive statement of critical theory, the book is obviously abortive, as the authors acknowledge and its curious structure attests. It consists of a preface, an opening chapter followed by two chapter-length "excursi," two more chapters, and, at the end, fifty pages of notes and drafts. Its odd organization almost seems to shout "incomplete," as did its initial title. It was first circulated in 500 copies as a typescript by the Institute for Social Research in 1944, under the title *Philosophische Fragmente* (philosophical fragments). It was then published in Amsterdam as *Dialektik der Aufklärung* in 1947, and after a long life in pirate versions, was republished in Germany in 1969. *DA* was finally translated into English in 1972, the same year that translated Adorno texts were circulated at the Birmingham Center for Contemporary Cultural Studies (Liu, 1999, p. 126). The culture industry chapter, abridged, was first published in an English-language media studies context in 1977 (Curran et al., 1977, pp. 312–13). The accompanying editorial note, though perhaps overemphasizing its elitism, sensitively captures the complexities of the argument, a sensitivity that would fade in general opinion as the Frankfurters became anti-populist villains in the 1980s (for critiques see, e.g., Collins, 1989; Thompson, 1990). The text has had little more than three decades of life in English-language scholarship, though it is twice that old.

As a self-proclaimed set of fragments, *DA* does not renounce its theoretical ambition; it signals its genre. The fragment is a standard mode in German philosophy and literature, dating at least to the late eighteenth century; it was practiced by such diverse favorites of critical theory as Marx, Nietzsche, and Benjamin. Horkheimer's and Adorno's fragments announce not the failure of their project, but rather its experimental character. Readers are invited to take the book as something to think with or against, not as a final vision of the world. Indeed, a first principle of critical theory is that thought is always historical and therefore provisional (p. ix/9).[1] "The Culture Industry" is a fragment within a fragment. The authors confess that the chapter is even "more fragmentary" (p. xvi/17) than any other part of the book, a stunning admission in light of the book's collection of notes and drafts. To use the clichés that ritually open academic presentations, the chapter truly is "part of a larger project" and a "work in progress."

DA is not only a fragment, but a composite. "The vital principle of the *Dialectic*," its authors say, "is the tension between the two intellectual temperaments conjoined in it" (p. ix/9). Adorno the aesthetician and Horkheimer the philosopher of critical social science (to put each in an inadequate box) pool their forces on every page, moving back and forth easily, dizzily, between love and industrialism, taboo and rationalization, culture and structure. DA consistently moves across both the sensuous experience of the individual and the world-historical development of science, technology, and political economy. The wedding of micro-feeling and macro-structure is a hallmark of critical theory.

The second barrier to understanding is cross-cultural. DA is extraordinarily wide-ranging, erudite in its leaps from one high-cultural topos to another to explain historical and contemporary conditions, and it presumes nothing less than an encyclopedic knowledge of European cultural and intellectual history. As Jameson (1990, p. 139) suggests, "The Culture Industry" is an installment of a well-known literary genre: the travelogue by literate Europeans bedazzled by American mores, such as Tocqueville, Dickens, Wilde, Gorky, and, more recently, Martin Walser and Martin Amis. Horkheimer and Adorno are often more than a little appalled at what they find in 1940s Los Angeles. It doesn't take much trolling through Adorno's prose to find howlers about American life: some critics will never forgive certain comments about jazz or jitterbugs. In turn, Anglo-American readers unacquainted with dialectical styles of argument can also be appalled: expecting reasonable exposition, they find seemingly know-it-all generalizations about society or history interspersed with goofily specific remarks about Donald Duck or Victor Mature. One of the intriguing and maddening things about reading DA is not knowing which statements are dialectical gambits meant to be unseated by what is coming next. DA is, in its way, a modernist text like *Ulysses* or *The Waste Land*, a chorus of voices, some of which are meant to be self-evidently absurd, others to be volleys of truth. One is never sure which sentence is wearing invisible quotation marks, self-evidently undoing itself – or establishing its truth – by its own extremity. Adorno's famous dictum counts for *DA*: "In Freud the only true statements are the exaggerations" (Adorno, 1974, p. 49).

A key to "The Culture Industry," as to *DA* generally, is the dialectical *modus operandi*. Over and over again our authors expose shotgun weddings between the real and the ideal. Suburban sprawl? "The false identity of the universal and the particular" (121/141). Style, spontaneity, amusement are likewise false summits, premature reconciliations. Horkheimer and Adorno are Hegelian Marxists in their relentless *exposé* of the fake totalities, which prevent people from attaining the only genuine totality: a just society. They respect facts as the concentrated deposit of social experience, but refuse to limit their thinking to things as they are. Such a failure of imagination is precisely what *DA* derides as "positivism," which does not mean simply a philosophy of science, but a more encompassing mode of concession to what it is that denies freedom. Imagination and enlightenment demand the right to be disloyal to reality in its present form. "Thinking is, indeed, essentially the negation of that which is immediately before us," as Frankfurt theorist Herbert Marcuse (1940, p. vii) quotes Hegel. The point is not that Horkheimer and Adorno are not responsible to truth, but rather that reading them requires an adjustment of sensibility. In dialectical thinking, a doctrine can be (and usually is) true and false at the same time – enough to make a commonsensical English-speaking reader's head swim.

The argument of the book

DA defies summation. Broadly, it is a philosophical history of domination, an archaeological dig through layers of civilization in a quest to understand what led to the disaster of the modern world. For Horkheimer and Adorno, Nazism was not an exception, but the consummation of logics already apparent elsewhere. The book's central question is how the original goal of human emancipation via enlightenment turned into "disaster triumphant" (3/19). The Enlightenment at first sought to disenchant the world – that is, to replace nature as an abode of unpredictable gods and demons with a rational universe governed by causal relationships. But what started as an effort to cast off the spell of inhuman powers embodied in myth turned into a suppression not only of parts of human nature, but also of people taken as either particularly enmeshed in nature (women) or opposed to it (Jews). The domination of nature went together with repression in the self and oppression of the other (showing the authors' characteristic pairing of psychological and sociological analysis). Some might find *DA*'s analysis too rarefied a way to go about explaining murder and hatred, but it remains one of the great statements confronting the mid-twentieth-century calamity.

One famous episode in *DA* clarifies the overall argument and also provides a critical context for the culture industry analysis: an original and idiosyncratic reading of Homer's *Odyssey*, especially the episode with the Sirens. Odysseus, in *DA* the prototype of the bourgeois man, ties himself to the mast of his ship in order to hear the song without ruin, while the oarsmen in the belly of the ship row away with wax plugging their ears. The song of the Sirens is the dangerous allure of primeval nature, a lure to return to the womb. All who heed it crash their ships on the rocks. *DA* thus offers a parable of class domination as well as of the self-sacrificial ego: the master suppresses his own passions; the slaves lack even that option and must dumbly toil. Inner and outer domination go together. Whatever its relevance for Homer (slight), this episode gathers the key themes of *DA*. The ego, like enlightenment itself, is bought at a price: the renunciation of primal unity with nature. High art (for that is what the Siren song has become) is riven with class division: Odysseus listening to the Sirens is basically "attending a concert" (34*/51) like a good bourgeois tied up in his coat and tails, while the toiling proles are not admitted to the hall. Art is separated from practice, specifically from life and death, and neutralized into an unanchored illusive beauty (*Schein*). Hence, contrary to rumor, *DA* regards high art not as salvation, but as both a distorting mirror of an unjust society and a cryptic text disclosing utopian tracings of a better world. The very fact that art is separate from life is both its scar and its strength today.

The culture industry chapter fits in the broader narrative of the book as a whole (as it were): mass culture serves as an organ of soft domination, as the latest twist in a tale of how the quest for emancipation enslaved us. Though the chapter specifically discusses film, music, radio, and advertising, its overall aim is to explain how the dream of enlightenment backfired: revolutionaries died to make us free, philosophers dreamed of reason, scientists fought calcified ideologies, all so that we could spend our time at the movies. Oh, what a being down!

The chapter's intellectual lineages

Three clarifications of intellectual lineage are important. First, though Adorno wrote on aesthetics and mass culture till his death in 1969, Horkheimer did not, which has led many scholars to treat Adorno as chief author of the chapter. Jameson (1990) and Curran et al. (1977), among many others, list authorship as Adorno and Horkheimer, which, although alphabetical, does not honor the authors' own choice. Horkheimer's essay "Art and Mass Culture" (1941) clearly anticipates many of the chapter's themes, and he deserves credit for much of the analysis.

Second, the analysis is not purely Marxist. The quality of Horkheimer's and Adorno's Marxism, like that of Benjamin, has been subject to endless debate. Seminar Marxism, or apolitical Marxism – whatever the label, my concern here is their intellectual sources, not their practical commitment. Their analysis of rationalization in the culture industry, its division of labor and specialization, is deeply Weberian – more specifically, the blend of Weber and Marx developed by Georg Lukács (1968). *DA* attacks the standardization of cultural objects, not commercial production of culture, which, as their Frankfurt colleague Leo Lowenthal (1961) showed, is a much older phenomenon. Whereas the fetish hides the process of *production* for Marx, in *DA* fetishism aids the *distribution* and *consumption* of cultural products. Fetishism envelops the product with glamour, rather than hiding the laborer's sweat behind the veil of exchange value. Neither economism nor ideology critique is *DA*'s direct method. Horkheimer and Adorno are more concerned with cynical reason than false consciousness (Sloterdijk, 1987). It is not simply that people are duped: they are active agents in their own duping. "The triumph of advertising in the culture industry is that consumers feel compelled to buy and use its products even though they see through them" (167/191). Here *DA* spots something trickier than class dominion: it is an active collaboration with industrialized culture, and hence closer to Gramsci and cultural studies than to traditional Marxism.

Third, though there are good grounds, as Paddy Scannell argues in chapter 4, for contrasting the positions of Adorno and Benjamin in the mid to late 1930s, Adorno was not simply a disdainer of the masses, nor was Benjamin simply a cheerleader of everyday rebellion. Benjamin had a massive lifelong influence on Adorno, whose last work, *Aesthetic Theory*, follows Benjamin in theme, vocabulary, and method. *DA*'s stated tactic of taking the promise of mass culture at face value is directly Benjaminian: "our analysis keeps to the products' objectively inherent claim to be aesthetic images which accordingly embody truth" (p. xvi/ 17). As Arato (Arato and Gebhardt, 1978, p. 215) correctly notes, "The authors of *Dialectic of Enlightenment* are as much Benjamin's followers as those of Lukács."

A redemptive reading

Perhaps what rankles most about "The Culture Industry" is its tone. Horkheimer and Adorno were, in Hannah Arendt's (1968) useful phrase, "men in dark times," and the text reflects murk and gloom overall. *DA* is, says Habermas (1985, p. 130), "their blackest book." Whatever other revisionist readings one might want to advance, no one can deny that its mood is not chirpy. Even so, two sentences about the culture industry chapter, found in the 1944 preface, are missing in later editions: "Large sections, long completed, await only a final edit. In them also the positive aspects of mass culture will be discussed" (Horkheimer and Adorno, 1944, p. viii). Many would never have guessed they had it in them, but here the Benjaminian face makes its appearance. What they actually had in mind with this teaser is unclear. The editors of Adorno's works suggest it was his essay entitled "The Schema of Mass Culture," which has the disadvantage of not being very positive; another possibility is *Composing for the Films* (1994), which Adorno wrote with Hans Eisler in 1947, which analyzes film music in a Benjaminian – even Brechtian – vein of discovering positive possibilities in mass culture.

Adorno's interest in culture as a site of resistance and rebellion clearly marks him as a forerunner rather than a foe of later cultural studies. His 1966 essay, "Transparencies on Film," even celebrates youth using film as an educator in forbidden practices.

> If today you can see in Germany, in Prague, even in conservative Switzerland and in Catholic Rome, everywhere, boys and girls crossing the streets locked in each others' arms and kissing each other unembarrassed, then they have learned this, and probably more, from the films. . . . In its attempts to manipulate the masses the ideology of the culture industry itself becomes as internally antagonistic as the very society which it aims to control. The ideology of the culture industry contains the antidote to its own lie. No other plea could be made for its defense. (Adorno, 1981–2, p. 202)

Likewise, Adorno's 1954 piece on television anticipates the notion of polysemy: "the heritage of polymorphic meaning has been taken over [from the high art tradition] by cultural industry in as much as what it conveys becomes itself organized in order to enthrall the spectators on various psychological levels simultaneously" (Adorno, 1991, p. 141). Though multilayered meaning structures in mass culture have more to do with latent and manifest psychological needs for Adorno than with semiotic guerrilla warfare, he is open to a politics of cultural interpretation. In his notions of (1) youth mimicking media to spite social authority and (2) polymorphic meaning, Adorno anticipates later populist moves, with the advantage that he doesn't kid himself about their political consequences.

True, much in the "The Culture Industry" suggests mass stupidity. Such statements as "Capitalist production so confines them, body and soul, that they fall helpless victims to what is offered them" (133/155) or "the product prescribes every reaction" (137/159) would seem to deny people any ounce of agency to think or interpret, let alone resist. People are perhaps the ultimate commodity produced by the culture industries. Yet Horkheimer and Adorno are better read as ancestors of political economic critics of audiences as an industrial category (Meehan, 1993) than as mandarin people-haters. They portray a supply-driven, not demand-driven, cultural economy. With much relevance for our age of teen pop and Internet cookies, they are pioneering critics of industrial structures that anticipatorily incorporate audience response into the product itself. Consumers are ancillary, a condition of the industry: as *DA* astutely notes, genre categories depend "not so much on subject matter as on classifying, organizing, and labelling consumers" (123/144). Film genres are thus not simply stylistic conventions, but ways of arranging populations. In his later essay, "Culture Industry Reconsidered," Adorno makes clear that "the masses are not primary, but secondary, they are an object of calculation; an appendage of the machinery" (Adorno, 1991, p. 85). Obviously Horkheimer and Adorno waste no love on the common folk (seeing the petit bourgeois male less as Homer's Odysseus and more as Homer Simpson), having long ago abandoned the hope of the proletariat as the subject of history. Their fundamental interests are production and product, not consumption; their aim is philosophical critique, not ethnographic research.

Yet even if their picture of the industry is too totalizing, it is worth remembering that *DA* was written at a time and place of unprecedented concentration in cultural production: Hollywood prior to the Paramount ruling of 1948, which forced studios to divest themselves of their theatrical holdings. 1940s Hollywood consisted of eight studios, which, at their peak, collectively produced 95 percent of all films exhibited in the United States. *DA*'s historical moment was "Hollywood at its most classical, American mass culture at its most Fordist" (Hansen, 1992, p. 46). What *DA* says about the culture industry reflects a historically specific mode of production of vertical integration. Its analysis is still relevant today (perhaps unfortunately), given massive concentration, the packaging of resistance, and the incorporation of audience preferences into the products themselves.

The chapter's great weakness is the conflation of culture and society. From the manufactured text, *DA* infers a manufactured audience. Its authors assume use from object. One could read their absence of social analysis charitably as a methodological choice. Less sympathetically, one could argue that they find questions of audiences and reception irrelevant, since they believe that social conditions simply mimic cultural and economic ones. *DA* often does read social homogenization (audiences) from cultural homogeneity (products), a major shortcoming for thinkers raised on Stuart Hall's claim that encoding and decoding need have nothing to do with each other. Moreover, *DA* can seem guilty of the indecency of telling people what they think or should think, of showing a basic lack of respect for what people might find in cultural objects.

Even so, when they do talk about audiences, little in their analysis suggests passivity. Consuming mass culture demands intense cognitive – even physical – activity. High involvement in media decoding is not incompatible with manipulation: "alert" reception can accompany an impoverishment of the imagination (127/148). (Lazarsfeld's and Merton's notion of the narcotizing dysfunction points to a similar disjunction between active cognition and passive action: see Simonson and Weimann, chapter 1). *DA* does not lament lack of activity in media use, but the vast expenditures of energy spent on distraction rather than liberation (Adorno, 1941, p. 48).

Further, *DA* discusses the "resistant public" (160/183) on which the culture industry foists its wares, even though the authors' sense of "resistance" is often closer to sullen truculence than to reading against the grain. If people don't fight the culture industry enough with their minds, according to *DA*, they do so with their bodies. Why do people go to the movies? "The unemployed in the great cities find coolness in summer and warmth in winter in these temperature-controlled locations" (139/161). The "message" of the film is quite extraneous. Similarly, "In spite of the films which are intended to complete her integration, the housewife finds in the darkness of the movie theater a place of refuge where she can sit a couple hours with nobody watching" (139*/ 161), a "disappearing act" that later feminist scholars would find resonant (Modleski, 1982). "The protest against the movies," as Horkheimer wrote Leo Lowenthal about the latter's "Biographies in Popular Magazines," "is not found so much in bitter critiques but in the fact that people go in and sleep or make love to each other" (Jay, 1973, p. 214). Horkheimer and Adorno certainly do not endow practices of bodily resistance with revolutionary significance, but they do recognize how audience needs and uses can overwhelm the manifest content of cultural texts. Contrary to rumor, they share this understanding with the Columbia tradition, uses and gratifications, and British cultural studies alike. So much for the Frankfurt school's supposedly omnipotent media.

To think that Horkheimer and Adorno only want the masses to read Kant and listen to Beethoven is absurd. *DA*'s complaint is not simply that the culture industry corrupts high art; it corrupts low art too. The crazy ambition of the culture industry is to fuse light and serious art into something easy; it destroys both the intellectual sublimation of high forms of culture and the physical release of low forms. In contrast to Beethoven's austerity or the carnival's raucousness, the culture industry offers only the sugar high of pop. Sensuousness and severity are dialectically inter-twined; industrial culture unhinges this balance. "The eccentricity of the circus, wax museum, and brothel is as embarrassing to [the culture industry] as that of Schönberg and Karl Kraus" (136*/157). How many other theorists dare to pair vulgar amusements with Viennese modern-ism? Low culture involves "rebellious resistance" and performance (Adorno, 1991, p. 85), whereas high art involves originality and tran-scendence. Like many German intellectuals (cf. films by Alexander Kluge and Wim Wenders), Horkheimer and Adorno romanticize the circus as a place of primordial rawness and social truth: they knew "the carnivalesque" long before it became the watchword of populists in social history and cultural studies. Mockery, cheekiness, rowdiness they approve of; they like folk art, "farce and clowning," Chaplin and the Marx Brothers (137/159), and "the self-justifying and nonsensical skill of riders, acrobats, and clowns" (143/165). The grotesque and the comic disclose fleeting moments of critique (142/164).

Horkheimer and Adorno favor erotic art at the one end and physical sexuality at the other, but the peek-a-boo world of Hollywood drives them batty. Eros is corrupted by the culture industry's prurient teasing: "The Hays Office merely confirms the ritual of Tantalus. . . . Works of art are ascetic and unashamed; the culture industry is pornographic and prudish" (140/162). "Mass culture," wrote Lowenthal in 1942, "is a total conspiracy against love as well as sex" (Jay, 1973, p. 214). For Horkheimer and Adorno the high and the low are authentic; the middling is a mass of repetition and adjustment.

Horkheimer and Adorno decidedly do not dislike pleasure, but they hate the way the culture industry turns it into boredom, making it a principle of necessity rather than freedom. Critical theory often laments that pleasure has become as hierarchical as any other good in a capitalist society (Marcuse, 1968, ch. 5). Its debasement is part of the dialectic of the enlightenment: "Pleasure is, so to speak, nature's vengeance. In pleas-ure men disavow thought and escape civilization" (105/126). At the level of hurt and joy lie the marks of rationalization. *DA* does not neces-sarily disdain escape from "civilization," about which its authors have very mixed views; rather, they think escapist entertainment escapes from the task of *genuine* escape. They are not Stakhanovites, but critics of the ruthless work ethic in Marx's thought. Amusement for them can be a surcease for the oppressed. In the festival and drunkenness lie many of society's most powerful wishes and dangers. Horkheimer and Adorno do not puritanically proscribe pleasure; they are annoyed that what is sold as pleasure is really the discontent of civilization. People have no chance for the delight that comes from encountering a successful aesthetic totality: a delight that is inseparable from the promise of a better world. That pleasure is a utopian protest against oppression is central to their argument. That they deny it could occur with Hollywood films or 1940s jazz does not mean that the principle is not relevant for us in a more sinuous, but no less powerful, mode of cultural production. A call for intensity in experience of art and culture is not a bad thing.

Assessment: what is living and dead in "The Culture Industry"?

In reading old texts, one needs principles of both charity and pruning. To be moved by *DA* is not to believe everything, or perhaps even very much of what it says. Thoughts may be rescued from their historic formulations; ideas need not be faithful – they rarely are – to their authors' intentions.

Perhaps deadest of all *DA*'s cultural analysis is what one might call the Hitler–Hollywood axis. Horkheimer and Adorno take mass culture as constantly evincing Fascist logics. For instance, "The quantity of organized amusement changes into the quality of organized cruelty" (138/ 160). Laughter at Warner Brothers cartoons is repressed sadism waiting to burst into riots and lynch mobs. These are readings in exile, cross-cultural illuminations, taking movies as Nuremberg rallies. This vision is, to a large extent, a historical husk of the 1940s. But before we write it off too quickly, we shouldn't forget the American flirtation with Fascism in the McCarthy era or the common sense that popular culture tends to celebrate the status quo. Media consumers in the biggest empire in the history of the world (the USA) might benefit from thinking more about the political dangers of their amusements. The principle of charity invites us to imagine truth where only the *passé* or *outré* seems to reign.

The culture industries today are more complicated; concentration of ownership can go together with decentralization of decision making, flexible production, and niche marketing. Homogeneity is less the rule than incorporation of irony and resistance. The notion of mass culture as a single bloc connecting industry, text, and audience is defunct (but watch Microsoft). But not *DA*'s sense of the interlocking of culture industries with others (banking, electricity); the push to product differentiation (the narcissism of petty differences); the micro-adjustment of production (pseudo-individuality) to audience tastes. *DA* never says that the culture industry simply produces trash; many of its wares are calculated perfection, corrupted by slickness, a rationalized signature meant to please and to soothe. Though one might shy away from Horkheimer's and Adorno's doctrine of a closed system of production, their sense of the ways in which feedback from audiences is built into production is more relevant today, with our focus groups and psychographics, than it was in the 1940s.

The confidence that there is a fixed canon of great works of culture is clearly dead – or at least more complicated – today. No question, both Horkheimer and Adorno were constitutionally elitist in their aesthetic attitudes; but they recognized, no less than their Hegelian cousin, John Dewey, that the problem lies not in works of art, but in the elitist institutions that keep them off limits. (On Dewey–Adorno resemblances, see Posnock, 1992.) Still, it is not outrageous to suggest (as we do in this book) that there are works, in whatever domain of culture, of such concentrated labor and thought that they legitimately claim people's precious time. Their vision of cultural policy in fact authorizes the project of this book. Excellence deserves sustained attention, as slop does not. Yes, we know: the sociology of culture (itself owing much to Frankfurt work) will say that there is no inherent quality but only prestige constellations. Perhaps; but there is a history of influence, and endurance across generations accompanied by genuine delight says much. Today one can say without blushing that Beethoven, Brahms, or Mahler is great, just as Duke Ellington, the Beatles, or Nirvana are great. Canons consist in part in their subsequent histories, the paths that old texts carve through new ones. The principle that excellence deserves honor can be extracted from the elitist historical limits placed on it by our authors.

DA is plainly a Eurocentric text, but with a difference: its aim is in large part to clarify and combat domination on grounds of class, gender, and race. Its orientation is European, but its authors' concern is humanity. As a privileged site in the domination of nature, gender serves *DA* as a crucial nexus for understanding the contradictory commands of a society that posts women ambiguously at one remove from the market. That women are both stunted and blessed by their political and economic deprivations is a point explored also in Horkheimer's 1930s work on authority and the family (Horkheimer, 1992). *DA*'s most creative readers have often been feminists grappling with its rich, but certainly not trouble-free, gender analysis. Horkheimer and Adorno are absolutely clear that Odysseus, in sailing past the Sirens, was renouncing the feminine. Despite the male-dominated authorship of early critical theory, critical theory's most important living exponents in the English language today are largely women, such as Seyla Benhabib, Susan Buck-Morss, Drucilla Cornell, Nancy Fraser, Miriam Hansen, and Shierry Weber Nicholsen. Nor is this affinity accidental. Similarly, *DA*'s account of anti-Semitism offers an uncommonly subtle treatment of what is now called "othering," which is quite relevant to very different sorts of racial or ethnic abuse. Though indisputably dead, European, and male, Horkheimer and Adorno are highly suggestive for grappling with the injuries and immunities of gender and race, however stumbling some of their formulations must ring to modern ears.

DA, in sum, is one of the few classics that make study of the media a world-historical problem, and does so with sweeping philosophical and historical learning. It treats the fate of culture in the modern world with an almost spiritual urgency and intensity. Its willingness to swing so sharply and probe so sensuously is consistently bracing. It is full of pungent observations about the texture of life and culture in one of the most interesting and strange periods of American history. Even its outrageous misfires offer perspectives through incongruity. The striking juxtaposition – brilliant and bathetic at turns – of high humanist reference points and popular cultural objects blurs cultural levels within their very text. (The practice of blending the canonic and the popular in media criticism is something McLuhan also learned from the high modernists, though his vision differs in many ways from *DA*.) Oddly, few critics have remarked just how funny *DA* is – like a Lenny Bruce who's read Hegel, as one of my students put it. The punchy timing, the unfailing eye for the ridiculous, the rapid shifting between macrocosm and microcosm, the slashing wit that is never far from tears, are classic marks of a black comic vision; all are here in abundance. For sheer intelligence, fascination, audacity, and stimulation, I know no text in the wobbly canon of media theory that can match "The Culture Industry" and *Dialectic of Enlightenment*.

Note

1   Citations of *DA* are given parenthetically. The number before the slash stands for the page in the English translation (Horkheimer and Adorno, 1994), an asterisk marking that I have altered the translation; the number following gives the page in the text in Adorno's collected works (Horkheimer and Adorno, 1981).

72 John Durham Peters

References

Adorno, T. W. (1941) On Popular Music. *Studies in Philosophy and Social Science*, 9, 17–48.

Adorno, T. W. (1974) *Minima Moralia: Reflections from Damaged Life*, tr. E. F. N. Jephcott. London: Verso. (Originally published in German in 1951.)

Adorno, T. W. (1981–2) Transparencies on Film, tr. Thomas Y. Levin. *New German Critique*, 24–5, 199–205. (Originally published in German in 1966.)

Adorno, T. W. (1991) *The Culture Industry*, ed. J. M. Bernstein. London: Routledge.

Adorno, T. and Eisler, H. (1994) *Composing for the Films*. London: Athlone Press. (First published in 1947, in English.)

Arato, A. and Gebhardt, E. (1978) *The Essential Frankfurt School Reader*. New York: Urizen.

Arendt, H. (1968) *Men in Dark Times*. New York: Harcourt, Brace & World.

Collins, J. (1989) *Uncommon Cultures: Popular Culture and Post-Modernism*. New York: Routledge.

Cook, D. (1995) *The Culture Industry Revisited: Theodor W. Adorno on Mass Culture*. Lanham, MD: Rowman and Littlefield.

Curran, J., Gurevitch, M. and Woollacott, J. (eds) (1977) *Mass Communication and Society*. London: Edward Arnold.

Fiske, J. (1989) *Reading the Popular*. London: Routledge.

Habermas, J. (1985) *Der philosophische Diskurs der Moderne: Zwölf Vorlesungen*. Frankfurt: Suhrkamp.

Hansen, M. (1992) Mass Culture as Hieroglyphic Writing: Adorno, Derrida, Kracauer. *New German Critique*, 56, 43–74.

Horkheimer, M. (1941) Art and Mass Culture. *Studies in Philosophy and Social Science*, 9, 290–304.

Horkheimer, M. (1992) *Critical Theory*. New York: Continuum.

Horkheimer, M. and Adorno, T. W. (1944) *Philosophische Fragmente*. New York: Social Studies Association.

Horkheimer, M. and Adorno, T. W. (1981) *Dialektik der Aufklärung: Philosophische Fragmente*. In T. W. Adorno, *Gesammelte Schriften*, vol. 3, Frankfurt: Suhrkamp.

Horkheimer, M. and Adorno, T. W. (1994) *Dialectic of Enlightenment*, tr. John Cumming. New York: Continuum.

Jameson, F. (1990) *Late Marxism: Adorno, or, the Persistence of the Dialectic*. London: Verso.

Jay, M. (1973) *The Dialectical Imagination*. Boston: Little, Brown.

Liu, H. (1999) The Project of the Culture Industry. Ph.D. dissertation, University of Iowa.

Lowenthal, L. (1961) *Literature, Popular Culture, and Society*. Palo Alto, CA: Pacific Books.

Lukács, G. (1968) *Geschichte und Klassenbewusstsein*. Neuwied: Luchterhand. (Originally published in 1923.)

Marcuse, H. (1940) *Reason and Revolution: Hegel and the Rise of Social Theory.* London and New York: Oxford University Press.

Marcuse, H. (1968) *Negations: Essays in Critical Theory.* Boston: Beacon Press.

Meehan, E. R. (1993) Heads of Households and Ladies of the House: Gender, Genre, and Broadcast Ratings, 1929–1990. In S. Solomon and R. W. McChesney (eds), *Ruthless Criticism: New Perspectives in U.S. Communications History,* Minneapolis: University of Minnesota Press, 204–21.

Modleski, T. (1982) *Loving with a Vengeance.* Hamden, CT: Archon.

Posnock, R. (1992) The Politics of Nonidentity: A Genealogy. *Boundary 2,* 19 (1), 34–68.

Sloterdijk, P. (1987) *Critique of Cynical Reason,* tr. Michael Eldred. Minneapolis: University of Minnesota Press.

Thompson, J. B. (1990) *Ideology and Modern Culture: Critical Social Theory in the Era of Mass Communication.* Stanford, CA: Stanford University Press.

4

Benjamin Contextualized: On "The Work of Art in the Age of Mechanical Reproduction"

———

Paddy Scannell

Introduction

Within any academic field the processes that determine which works achieve canonical status are partly determined by the history of the field itself. Marx pointed out that when men determine to make a revolution, they look to the past to provide them with roles and models. Likewise, more prosaically, emerging academic disciplines also consult the past for guidance and inspiration as they seek to clarify their concerns and stake out a distinctive domain of inquiry. One text that speaks eloquently from the past to later generations of academics concerned with media and communication is "The Work of Art in the Age of Mechanical Reproduction" by Walter Benjamin. He wrote this essay in 1936 as a contribution to an ongoing debate, within a small but distinguished circle of intellectuals, about the status and role of art in the then new circumstances of "mass culture." Four years later, Benjamin, a German Jew, committed suicide after being refused permission to enter Spain, fearing he would fall into the hands of the Nazis. His collected works were not published until the mid-1950s in Germany, where they had an immediate impact, and he was unknown to Anglo-American readers until a collection of his essays was translated into English, with a brilliant introductory essay by his friend and admirer Hannah Arendt.

This collection, *Illuminations*, published in 1968, includes the essay on mechanical reproduction, and is the basis of Benjamin's worldwide reputation today.

Illuminations contains selections made from the two-volume German *Schriften*, edited and introduced by Theodor Adorno and published in 1955. Arendt's "chief purpose" in making her selection was "to convey the importance of Benjamin as a literary critic" (Benjamin, 1968, p. 267). Most of the essays in the collection are about either literature (Baudelaire, Proust, and Kafka) or related topics (translation, book collecting), with the exception of the celebrated "Theses on the Philosophy of History" (pp. 255–66). "Mechanical Reproduction" thus stands in some isolation from the rest of the collection. What makes it distinctive, apart from its subject matter, are certain aspects of Benjamin's interests and concerns, notably a political engagement with questions concerning art and commodity production from a (loosely) Marxist perspective. That perspective provides the thread that links the text with its resurrection, several decades later, in circumstances hugely different from those in which, and for which, it was originally written. This essay thus has two tasks: first, to account for the original circumstances that gave rise to "Mechanical Reproduction" and the debate to which it made a central contribution, and second, to explain briefly the reasons for its posthumous fame when it became available to English-speaking readers nearly 40 years later.

Art and politics in the 1930s

The period between World Wars I and II was one of profound economic, political, and cultural change in Europe and North America. What we now call "consumer capitalism" was decisively established in the West in the interwar period, when mass markets were created for a whole new range of domestic and leisure consumer goods. Intimately linked to this was the wide social penetration of new electronic forms of communication (telephone and radio) and of "mass" entertainment (cinema and the record industry). "Mass society," "mass politics," "mass production," and "mass culture" were key concerns in contemporary political, social, and cultural debates. On the whole, European intellectuals were hostile to the masses (the urban, industrial working classes) and to the new forms of mass culture that catered to their tastes. Artistic modernism, buttressed by theories of the avant-garde, ensured that the arts were "difficult" and beyond the grasp of the great mass of ordinary women and men whose "low-brow tastes" threatened to swamp and destroy "high-brow" standards of taste and ways of living – or so it

seemed to many artists and intellectuals at the time (Carey, 1992). This
was one aspect of the debate around the role of art and its relation to the
masses to which Benjamin's essay contributed. But it had a more urgent
political dimension in light of the deepening political crisis that grew
directly from the economic crisis of 1929, which triggered the rise of
Fascism in Europe in the 1930s and ultimately the outbreak of World
War II.

A crucial issue concerned the implications of mass culture. Was mass
entertainment yet another instance of the exploitation of "the masses,"
or was it a potential means for their emancipation? The effect of economic and political crisis was to politicize culture and raise again the
question of whether art could, or should, be directly involved in contemporary life and affairs. The question of political commitment for art and
for the artist was intensely debated throughout Europe and the United
States. In the Soviet Union, writers and intellectuals were called upon to
be "engineers of the soul": to throw themselves wholeheartedly behind
the new Communist society and produce artistic representations of the
men and women of the new Russia. A whole new genre of "socialist
realism" in art and literature came into being to celebrate the achievements of the socialist revolution. In Britain, the intellectuals marched
sharply to the left. They were deeply concerned with the prolonged social
fallout of the economic crisis that created long-term unemployment
in the industrial heartlands of the United Kingdom. They espoused new
popular movements: for peace, for the republican cause in the Spanish
Civil War (Hynes, 1966). In the USA, intellectuals became enthusiastic
recruits to the New Deal administration and made films, photographed,
and wrote about the impact of the Depression and the heroic efforts of
the New Deal to counter it (Stott, 1986).

In Germany, those intellectuals who were hostile to National Socialism, or whose lives were threatened, fled when Hitler came to power in
1932. Among them was a group of academics who were members of the
Institute of Social Research, an independently funded research center
attached to the University of Frankfurt, later known universally as the
"Frankfurt school." Two of its leading figures were Max Horkheimer
(the institute's director for most of its history) and his close friend Theodor
Adorno. Attached to the institute as an associate fellow on a tiny stipend
was Walter Benjamin. Shortly after Hitler came to power in 1933, the
institute's offices were searched by the police, and were later seized and
confiscated for being "Communist property" (Wiggershaus, 1994, p. 128).
Adorno and Horkheimer eventually reestablished the institute in the USA,
attached to Columbia University. They remained in the United States,
German-Jewish émigrés in exile, until after the war, when they returned,

with much honor, to Frankfurt. Benjamin left Germany, but remained in Europe. He was in Paris when the German army invaded France in 1940, and fled south to the Spanish border hoping to escape capture.

It was this situation – the apparently irresistible rise of Fascism, the impact of mass production on art and culture, the accompanying new forms of art and entertainment (film, photography, radio, and gramophone records) – that Walter Benjamin addressed in "The Work of Art in the Age of Mechanical Reproduction." I consider his essay here, not as an autonomous text, but in relation to what inspired it and the responses to which it gave rise. Thus I argue that Benjamin's essay makes a persuasive case for the emancipatory potential of new forms of "mass culture," but also present Adorno's powerful criticism, "On the Fetish Character in Music and the Regression in Listening," which was written in direct response to Benjamin's essay and published two years later, in 1938. My aim is not to adjudicate the outcome of this interchange, but rather to show the complexity of the issues it raised about the social and political role of art and its enduring relevance; for it was the return of this question in very different circumstances four decades later that prompted the resurrection of the texts under review here. I also present some key sources of inspiration drawn upon by both sides in the argument. In particular, I will show the importance, for Benjamin, of his friend Bertolt Brecht, whose ideas about theater and politics underpin his thoughts about the contemporary situation of art. I will likewise highlight the contribution that the concepts of Georg Lukács made to Adorno's response. In all this I aim to show how and why the question of art and politics mattered at the time. Far from being of merely academic interest, the issues that concerned Benjamin and Adorno, Brecht and Lukács, were compelling ones that intimately and fatefully touched their lives in different ways.

Art, reproduction, and the loss of aura

The central thesis of Benjamin's essay is that in modern conditions, art has lost its aura, which is destroyed by mechanical reproduction, or mass production. The meaning of "aura" is central to understanding the essay and to Benjamin's thinking in a wider sense. The Latin word *aura* means "breeze." It is used as a metaphor for the subtle emanation that things give off as the mark of their distinctiveness. In European painting, for instance, the aura of sanctity is represented by a halo around a saint's head, or a subtle glow around the figure of the Madonna. For Benjamin, Art is invested with and surrounded by aura, a halo of significance that distinguishes it from non-auratic, everyday things. In modern societies art proclaims itself as Art by its *uniqueness* and *distance* from daily life and its affairs – the two key marks of auratic art. There is only one *Mona Lisa*, for instance, and its significance as Art is caught up to a considerable extent in its status as a unique, singular thing. Art is also marked by its distance from everyday life, retreating into the museum, the gallery, the theater, or the concert hall.

In pre-modern times this was not the case. Art was embedded in the very fabric of society. It embodied and expressed a society's most intimate values and beliefs, its sense of its history and place in the world. As such, what we now call Art had a very different function then, and was closely linked to religion, magic, and ritual. In a beautiful essay called "The Storyteller," Benjamin (1978) reflects on the decline of storytelling in modern societies, displaced on the one hand by the novel, and on the other by the newspaper. The former testifies to the collapse of tradition, the latter the extent to which experience has been displaced by information. Storytelling, Benjamin argues, is at the heart of traditional societies. It embodies and expresses the tradition; indeed, it *is* the tradition. The authenticity of the tradition (its living quality, its aliveness, its aura) is preserved in the practice of storytelling. But modern, secular rationality destroys tradition, ritual, magic, and religious beliefs. The Age of Reason invented a new thing, Art, which it invested with an invented tradition – Creativity, Genius, Beauty – to stand as timeless reminders of the human spirit. The aura of, let us call it, "Gallery Art" (which is what we mean by Art in modern times) is a secular mystique, and the "worship" of great art is a secular ritual practiced largely by the European bourgeoisie and its intellectuals.

Mass production destroys Art's aura, because it destroys its twin characteristics of uniqueness and distance. Photography and cinema multiply the image *ad infinitum*. There may be one *Mona Lisa*, but there are umpteen photographic reproductions of it in all sorts of contexts, including the downright vulgar. At the same time, mass reproduction destroys the *distance* of the art object. No longer the unique original to which we must all go in reverence if we wish to see it, it is pried from its shell. It goes out into the world, where it circulates in many forms. It comes to us. The sense of reverence for the auratic art object is shattered. In the concert hall or at the art gallery we display our reverence by our concentrated and silent attentiveness to the performance or exhibition. But the mass publics for new forms of mass culture take a more relaxed attitude. They do not have to concentrate on the auratic experience. They can watch in a state of distraction. They can listen to music on the radio or gramophone and do other things at the same time.

What are the implications of the destruction of aura? For Benjamin, it is the *democratization* of art. What was once for the select few is now available for the many. Modern technologies of visual reproduction (Benjamin had in mind photography and cinema in particular) can become art forms for the millions. Moreover, they bring about transformations in how we perceive reality, offering us new perspectives on the world. The camera is deeply enmeshed in the web of reality. It can go to places that were hitherto inaccessible to most of us. Movement can be speeded up or slowed down to reveal the beauty of things not available to ordinary perception – say, the moment of impact of a drop of water. The cinematic close-up creates a new kind of intimacy in public, allowing millions access to the look on a human face that was formerly reserved for lovers or for parent and child. In all this, what Benjamin calls the "theology of art" – its ritual or cult value as a thing of beauty and a joy forever, the *worship* and canonization of art by its ideologues, the intellectuals – is put in question. Mass reproduction destroys the unique authenticity of the original work, which can no longer be worshipped as such. "The total function of art is reversed. Instead of being based on ritual, it begins to be based on another practice – politics" (Benjamin, 1978, p. 226).

Like many European intellectuals at that time, Benjamin still believed in the revolutionary potential of "the masses." His views on the relationship between the masses and new modes of production were spelled out in a 1934 lecture he gave in Paris to the Institute for the Study of Fascism, published three years later in essay form as "The Author as Producer." Here Benjamin argued that the revolutionary potential of new technologies depended on the role in the production process of the intellectual (writer, author), who must align himself with the masses. It is no use invoking the autonomy of the poet, his freedom to write whatever he pleases (Benjamin, 1978, p. 255). Art is not about *self*-expression: the author must serve the interests of the people. At the same time, in new "mass" forms of writing such as newspapers, there is a greater opportunity for readers to play an active part, rather than being mere consumers. They can write letters and influence editorial opinion. In the new, post-revolutionary Russian cinema, Benjamin points out, ordinary Russians are used instead of actors to portray "the masses." Thus, new forms of mass communication may transform consumers into active participants. Benjamin is arguing for a new relationship between authors, products, and audience. Not the worship of the author (as Genius) or of the work (as Truth and Beauty) by an adoring audience, but a more equal and collaborative relationship in which the author gets down from his pedestal and aligns himself with the audience (the masses), takes their point of view, and gives it expression in his work.

This was the kind of theater that Bertolt Brecht tried to create. For Brecht, the dominant theatrical tradition – the whole commercial *business*, or "apparatus" of theater – served primarily to confirm middle-class audiences in their good opinion of themselves. It did nothing to make them confront contemporary reality or question their own social attitudes and values. Brecht thought of this kind of theater as "culinary consumption" – pleasant, bland food dished up for bourgeois audiences who wanted nothing more than a comforting, self-affirming, emotional theatrical experience. He, by contrast, wanted to create theater for new, non-bourgeois audiences who did not ordinarily go to the theater. He wanted a theater that a working-class audience would enjoy, where people would feel at ease and not constrained to be "on their best behavior." Going to the theater could be fun. It could also be a learning experience, inviting audiences to think about the contemporary world and their position in it. It should therefore be *realistic* in a double sense: with respect to what is *actually* going on in the world, and how this affects those for whom the tale is told (i.e. working-class audiences). To do this, Brecht argued, the new theater must employ new techniques and methods: "Reality changes; to represent it the means of representation must change too. Nothing arises from nothing; the new springs from the old, but that is just what makes it new" (1978, p. 110). In all this, the aim was to achieve a new kind of involvement for a new kind of audience – not the cozy, self-affirming emotional involvement that bourgeois theater offered its audiences, but active, conscious political involvement. Theater that would make people think, that might change their attitudes; theater that could play a part in social change rather than merely reaffirming the existing order.

Brecht's ideas about theater underlie much of Benjamin's thinking in both essays under discussion here. In "The Author as Producer," Benjamin makes the links between his and Brecht's ideas explicit (Benjamin, 1978, pp. 261–2, 265–7). He also makes clear that he is discussing the role of art in relation to class struggle. The instruments of production are in the hands of the enemy – the newspaper, for instance, "belongs to capital" (p. 259). The new technologies have no revolutionary potential in themselves, but are put to reactionary use in reactionary hands. Consider the case of "art" photography: "It is unable to say anything of a power station or a cable factory other than this: what a beautiful world! . . . It has succeeded in making even abject poverty, by recording it in a fashionably perfected manner, into an object of enjoyment" (pp. 262–3). This is what Adorno meant by "the barbarism of perfection" (1978, p. 284). Technically perfect images dished up for culinary consumption, that aestheticize the world and thereby close off the possibility of any critical perspective on a less-than-perfect reality. In "The Author as Producer," Benjamin calls on intellectuals (writers, journalists, photographers, etc.) to work within cultural institutions to subvert their functions. They must change their practices and use the new instruments of communication for politically progressive purposes, making them work in the interest of the masses rather than against them: "Technical progress is for the author as producer the foundation of his political progress" (1978, p. 263).

In "Mechanical Reproduction" Benjamin takes a less explicitly political line. He no longer calls on intellectuals to change the apparatuses of cultural production from within. Rather, in contradiction to his argument in "The Author as Producer," he seems to see the technologies of mass cultural production as having an intrinsic emancipatory potential. By transforming the scale of cultural production and distribution, he argues, they play a democratizing role, bringing culture to the millions and shattering the aura of culture as something for "the happy few." And by transforming the nature of perception, they offer new perspectives on contemporary reality that were hitherto unavailable.

This begins to sound like technological determinism, a questionable line of thinking that treats technological innovation as an instrument of social change irrespective of the uses to which it is put. In "The Author as Producer," Benjamin argued (quite rightly) that photography, when put to modish use, had a flatly reactionary social function. In "Mechanical Reproduction," however, he appears to believe the camera *per se* can change perceptions of reality. But Benjamin is alert to the possibilities of *fake aura*, by which he means the reappropriation of mass culture for ritual purposes:

> Fascism sees its salvation in giving the masses not their right, but instead a chance to express themselves. The masses have a right to change property relations. Fascism seeks to allow them expression while preserving property. The logical result of Fascism is the introduction of aesthetics into political life. The violation of the masses, whom Fascism, with its *Führer* cult, forces to its knees, has its counterpart in the violation of an apparatus which is pressed into the production of ritual values. (1978, p. 243)

A socialist politics is committed to revolution on behalf of the masses, in order to eliminate the inequities of property relations in capitalist societies. It therefore seeks to rouse the masses to the overthrow of the existing social and political order. Fascism, by contrast, is committed to preserving unequal economic and social relations. It recruits the masses to politics, not to mobilize them for social change, but to allow them to express themselves, "to let off steam." This is why Fascism aestheticizes politics. It transforms politics into theater, a spectacle in which participants can participate directly in political life, but cannot effect change. It does this through the fake aura of the mass rally with its ritual pomp and pageantry, and the cult of Führer worship which is given charismatic expression on such occasions. The forms of mass culture (cinema, radio) are harnessed to the purposes of propaganda and the cult of the event. All this leads to one thing: war. Against the aestheticization of politics by Fascism, socialism responds by politicizing art. This was the objective of Brechtian theater, and the final point of Benjamin's essay.

The fetishization of music

Benjamin sent a copy of "Mechanical Reproduction" to Adorno for comment. He hoped that Adorno would publish it in the institute's journal, *Zeitschrift für Sozialforschung* (*Journal for Social Research*). Adorno, however, was displeased by two aspects of the article: first, the "flatly reactionary position" assigned to auratic art and the progressive role assigned to new technologies of mechanical reproduction; second, and relatedly, the presence in the essay of Brechtian themes concerning art and politics.

Adorno set out his immediate responses in an exchange of letters with Benjamin and, in a more considered way, in an article entitled "On the Fetish Character in Music and the Regression of Listening" (1978), which put forward a detailed counter-argument to the case for mass culture that Benjamin had advanced. In his essay, Adorno attacked the impact of the industrialization of music on contemporary musical life. Two related technical developments at the end of the nineteenth century had an enormous impact on every aspect of musical life in the early twentieth century. These were sound recording and the radio, both major instances of the mechanical reproduction of sound. Before the gramophone and the radio, music was necessarily a live art, in which the performance itself was central to the experience. It was thus a social activity, involving players and audience in the production and experience of the musical event. But the record and the radio shattered the immediate social relations of musical life by their destruction of the performed event. Music now had two separate and unconnected moments: the moment of production (the recording, the radio transmission) and the moment of consumption (listening via radio or gramophone). What connected these two moments was the musical "product." These two new "social technologies of sound" had the effect, Adorno argued, of *reifying* music.

This concept was drawn from Georg Lukács's influential essay entitled "Reification and the Consciousness of the Proletariat," written in 1923, which aimed at expanding the implications of commodity fetishism outlined by Marx in 1867 in a famous section of *Capital*, "The Fetishism of the Commodity and its Secret" (1976, pp. 163–77). A fetish is an object endowed with magical properties – for example, a charm purchased to protect oneself from harm or misfortune – and fetishism is the worship of such objects. Marx treated commodities, especially money, as fetish objects. The magic of money is the riddle of the commodity fetish (p. 187). The fetishization of commodities (manufactured goods) is the *object*ification of the social relations of production into relationships between *things*. This process displaces and devalues human social life. When manufactured commodities realize their value *as* commodities in exchange for the universal commodity (money), they do so at the expense of those who made the commodity but have no control over the objects of their labor and derive little benefit from it. If labor is, as Marx claimed, the expression of our common human nature, then the fate of labor under capitalist conditions indicates that "[t]he *devaluation* of the human world grows in direct proportion to the *increase in value* of the world of things" (Marx, 1992, pp. 323–4).

Lukács extended the implications of Marx's analysis to include all aspects of social, cultural, and intellectual life, via the concept of *reification*. "Reification" is rooted in the Latin word *res* ("thing") and means, literally, "thingification." Lukács argued that the commodity structure had penetrated all aspects of society, both inner and outer, and remolded it in its own image. Thus, the reified commodity-thing becomes "the universal category of society as a whole." Adorno, in turn, applied Lukács's analysis of the reified world to contemporary musical life. It was not simply that music was reified as a marketable commodity-thing in the form of a gramophone record. It was fetishized (glamorized, worshipped) in all sorts of ways that combined to conceal the fate of music in modern times – namely, the loss of its social, sociable character and, with that, the accompanying possibility of true musical pleasure. The first part of Adorno's essay explores the many ways in which reified music exhibits its "fetish character" through the fetishization of performance, the stylization of production, and the fetishization of consumption. All three aspects – production, product, and consumption – bear the stigmata of reification.

The fetishization of performance shows up in various ways. First, there is the worship of "the beautiful voice." Then there is the fetishization of the great composer or conductor, particularly the latter. Finally, there is the notion of the authentic (great, "true") performance, a tendency greatly enhanced by the professionalization of music playing and the notion of the "definitive" recording. This shows up in popular as well as classical music, as has been astutely analyzed by Simon Frith (1986). The fetishization of authenticity (the great voice, the great performance, the great conductor) is an aspect of a total standardization and conformity that allows no place for imperfection. The professionalization of music (itself an accelerated consequence of new technologies) devalues all other music making, which is now relegated to the inferior status of "amateur" performance. In a telling phrase borrowed from Eduard Steuermann, Adorno wrote of "the barbarism of perfection," which he regarded as the definitive reification:

> The new fetish is the flawlessly functioning, metallically brilliant apparatus as such, in which all the cogwheels mesh so perfectly that not the slightest hole remains open for the meaning of the whole. Perfect, immaculate performance in the latest style preserves the work at the price of its definitive reification. It presents itself as complete from the very first note. The performance sounds like its own phonograph record. (1978, p. 284)

The stylization of production means its standardization into something like an assembly line sound. Adorno detected this development in the emergence of the pop song. The standardization of music meant its transformation into "easy listening," something that was instantly and effortlessly consumed, epitomized by the catchy tune or refrain and the standardized rhythm (four beats to the bar). This mass-produced music pointed, Adorno argued, to the fateful separation of music into two distinct categories, "serious" and "popular." He traced this division back to the eighteenth century, claiming that Mozart was the last composer who effortlessly combined both elements in his music. Thereafter, music diverged increasingly in two separate directions, a tendency finally sealed by its commodification as the three-minute recording aimed at maximizing profit in the quest for a hit.

All this loses sight of the intrinsic pleasure of music, which is in performance. It has regressed to an isolated pleasure for an isolated listener, who fetishizes the act of listening but loses sight of what is listened to. This shows, Adorno argued, in the peculiar obsessions of equipment freaks who fetishize *sound* as an abstract thing independent of what is being played. Adorno pointed to radio hams as an instance of this process. We might point to hi-fi freaks and the fetishization of perfect acoustics. It also shows in the phenomenon of the fan who knows everything there is to know about the fetishized object, who writes to radio stations demanding more airtime for the object fetish, and who is lost in fake ecstasy at live performances. In all such ways the fan is in thrall to the "star" fetish object.

Yet no one *really* listens to music any more, Adorno argued. More music is available on a daily basis than was ever possible in earlier times. In fact, thanks to the music industry, it is almost impossible to escape from music nowadays. But the more there is, the less people listen. The reification of music is indicative of music's regression from a worldly, social pleasure to an inner state of mind, a matter of subjective taste ("I know what I like"). Reified music is, first and last, in the head of the isolated, individual consumer of music.

Adorno saw all these aspects of reified, fetishized music as indicative of the *regression* of listening. This term, taken from Freudian psychoanalysis, means a reversion to an earlier childlike state. What Adorno meant by this is that listening to music no longer has an adult character; it has lost any critical, rational function. "Regressive listeners behave like children. Again and again and with stubborn malice, they demand the one dish they have once been served with" (p. 290). The reification of music produces a kind of mass infantilism in listening publics, who no longer listen any more. What is thus lost is the possibility of resistance or criticism and, beyond that, the possibility of *autonomous art*: art as the expression of human autonomy, independence, and freedom.

Autonomous art

Adorno believed in the redemptive possibility of what he called "autonomous art." "Autonomy" (Greek: *autos*, "self"; *nomos*, "law") means self-government. In a philosophical sense it means that human beings, by the exercise of their will, are self-determining. Human freedom, in principle and in practice, presupposes individuals as autonomous, self-ruling agents who are free from *heteronomous* constraint (the constraints of externally imposed law or rule). Autonomous art is thus the free expression of a self-determining, creative "author" who produces the art work. More crucially, this integral artistic freedom is embodied in the autonomy of the form and content of the art work itself. Art, in other words, obeys its own laws. As such, it stands in opposition to mass culture, which is governed by heteronomous factors, most obviously the profit motive. The heteronomy of mass culture reveals itself in the search for mass audiences. In order to reach large and diverse audiences, the form and content of cultural products must be simple, accessible, and easy to understand. Thus, the *forms* of mass culture are determined by heteronomous factors. It follows that the autonomy of autonomous art must reveal itself in forms and content that resist the pull of heteronomous forces.

If heteronomous culture offers easy, accessible, simple pleasures, then autonomous art can be none of these things.

Adorno accepted and defended autonomous art as "difficult." It is meant to be. That is how it resists easy "culinary" consumption. Autonomous art demands real effort and commitment on the part of the reader, listener, or viewer. Benjamin might defend the "distracted attention" of mass audiences, but Adorno would have none of it. The concentration demanded by modern art was the mark of its negation of the culture market. In an exchange of letters on the topic, Benjamin tactfully conceded, "I have tried to articulate positive moments as clearly as you managed to articulate negative ones" (Taylor, 1980, p. 140).

But Adorno also rejected the political stance of Benjamin and Brecht. Art for art's sake, he declared, was in need of defense and rescue from "the united front which exists against it from Brecht to the [Communist] Youth Movement" (Taylor, 1980, p. 122). Adorno (1978) made his views on this matter plain in an essay on "Commitment" written many years later, criticizing Jean-Paul Sartre, Lukács, and Brecht, all of whom defended the position that writers should be politically "engaged" and express this commitment in their work (Taylor, pp. 300–17). Adorno does not wholly reject their position. But he points out that Lukács's defense of socialist realism against modernism served to prop up the dreadful Stalinist tyranny. As for Brecht, it is easy to prove the discrepancy between his ideas about theater and his theatrical practice. Indeed, Brecht himself conceded that what he really cared about was the theater itself, irrespective of politics. The case against commitment is that it can too quickly collapse into heteronomy. When it turns into propaganda, as it so easily does, it betrays it own cause and commitment – namely, truth. That was the sticking point for Adorno. He defended to the last the autonomous work of art for its stance against its betrayal by contemporary economic and political life. If it offered few pleasures, if its appeal was limited, it was nevertheless true to itself. Its negativity exposed the essentially negative character of dominant forms of economic, political, and cultural life, even as they thought of themselves as affirmative.

Aftermath

When Benjamin's work became available in English in the 1970s it played into a time in which, as in the 1930s, culture was repoliticized – not by a downturn in the global capitalist economy and its political consequences, but by the new social movements of the 1960s, especially civil rights and feminism, and the American war in Vietnam. The French "cultural revolution" of May 1968 had ramifications throughout Europe, which showed in concerted attempts to repoliticize mass forms of entertainment, particularly cinema (again) and the newer mass medium of television. In this context Brecht's ideas for a revolutionary theater were taken up again and applied to filmmaking and television drama production. Benjamin too appeared in these debates, but usually as a supporting player (Harvey, 1980; Walsh, 1981).

In the 1970s, British cultural studies was redefining itself under Stuart Hall's directorship of the Centre for Contemporary Cultural Studies at Birmingham University. In its concern to retheorize the meaning of culture, the center looked outside Anglo-American empiricism, of which it was deeply suspicious, and turned to Continental theory for support. As part of this general process, the newly available work of Benjamin was taken on board within the overarching frame of Western Marxism (New Left Books, 1977), as Hall (1980) noted in a synoptic review of the development of cultural studies:

> It was therefore of the utmost importance that at precisely this moment [the early 1970s] many of these long-forgotten or unknown "Western Marxist" texts began to appear in translation, largely through the mediation of New Left Books and Merlin Press. English Cultural Studies thus had to hand, for the first time, an alternative source of theorizing within Marxism about its characteristic problems: in Lukács' literary historical work, Goldmann's *Hidden God*, the first translations of Walter Benjamin, the early texts of the "Frankfurt School" (known previously only because American "mass society theorists" were taken to have successfully refuted Adorno's pessimistic critique), Sartre's *Question of Method*. (p. 25)

Yet, within this essentially political agenda, whose primary objective was to rethink Marxism, Benjamin was, at best, a warmly admired but marginal figure (McRobbie, 1994, pp. 96–9). He was always a somewhat eccentric Marxist (he had little faith in "progress"), and his overtly political writings of the 1930s, with their Brechtian motifs, reflected only one strand in the thinking of this complex, melancholy "man of letters."

In the post-Marxist 1980s, attention turned to other aspects of Benjamin's thinking, and he was read as a pioneering cultural analyst of "modernity" (Frisby, 1985), this problematic now being raised in debates about its supersession by "postmodernity." A long-term project, uncompleted at his death and largely unpublished, was the study of nineteenth-century Paris and its culture – the everyday life of a great city – as emblematic of the experience of modernity. Benjamin's notes on this topic were published in German in the 1980s and made available in English by Susan Buck-Morss in 1989. Literary and cultural theory became increasingly interested not only in the subject matter of Benjamin's project, but also in how he went about it: the fragmented, allusive style of writing; the concern with the meaning of history as crystallized in everyday experience, in marginal things, and in exemplary urban types, most famously the *flâneur* who strolls the city streets (McRobbie, 1994).

In the 1990s "Mechanical Reproduction" had another rebirth, this time in relation to the impact of digital media and the rise of the Internet. Benjamin had emphasized the impact of new technologies on the visual arts. The digitization of the image reopened old questions about the "truth" and "authenticity" of the original, especially in relation to photography. Out there in cyberspace, students in film/TV programs write essays on "Art and Authenticity in the Age of Digital Reproduction," while contemporary artists explore the convergence of text, sound, and visual images. Today, references to Benjamin's essay crop up all over the place. It has become an essential reference in an increasingly diverse set of academic discussions concerning cultural and media studies; feminist writing; film, photographic, and art theory; literary and social theory; history and technology. It is interpreted in a variety of ways, with less emphasis on its overtly Marxist concerns and more on the general questions it raises concerning art and the political and cultural implications of today's new technologies. Clearly Benjamin attempted a redemptive reading of the then new media of film and photography, arguing against the grain of prevailing intellectual opinion so forcefully expressed in Adorno's critical response. Those who see the Internet as offering the possibility of the "global" rather than the "mass" democratization of politics and art invoke the spirit of "The Work of Art in the Age of Mechanical Reproduction."

In his own time, Benjamin sought to find a framework and a vocabulary with which to make sense of newly emergent technologies and their social and political potential. This could only be done, as he well understood, within the context of the tradition in which the present is, at any time, embedded. A canon serves, in part, as a collective *aide-mémoire*, a reminder that what we encounter today was once experienced by others and, at the same time, as a resource for making sense of the enigmas of the future as they emerge into the present light of day.

References

Adorno, T. (1978) On the Fetish Character in Music and the Regression in Listening. In A. Arato and E. Gebhardt (eds), *The Essential Frankfurt School Reader*, Oxford: Blackwell, 270–99.

Benjamin, W. (1968) *Illuminations*, ed. and tr. H. Arendt. London: Fontana/ Collins.

Benjamin, W. (1978) The Author as Producer. In A. Arato and E. Gebhardt (eds), *The Essential Frankfurt School Reader*, Oxford: Blackwell, 254–69.

Brecht, B. (1978) *Brecht on Theatre*, ed. and tr. John Willett. London: Eyre/ Methuen.

Buck-Morss, S. (1989) *The Dialectics of Seeing: Walter Benjamin and the Arcades Project*. Cambridge, MA: MIT Press.

Carey, J. (1992) *The Intellectuals and the Masses, 1880–1939*. London: Faber.

Frisby, J. (1985) *Fragments of Modernity*. Cambridge: Polity.

Frith, S. (1986) Art Versus Technology: The Strange Case of Popular Music. *Media, Culture & Society*, 8 (3), 263–80.

Hall, S. (1980) *Culture, Media, Language: Working Papers in Cultural Studies, 1972–1979*. London: Hutchinson.

Harvey, S. (1980) *May '68 and Film Culture*. London: British Film Institute.

Hynes, S. (1966) *The Auden Generation: Literature and Politics in England in the 1930s*. London: Faber & Faber.

Lukács, G. (1970) Reification and the Consciousness of the Proletariat. In *History and Class Consciousness*, London: Merlin Press, 23–67.

Marx, K. (1976) *Capital*, vol. 1. Harmondsworth: Penguin.

Marx, K. (1992) *Early Writings*. Harmondsworth: Penguin Classics. (Originally published in 1844.)

McRobbie, A. (1994) The *Passagenwerk* and the Place of Walter Benjamin in Cultural Studies. In *Postmodernism and Popular Culture*, London: Routledge, 96–120.

New Left Books (1977) *Western Marxism: A Critical Reader*. London: New Left Books.

Stott, W. (1986) *Documentary Expression and Thirties America*. Chicago: University of Chicago Press.

Taylor, R. (ed. and tr.) (1980) *Aesthetics and Politics: Debates between Bloch, Lukács, Brecht, Benjamin, Adorno*. London: Verso.

Walsh, M. (1981) *The Brechtian Aspect of Radical Cinema*. London: British Film Institute.

Wiggershaus, R. (1994) *The Frankfurt School*. Cambridge: Polity.

5

Redeeming Consumption: On Lowenthal's "The Triumph of the Mass Idols"

Eva Illouz

A canon, to paraphrase Marx, is something we are normally born into, not something we discuss, let alone establish. Indeed, canons are strange sociological phenomena that seem to be established, not by explicit volition or public debate, but by a tacit accord among various tastes and positions. Given that canons have often been debunked as representing particular and partial interests, it may seem somewhat ironic to offer a canon in communications, a field that rehabilitates the unholiest aspects of our culture – the "kitsch," the "ephemeral," the "disposable." This has made it harder for communications to create the institutional dynamics of reverence essential to the canonization of texts and disciplines (media events and other such highly ritualized abstractions are exceptions). Distinguished universities like Harvard, Princeton, and Yale have yet to create departments of communication, thus maintaining the perception that the field belongs to the middle rather than the high-brow segments of academic hierarchy. If canons embody authority, permanence, and reverence, they should not be easily compatible with a field that has done more than others to rehabilitate the transient and disposable aspects of our culture. All this might suggest that there is something intrinsically paradoxical, even self-defeating, in trying to establish a communications canon. Nevertheless, I will explain in this chapter why a text like Lowenthal's "The Triumph of the Mass Idols" should be read and reread by current and future generations of communications students.

In the academic world, the disciplines in which no canon exists are those which are defined as most "scientific." In the social sciences this is clearly the case for experimental psychology and economics, which are closer to the scientific end of the spectrum. Interpretive sciences like sociology and anthropology, on the other hand, rely strongly on a canon of texts and authors. These canons are somewhat ambiguous entities: on the one hand, they point to and enact a form of intellectual agreement on the foundations of a discipline to be found in the works of "classical singular authors" (e.g. the familiar quartet of Marx, Weber, Durkheim, and Simmel in the field of sociology). Yet, at the same time, what makes canons function is the fact that each classical author offers a singular set of metaphors for grasping the world that either ignores or rejects another set of metaphors. We can thus say that the canon of such interpretive disciplines is structured by paradigmatic disagreement. I would thus define a canon as *an agreed-on set of texts that fundamentally diverge from one another.*

It follows from the above that a text can become canonic when it offers a radically new set of metaphors for grasping social reality and reorganizing our understanding of how the social world works. Canonic texts are crucial to interpretive sciences, because they offer singular metaphors and language games for understanding reality. It would be unhelpful to view Marx as more advanced than Confucius, or Donna Harraway as more advanced than Simone de Beauvoir. Each opens up a field of vision that takes us neither forward nor backward, but simply offers new handles with which to grasp reality. Weber will never outdo Marx, despite the fact that both examined the causes and effects of capitalism.

A canon is thus characterized by the *intractability of the various positions it offers*. To take this point even further, I would say that a canonic text is one on which new and contradictory evidence has little or no effect. Historians have successfully contested Marx's vision of the French Revolution as the result of a class struggle and Weber's causal relation between Protestant asceticism and capitalism. Yet it is Marx and Weber who will – and ought to – remain in the canon, not the distinguished historians who have shown their historical claims to be questionable, because the former offered language and theoretical "vision" to grasp reality, while the latter offered, at best, facts and methods. Similarly, we now know that readers can, and occasionally do, decipher mass media texts in all kinds of creative and resistant ways; yet Horkheimer's and Adorno's statements on the culture industries will remain canonic for the field of communications even if they overlooked what has become common knowledge. This is because when we establish canons, we are concerned less with establishing factual verities than with generating conceptual tensions between texts, concepts, and fields of vision. A text becomes canonic when it creates a strategic conceptual tension with other texts and opens up a new way of thinking about the world.

We should value these texts not because of their "originality" or "excellence" – as is often claimed in defense of canons – but rather because they help mobilize and organize communities of knowledge, and more especially intellectual disagreement, in a very efficient way. For example, Gramsci, Foucault, Derrida, and Bourdieu each provided their own set of metaphors to deconstruct the assumptions that animate the traditional literary canon and to discuss the ways in which social and cultural value is constructed. Yet, in appropriating these authors to demolish the traditional canon, such disciplines as English, cultural studies, and communications ironically created a new canon, one that theorized the opposition to established canons by the incipient disciplines. By appropriating these texts, new paradigms of knowledge could be quickly organized (into, say, "cultural studies") to produce new ways of talking about the entanglement of politics with value (e.g. through such metaphors as "hegemony," "discourse," "deconstruction," or "cultural capital"). Foucault's, Derrida's, and Bourdieu's critiques of the foundations of the Western canon could produce new knowledge paradigms because they themselves became an essential part of the current canon of social sciences. This suggests, in turn, that canons bind members of communities of knowledge together around certain texts, because they can generate disagreement around a common set of problems (e.g. the relation between "culture" and "power"). In short, canons help us generate the conceptual tensions from which knowledge paradigms evolve.

The more interpretive a discipline is, the more it needs a canonic organization of knowledge in order to communicate and exchange points of view. Communities of knowledge need an agreed-on set of rules and/ or references; otherwise they risk becoming shapeless or being forced to rely exclusively on scientific modes of gathering and discussing data, which threaten the ways in which interpretive knowledge is normally generated. I would even argue that a canon offers the best way to make a virtue of the necessities to which we are condemned in the social sciences. Because we cannot claim any privileged method or royal road to comprehending the social world, we must make do with what Nietzsche called a "perspective" – a particular point of view from which we come to know an object. A canon is an ensemble of perspectives and, as such, allows us to seize a single object through a variety of viewpoints and positions. Thus, when we teach our students about "culture and power" from Marx to Derrida via Althusser, we are really teaching a set of perspectives that are in dialogue and in tension with each other.

If I am a staunch defender of canons, it is not because I want to defend "excellence" or "permanence" – I reject both – but because I think communities of knowledge are better organized when they make available a panoply of distinct conceptual perspectives as well as the tensions between them. In approaching Lowenthal's piece, I ask whether or not it offers a "singular perspective," and whether this perspective is able to generate some of the conceptual tensions central to communications. Even though his findings have been largely contested by recent research, Lowenthal's approach to cultural material remains canonical to our field, because his text is still inscribed in fundamental conceptual tensions. What makes a text "canonic" is not its ability to prophesy the present – Lowenthal was, in my opinion, wrong on most counts – but rather its ability to invoke dilemmas that are still central to our field.

"The Triumph of the Mass Idols"

As the title of Lowenthal's piece indicates, the triumph of consumption marks the resounding failure of culture. When the article was published in 1944, Lowenthal was, like other members of the Frankfurt school, living on the East Coast in the USA. Like them, he was baffled by the enormous power wielded by the culture industries and interested in understanding their broad social and political implications. Like them, he was appalled by the "entertainment ethic" he found reigning in the USA. And, like them, he engaged in the systematic empirical investigation of the forms and effects taken by the new culture industries. In this investigation he examined biographies of people that appeared in book form and in magazines during the period from 1940 to 1941. He also analyzed the themes of biographies over a period of 40 years, from 1901 to 1941.

Lowenthal grouped the biographies into three categories: those of people who belonged to political life, to the realm of business, and to the realm of entertainment. He found that prior to World War I there had been a very high interest in political figures, and that biographies of business and professional men were nearly equal in number to those of politicians, a state of affairs which changed dramatically after the war. Indeed, the political biographies were cut by 40 percent, and marked a considerable decrease of people from "the serious and important professions and a corresponding increase of entertainers." When Lowenthal further analyzed the composition of the entertainment category, he found that while at the beginning of the century three-quarters of the entertainers were what he called "serious" artists and writers, this class of people had been reduced by half 20 years later and disappeared completely over time. While two decades earlier people from the realm of popular entertainment had barely been present in the biographies, they now formed the largest group. For example, not a single figure from the world of sports was featured in the earlier samples, but by the 1940s such figures ranked close to the top of favorite selections.

According to Lowenthal, the heroes of the past embodied a now defunct ideal of production, while present-day magazine heroes were "idols of consumption," all of them related to the realm of leisure. So the ordinary citizen is faced with the grotesque result that at a time when industry is producing with maximum speed and efficiency, the idols of the masses are not, as in the past, the leading names in the battle of production, but the headliners of the movies, ball parks, and night clubs. If in the 1900s and even the 1920s the vocational distribution of magazine heroes accurately reflected the nation's trends, such hero selection now led to a dreamworld of the masses, who could no longer use biography as a means of orientation, education, and social mobility. This is an ominous transformation for several reasons: first, because the new heroes embody a kind of wealth that is not directly tied to society's needs; second, because culture no longer adequately reflects the real engines of economy and society; and third, because the new heroes no longer guide and instruct us morally, but rather entertain us – that is, lure us into a world of illusions, facile pleasures, and mindless passivity. While the heroes of the past offered some kind of guidance toward the path of social mobility, the contemporary heroes of consumption and entertainment make of "success" another item of consumption, with the result that they in fact take us further away from *real* social mobility. Lowenthal goes as far as suggesting that these biographies exert a subtle but definite psychic terror on their readers.

A critical approach to culture

Wayne Booth's (1961) classic distinction between "telling" and "showing" contrasts the position of an all-knowing narrator, who goes behind the characters' backs and tells the reader what they really think, with that of the narrator who lets the characters speak and act without comment. In order to "tell" – that is, to go behind the backs of social actors – the analyst of culture frequently uses a *critical theory* (e.g. Gramscian, Foucauldian, communitarian, etc.) which enables the narrator to tell us what social actors *really* mean, feel, experience, or think. This is Lowenthal's own position, claiming, for example, that "the worship of heroes of consumption derives from the search for an authority figure" or from "a reified consciousness." In those moments of his narration when Lowenthal tells us what his main protagonists – the biographies and the readers – "really" mean or feel, he is using a critical approach to culture, which makes the meaning of a text depend closely on the critic's set of political and moral assumptions about the social order. Those aspects of the text where the narrator "shows" us the characters without (seeming to) comment on them can be found in his methodology.

Even if Lowenthal's article subsumes his methodology and findings into a single authoritative "telling" voice that overinterprets the social significance of the biographies, there exists a tension between "telling" and "showing," which makes this piece a very fertile one. We have become far more wary about inferring the social effects of texts from their structure. Such analyses open the doors of the study of culture to any prophet of doom. Yet, despite its many mistaken strategies, I believe this text is canonic for the field of communications, because it lays out the main strategies of cultural studies.

To begin with, Lowenthal's study has a quality which, even today, is too rarely encountered: it freely borrows from quantitative and qualitative methods, and from historical as well as sociological methods. Whereas we have become entrenched in sterile quarrels over the superiority of one method of analysis over another, Lowenthal's piece can still teach us one or two things about the "methodological imagination" so crucially needed in a field that must juggle and hold together the many balls of the cultural process. Moreover, Lowenthal views biographies as *models of* and *models for* – as mirrors of social life as well as guides for social behavior – thus not only foreshadowing Clifford Geertz's famous distinction, but also paving the way for the sociology of culture, which precisely investigates this double-edged character of symbols.

Second, because biography is a middle-brow genre, Lowenthal could legitimately make use of analytical techniques borrowed from literature, thus involuntarily mixing cultural segments and collapsing cultural hierarchies – a move that would later on become the hallmark of cultural studies. To the best of my knowledge, at the time Lowenthal was writing, using methods of literary analysis to understand items of popular culture, or at least of "middle-brow" culture, was highly innovative (see his analyses of his characters' personality, the techniques of their presentation, their relations to other characters, and their physical surroundings). Implicit in this methodology (even if Lowenthal probably did not will it) is the key claim that *a common methodology can and should be applied equally to the realms of literature and popular culture.* Again, this is a fundamental claim of cultural studies which have systematically overlooked cultural hierarchies to look for meaning patterns across cultural formations.

Third, the choice of biographies as a category of analysis to document social change is remarkable in yet another respect. Biography is a symbolic form that has the characteristic of being "betwixt and between": between fact and fiction, history and literature, neither high-brow nor low-brow. It is properly a middle-class cultural genre that mixes codes of historical realism with codes of fictional narrative. In this respect biographies are likely to exert a significant cultural influence, for they elicit the same mechanisms of identification as the novel, but can more effectively guide behavior because they describe real rather than fictional lives. Moreover, the choice of biography as a "cultural indicator" is particularly judicious in light of the fact that, as research of the last 20 years has shown, our relationship to our environment and our sense of self are constructed and negotiated in essentially narrative categories. As Giddens (1992) and Beck and Beck-Gernsheim (1995) have suggested, modernity has been marked by the transformation of identity into a biographical project. Inasmuch as biography is a narrative of selfhood that leans on, and draws from, what Sherry Ortner calls "key cultural scenarii," it is both collective and exemplary. However, Lowenthal's main goal was to show that the transformation of such exemplary biographies is indicative of a new *inability* to shape valuable selves and biographies.

It is ironic that such a remarkable methodological apparatus as Lowenthal's was mobilized to make so many statements which have since been largely disproved. For one thing, it can easily be shown that the heroes of consumption, who Lowenthal saw as threatening the old industrial order, were in fact the representatives and carriers of the "third industrial revolution," based on knowledge, information, and electronic technology, and that the shift from production to consumption has generated far more wealth and self-made men than the "second industrial revolution." If biographies of sports or movie stars have so easily supplanted the biographies of the old industrial elites, it is because these stars and the realm in which they move have generated the most extravagant sources of wealth in the history of capitalism. Moreover, information-based capitalism, aptly dubbed "techno-capitalism" by Douglas Kellner (1989) has given rise to a new form of social mobility through the channel of education. Indeed, professionals and "new cultural intermediaries" constitute a relatively wide middle and upper-middle class, which has provided a much greater channel of social mobility than the nineteenth-century Darwinist conceptions of leadership and merit could allow for (Bendix, 1956; Whyte, 1957).

As well, far from auguring the decline of work, the culture of leisure has in fact been accompanied by a steady, massive increase in working hours, as Judith Schor (1991) has shown very well in her historical analysis of the working patterns of Americans. And, as Arlie Hochschild (1997) has demonstrated, people increasingly flee their homes, preferring to take refuge in the orderly environment of their work, which they view as a liberation from the hard work of their leisurely homes. Indeed, consumer capitalism grew on the shoulders of Fordism, which was characterized by its intensive organization to make work more efficient and rational, in order to increase production. The difference between the early (so-called industrial) capitalism and the later "consumer" capitalism is that work on the self has migrated to a different site. In consumer capitalism, the body has become the object of constant hard work, and the glamour and fun are undergirded by a fundamentally anxious attitude vis-à-vis one's self: a far cry from the mindless hedonism that Lowenthal attributes to it.

Lowenthal's text resonates deeply with the set of questions and dilemmas that still preoccupy us. In particular, it offers an important perspective for understanding the relationship between culture and economy, which we must still confront, for we have not yet finished understanding our ambivalent relation to capitalism. In more than one way, Lowenthal's piece is a witness to such ambivalence and to our difficulties in interpreting the role that culture should assume in such an economic and social order.

With the extraordinary acumen that characterized the work of the Frankfurt school, Lowenthal saw that the idiom of consumption and leisure marked a significant departure from nineteenth-century culture and economy. More dramatically, he debunks in his famous article what would make Daniel Bell (1976) one of the most famous American sociologists of the 1970s and 1980s: namely, the contradiction between two idioms of capitalism, the idiom of production and the idiom of consumption, and between the work ethic and the hedonism encouraged (and even required) by the sphere of consumption. Like other sociologists, Lowenthal preferred the culture of industrial capitalism even if he did not like its social injustice, because at least it offered guidance, and valued and rewarded moral character. In short, what industrial capitalism could offer was a cultural order organized by moral hierarchies.

Lowenthal's study is based on two assumptions: the first is that culture ought to emanate from a higher moral order. The second, which follows from the first, is that cultural analysis of texts can be a substitute for, or at least an introduction to, political analysis. These assumptions still largely guide cultural analysis.

From his analysis of texts, Lowenthal concludes that readers worship the idols of consumption, that the biographies examined point to massive cultural and moral losses, and that they mark the disappearance of individuality and the triumph of the shapeless, directionless masses. He maintains that "[s]uccess has lost the seductive charm which once seemed to be a promise and a prize for everybody who was strong, clever, flexible, sober enough to try" (p. 129). His strongest claim is that biographies no longer play an educational or informative role. Culture does not elevate and guide us; it merely amuses us, and in the process can no longer help us to become self-made, successful men and women.

I am unsure whether Lowenthal mourns only the *charm of the promise* – which could remain unfulfilled as long as it was charming – or a lost age in which promises were delivered and one was rewarded for one's merit. If he is mourning simply the disappearance of the charm of success, he can be reassured, because the charms of the heroes of consumption are as powerful as those of Ulysses' Sirens: it would take nothing less than binding ourselves to the mast to resist the "song" of movie, music, or sports stars. But Lowenthal's regret that merit is no longer rewarded is puzzling. How could Lowenthal, a member of the last serious Western European Marxist school of thought, really believe that success rewarded whoever was clever, flexible, or sober enough? Richard Bendix's study of the rise of industrial capitalism showed clearly that social mobility was probably lesser in the past than in the present; nor was it necessarily based more on merit. Lowenthal betrays here a very German axiomatic admiration for endless Faustian striving, for activities with unattainable goals; a Marxian axiomatic ennoblement of work as the only dignified human activity; and a strong reluctance to accept the cultural decline of industrial elites.

Like that of so many other cultural analysts, Lowenthal's critique is based on the cardinal assumption that culture must be subordinate to a higher social and political vision, thereby elevating us. He would much rather have us admire the Carnegie Mellons, the Morgans, or the Schwabs (who all made their fortunes during the second industrial revolution) than, say, Denzel Washington or Oprah Winfrey, because the former embody a moral superiority that Lowenthal identifies as the vocation of culture. Indeed, the old industrial elites worked very hard to legitimize their wealth by wrapping their success in an aura of gravity and sobriety – a far cry from the aura of careless glamour and fun in which the new heroes of consumption dress themselves. What these idols of consumption are really guilty of, I think, is desecrating the magical aura of seriousness in which the nineteenth-century economy and culture were carefully sealed to protect them from the contaminating influence of "the masses."

In the end, and ironically so, Lowenthal erects another idol: the idol of work and production. For, as Max Weber brilliantly showed, the rationality of production is fundamentally *irrational*. Endless production is no more rational or elevating than endless consumption. It presents itself as a noble and legitimate activity only at the price of a mystification that makes Lowenthal and many proponents of critical theory the real idol-worshippers. What is so astonishing about mass consumption, in fact, is not that it erects idols, but rather that it has properly *no* god. Consumption lacks transcendence, is restless, and, as Lasch (1979) noted long ago, fundamentally narcissistic. We are not yet able to understand or analyze the meaning of a culture whose vocation is not "moral" or oriented toward the achievement of higher values, but rather toward *self-fashioning*.

For Lowenthal, as for most members of the Frankfurt school, the emergence of the sphere of consumption meant the passage from an age of individuality to the age of the anonymous homogeneity of the mass. But the contrary interpretation is far more plausible. As Zygmunt Bauman put it, "production is a collective endeavour. Consumption is a thoroughly individual, solitary and in the end, lonely activity" (1998, p. 30). Indeed, far from promoting greater individuality and strength of character, the factory was a far more homogenizing cultural force than consumption, a tendency which has only accentuated with time (Kunda, 1992). According to Lowenthal, consumption-man strives for a kind of social adjustment that makes him supremely conformist. But here again I would argue the opposite view. The extraordinary grip exerted by consumer capitalism is found in the fact that it sells on the basis of infinitesimal differences; consumption summons us as consumers primarily by inviting us to be thoroughly original, individual, and "true to our true self" (Lears, 1981; Marchand, 1985; Illouz, 1997). Anyone who has seen an American corporation or has read C. Wright Mill's study *White Collar* (1951) knows that few places demand such thorough adjustment and conformism as the capitalist workplace. By contrast, consumption marks the apotheosis of individuality, which is precisely why it departs radically from social visions based on community and hierarchy of values.

But consumption is far from being the smooth, well-adjusted behavior that Lowenthal makes it out to be, for it reflects a fundamentally worried, restless, dissatisfied attitude, in perpetual motion and striving. Ironically, the very Faustian ideal of endless striving that Lowenthal seems to long for in the defunct production heroes is much better embodied in the realm of consumption, in which one literally never finishes aiming at a target in perpetual motion. For Lowenthal, the past heroes of production offer a higher model of personhood because, as he put it, "the individual ha[d] to find himself in the soliloquy of the mind," as opposed to the present day, where action, development, and self-making have been rendered obsolete. However, I would suggest that, on the contrary, consumption calls for an endless, Sisyphean project of self-making. The dubious, but very successful, marriage of consumption with psychology makes us responsible for fashioning the innermost crannies of our self and our psyche (Lears, 1981). We have never been so thoroughly engaged in a perpetual soliloquy of the mind to find out who we are. There *is* a difference between the heroes of production and the heroes of consumption, but it is not the one Lowenthal offers us. True: heroes of consumption do not encourage virtue or strength of character, and target the self more than "action" proper. But this is not because we have become more indoctrinated, but rather because (in the most ironic twist on Lowenthal's claims) we now direct all our energies toward fashioning our own biographies, in the form of our CVs and personal lives. If the biographies of others no longer serve us as guides, it is because we have become not too little, but too much, preoccupied with our own biographies – biographies which in turn are supposed to reflect the deepest, most inaccessible part of our own selves.

Lowenthal's critique of consumption is waged in the name of a specter that haunts many critiques of modern life: namely, the golden age of an ethical community (*Sittlichkeit*) that could form individuals and provide them with character and virtues. Far from seeing the constant work demanded in the sphere of consumption, Lowenthal claims that consumption makes us, quite literally, inanimate objects: "Behind the polished mask of training and adjustment lurks the concept of a human robot who, without having done anything himself, moves just such parts and in just such directions as the makers wished him to." But robots, in fact, stand for the opposite of what consumer society creates: namely, desire, and the desire to desire. It was Foucault's major contribution to show that modernity marks the height of a long-term project of self-fashioning (of which consumption is one of the main vectors) defined by the pursuit of pleasure and desire. The modern individual does not cultivate moral dispositions, but an "aesthetic way of life" oriented toward pleasure, satisfaction, and the art of everyday living.

This is not to say that we should not criticize the sphere of leisure and consumption. I am very wary of the happy post-modern endorsement of contemporary culture. It remains the exceptional legacy of the critical theorists to demand relentless attention to the many cultural and economic forms that barbarity takes. Like them, I think our main task is, and remains, critique. But how should we wage this critique? I believe we must learn to criticize the many seductions of consumption outside the compass of nineteenth-century categories. If the media–consumption nexus raises such difficulties for analysis, it is because many scholars cannot transcend the categories from which the social sciences were born: worries about the decline of the ethical way of life and the rise of the aesthetic way of life; individualism and individuality versus the bounded community; a model of culture based on tradition and reverence. In order to succeed in our goals, we must reflect on the remarkable gains of a more democratic and unavoidably more chaotic and insipid cultural sphere, and on the limits we are willing (or not) to impose on this process of democratization. Thus, a critique based on nineteenth-century models of community, of ethical conduct, and of an auratic view of culture is fated to become a "prophecy of doom," and to miss the extraordinary intellectual challenges posed by the conjunction of mass media and the sphere of consumption. It is these challenges that Lowenthal's article invites us to measure up to.

References

Bauman, Z. (1998) *Work, Consumerism and the New Poor*. Buckingham: Open University Press.

Beck, U. and Beck-Gernsheim, E. (1995) *The Normal Chaos of Love*. Cambridge: Polity.

Bell, D. (1976) *The Cultural Contradictions of Capitalism*. New York: Basic Books.

Bendix, R. (1956) *Work and Authority in Industry: Ideologies of Management in the Course of Deindustrialization*. Berkeley: University of California Press.

Booth, W. C. (1961) *The Rhetoric of Fiction*. Chicago: University of Chicago Press.

Giddens, A. (1992) *The Transformation of Intimacy: Sexuality, Love, and Eroticism in Modern Societies*. Stanford: Stanford University Press; Cambridge: Polity.

Hochschild, A. R. (1997) *The Time Bind: When Work Becomes Home and Home Becomes Work*. New York: Metropolitan Books.

Illouz, E. (1997) *Consuming the Romantic Utopia: Love and the Cultural Contradictions of Capitalism*. Berkeley: University of California Press.

Kellner, D. (1989) *Critical Theory, Marxism, and Modernity: Development and Contemporary Relevance of the Frankfurt School*. Cambridge: Polity.

Kunda, G. (1992) *Engineering Culture*. Philadelphia: Temple University Press.

Lasch, C. (1979) *The Culture of Narcissism: American Life in an Age of Diminishing Expectations*. New York: W. W. Norton & Company.

Lears, T. J. J. (1981) *No Place of Grace: Antimodernism and the Transformation of American Culture, 1880–1920*. New York: Pantheon Books.

Lowenthal, L. (1961) The Triumph of the Mass Idols. In *Literature, Popular Culture, and Society*, Palo Alto, CA: Pacific Books, 109–36.

Marchand, R. (1985) *Advertising the American Dream: Making Way for Modernity, 1920–1940*. Berkeley: University of California Press.

Mills, C. W. (1951) *White Collar: The American Middle Classes*. New York: Oxford University Press.

Ortner, S. (1990) Patterns of History: Cultural Schemas in the Foundings of Sherpa Religious Institutions. In E. Ohnuki Tierney (ed.), *Culture through Time: Anthropological Approaches*, Stanford, CA: Stanford University Press, 57–93.

Schor, J. (1991) *The Overworked American: The Unexpected Decline of Leisure*. New York: Basic Books.

Thurow, L. C. (1984) *Dangerous Currents: The State of Economics*. Oxford: Oxford University Press.

Whyte, W. H. (1957) *The Organization Man*. Garden City, NY: Doubleday.

PART III
The Chicago School

———

Introduction

"Chicago," wrote Henry Adams, "asked in 1893 for the first time the questions whether the American people knew where they were driving. . . . Chicago was the first expression of American thought as a unity; one must start there" (Adams, 1931, p. 343). Though he was not referring to the University of Chicago's Department of Sociology, he could have been. The city's convulsive modernity – with industrialization, urbanization, and immigration exploding at a speed unparalleled anywhere in the nineteenth century – found voice in an influential body of social thought and research that set the tone for American sociology from World War I to World War II. Out of ethnic mixing, class conflict, and social disorganization, two generations of sociologists brewed a social theory that saw communication as the prime mover of social order. Though mass media *per se* were only occasionally the primary focus at Chicago, communication always was, whether the population under study was gangs, taxi-dancers, or Polish peasants. For Chicago, communication was the primary mode by which human ties are made; as such, it was the primal element of social life (Depew and Peters, 2001).

Communication was a productively ambiguous concept for the Chicagoans: both empirical and normative, small-scale and large-scale, material and ideal. Communication could refer to empirical practices such as journalism or correspondence between America and the old country, but it could also serve as a normative criterion for judging human association. Though Chicago sociology prided itself on its non-moralistic approach to subcultures and so-called deviance, it clearly didn't lack ideas about what a good society needs: fair chances for all citizens to take part interactively in determining their common conditions. Interaction is a key term: in both research method (participant observation) and theory of democracy (participatory), Chicago sociology delights in the shoulder rubbing of diverse people. It posits a serendipity in public interaction, crowds milling about, and the encounter with strangers. The Chicago school prizes the newspaper for orchestrating a crisscrossing of social worlds in its pages. Interaction could now be extended over a new scale of distances, as space and time collapsed with the growth of modern transportation and communication. The more normatively minded (Cooley, Dewey) found this an exciting possibility for the founding of a great community, but also worried about its dark side: the depreciation of local, face-to-face life. If communication creates community, what of communities consisting purely of symbolic interaction, without a local anchor?

Our three selections are perhaps unrepresentative by date, but not by argument. Wirth reproduces some classic principles of Chicago social thought. Similar visions of community, of a civic-minded social science, of the potential dangers and delights of large congregations of people can all be found in Dewey's essays of the 1890s, Park's 1904 dissertation on *The Crowd and the Public*, and Mead's lectures and political journalism in the 1910s. Lang and Lang and Horton and Wohl both offer variations on old Chicago themes. Lang and Lang give us a classic Chicago object: a co-present urban congregation. But the grouping along MacArthur's parade route is neither a dangerous crowd nor a democratic public, but a prop in a staged event for another audience, one that has retreated from the streets. Here the authors reaffirm one of the ambiguities of modern communication: participation at a distance may displace or transform the elbow-bumping interaction of local sociability. Horton and Wohl likewise trouble the old communication–community equation. In the formative accounts of communication of Cooley and Mead, interaction at a distance enhanced democracy. Para-social interaction is an ironic commentary on this optimistic dream. The radio listeners who imagine themselves the intimates of "the Lonely Gal," for instance, look more like losers than good citizens. Here interaction is not a real encounter with strangers, but a projection of fantasy. Horton and Wohl fit the Chicago lineage of nervousness about media forms that appeal to fantasy and undercut the potential for co-present interaction (clear, for instance, in Blumer's studies of movies (1933)).

For scholars interested in the media and their social, cultural, and political meanings, Chicago is something of a Mecca. For later scions of the Frankfurt school such as Jürgen Habermas, Chicago social theory, especially that of Mead, has been an inspiration for discovering the normative basis of democracy. By the 1950s, Chicago and Columbia traditions were cross-fertilizing; and even Harold Adams Innis studied at the University of Chicago. Though Chicago may have overestimated the relative importance of communication in the creation of social life, it will remain a way station for those who seek light on how we symbol-using animals manage to interact up close and far off.

References

Adams, H. (1931) *The Education of Henry Adams*. New York: Modern Library. (Originally published in 1918.)

Blumer, H. (1933) *Movies and Conduct*. New York: Macmillan.

Depew, D. J. and Peters, J. D. (2001) Community and Communication: The Conceptual Background. In G. J. Shepherd and E. W. Rothenbuhler (eds), *Communication and Community*, Mahwah, NJ: Erlbaum, 3–21.

6
Community and Pluralism in Wirth's "Consensus and Mass Communication"

Eric W. Rothenbuhler

In mass communication we have unlocked a new social force of as yet incalculable magnitude. In comparison with all previous social means for building or destroying the world this new force looms as a gigantic instrument of infinite possibilities for good or evil. It has the power to build loyalties and to undermine them, and thus by furthering or hindering consensus to affect all other sources of power. By giving people access to alternative views mass communication does of course open the door to the disintegration of all existing social solidarities, while it creates new ones. It is of the first importance, therefore, that we understand its nature, its possibilities and its limits and the means of harnessing it to human purposes. (Wirth, 1948, p. 12)

Louis Wirth's "Consensus and Mass Communication" is an interesting nominee for canonic status for several reasons. Not least among them is that Wirth presents the piece as timely rather than timeless, thus reminding us of the very different ways in which we use the word "canon" in social-scientific and religious contexts. Written as a speech for an academic occasion – Wirth's presidential address to the American Sociological Society in December 1947 – "Consensus and Mass Communication" is a communication in the narrow sense of the noun, from one professor to some others present before him as an audience. If we receive it now as having relevance outside the context of its original delivery – without any claim of God or Truth – that value must depend on our own reading as much as on the text as such. I read the work under the influence of much that came after it, and I put Wirth's work in dialogue with older texts and other aspects of intellectual history selected according to our agenda as much as his own.

"Consensus and Mass Communication" remains valuable reading because it provides a view on the history of the field that is unusually useful for contemporary concerns. This chapter is organized according to those concerns, under a series of topical headings. Throughout I will also show how Wirth's paper serves as an example of Chicago sociology, and thus as a useful window on that part of our field's history.

Wirth's essay begins by invoking the threat of nuclear annihilation and the corresponding need for knowledge to control the social uses of knowledge. He proposes to concentrate on consensus as "both an approach to the central problem of sociology and to the problems of the contemporary world" (1948, p. 2). Communication is presented as both the means and the product of consensus, with mass communication as the analogue of mass consensus. Progress on problems of consensus in mass society will also be progress toward the goal of inclusive demo-cracy, in his analysis. The ultimate goal would be world consensus, to "allow the fullest use of the world's resources to meet human needs under freedom and order and in peace" (p. 14).[1]

A communication-centric conception of sociology

Wirth defines sociology as working "to understand the behavior of men insofar as that behavior is influenced by group life. . . . the capacity of [society's] members to understand one another and to act in concert toward common objectives and under common norms" (p. 2). Com-munication is the process that supports this capacity to understand and act in concert: "If men of diverse experiences and interests are to have ideas and ideals in common, they must have the ability to communicate" (p. 4). Wirth quickly complicates this appeal to commonality, but begin-ning with the centrality of communication indicates his grounding in the Chicago school of sociology.

From theoretical debates about symbols and reality to studies of news-paper circulation and public opinion, communication in its various forms was a recurrent topic for the Chicago sociologists, Wirth among them. Communication appears at three different levels of analysis in their work. Most generally, communication is central to the pragmatist philosophy on which their work was founded. William James (with whom Robert Park, one of the leaders of Chicago sociology, had studied at Harvard); John Dewey, who taught at Chicago from 1894 to 1904; and George

Herbert Mead, with whom generations of Chicago sociologists studied, provided a conception of human being, knowledge, truth, value, and action founded in symbolic exchange. (The debates about how best to interpret the various positions of these three philosophers are not essential in this context; see e.g. Kurtz, 1984.) Mead's courses were essentially required of sociology students at Chicago, and the pragmatist conception featured prominently in "the green bible," the graduate textbook *Introduction to the Science of Sociology*, compiled by Park and Burgess. For the sociologists, the pragmatist conception of pluralist realities and the emphasis on experience yielded a body of methods, presumptions, questions, and explanations about social life in which people's perspectives were as important as any material, non-perspectival facts. Sociology, informed by pragmatism, was concerned with people as positioned in communication networks, flows, and interactions, defined by symbols and meanings as much as by geography, demography, and social organization. (Georg Simmel's influence was also crucial here; Park had studied with Simmel briefly in Germany, and excerpts of Simmel's work were prominent in Chicago teaching and in the *Introduction*.) As one small example, consider the concluding sentence of an article based on Wirth's doctoral dissertation: "The ghetto . . . can be completely understood only if it is viewed as a sociopsychological, as well as an ecological, phenomenon; for it is not merely a physical fact, but also a state of mind" (Wirth, 1964a, p. 98). (This quotation echoes both Park – the city is "a state of mind, a body of customs and traditions," as well as an agglomeration of people, institutions, and built environment (1925a, p. 1) – and Simmel's "The Metropolis and Mental Life" (1964).)

The Chicago sociologists saw communication processes, technologies, and institutions as fundamental to modern society. The study of the newspaper, public opinion, attitudes, transportation and communication infrastructures and flows, networks, group interaction, and sociometry were all pioneered by Chicago sociologists, because each was defined as an essential topic. Sociology could not be without them. Ogburn posited "that communication and transportation 'constitute the second phase of the industrial revolution' (1935)" (in Kurtz, 1984, p. 68). The *Introduction* includes multiple chapter subheadings on communication, 25 index entries, and cross-references to language, newspapers, and publicity. (See Depew and Peters, 2001.)

At the most specific level the Chicago sociologists derived a variety of propositions, hypotheses, methods, and indicators from their conception of the fundamental nature of symbol and communication. These include Thomas's aphorism, "If men define situations as real, they are real in their consequences," as well as the methodological dependence on letters in Thomas and Znaniecki's (1918) classic study *The Polish Peasant in Europe and America*. Park's studies of newspaper history and circulation (e.g. 1925b, 1929–30), as well as McKenzie's (1968) use of newspaper circulation as an indicator of the geography of urban influence, are specific adaptations of the general principle of the importance of communication. For the same reasons Chicago neighborhood studies often included maps, diagrams, and tables of who talked to whom, of overlapping group members, of newspaper circulation, and so on (see Burgess and Bogue, 1964; Short, 1971; Whyte, 1955, for examples).

For Wirth, then, this intellectual background supports the proposition of his essay "Consensus and Mass Communication" that mass communication is a phenomenon of equal importance to atomic energy, and its study and control a necessary counterbalance to the unleashing of the destructive potential of atomic energy. Generations later, post-modernists would strive to scandalize their readers with such extreme claims, but Wirth reports it as plain fact: "Mass communication is rapidly becoming, if it is not already, the main framework of the web of social life. . . . We live in an era when the control over these media constitutes perhaps the most important source of power in the social universe" (p. 10). Wirth, though, took this as a call for social scientists to work toward understanding the media and mass communication, with the aim of ameliorating their results. He believed in knowledge and its uses.

Culture and everyday life

The study of everyday life in the modern city, among differing ethnic, racial, national, and religious groups, differing classes, neighborhoods, workplaces, and leisure settings is another of the major contributions of Chicago sociology. "Consensus and Mass Communication" can provide students with a gateway to that contribution, though they will have to look elsewhere to find it discussed more explicitly. Today Raymond Williams is almost universally credited with authoring the intellectual shift to culture as a whole way of life that founded cultural studies. This move grew out of his study of the English novel and drew on the sensibilities and methods of anthropologists (e.g. Williams, 1983; and see Peters, chapter 11 below). Consider this from Wirth's teacher Robert Park in 1915 (quoted here from the slightly revised 1925 reprint):

> The same patient methods of observation which anthropologists like Boas and Lowie have expended on the study of the life and manners of the North American Indian might be even more fruitfully employed in the investigation of the customs, beliefs, social practices, and general conceptions of

life prevalent in Little Italy on the lower North Side in Chicago, or in recording the more sophisticated folkways of the inhabitants of Greenwich
Village and the neighborhood of Washington Square, New York.

   We are mainly indebted to writers of fiction for our more intimate knowledge of contemporary urban life. But the life of our cities demands a more
searching and disinterested study than even Émile Zola has given us. (Park,
1925a, p. 3)

Chicago sociology was centered on attention to the structures and
practices of everyday life and produced a rich literature on neighborhoods, gangs, night clubs, working-class life, racial differences and relations, immigrant life, and more (see Burgess and Bogue, 1964; Short,
1971, for examples). Wirth's work on the ghetto as a social form, his
essay "Urbanism as a Way of Life," as well as his community studies
and essays on cultural conflict and city life all contribute to a historically
informed, conceptually sophisticated, empirical sociology that anticipates
cultural studies (Wirth, 1964a, 1964b, 1964c; see also Park, 1925a).
The missing elements are an explicit argument about the definition of
culture, the neo-Marxist conceptions (though Wirth was active in Marxist antiwar activities as an undergraduate (Sheldon, 1968; Wirth Marvick,
1964)), and attention to spectacular popular entertainments and youth
cultures. The Chicago approach – Wirth in particular – is more concerned with the normal than the unusual, the group than the individual,
the adult than the young, and work life than leisure life. In any case,
both Chicago sociology and contemporary cultural studies view culture
and communication as inherently intertwined. "Communication as I
understand it is, if not identical with, at least indispensable to, the cultural process" (Park, 1972b, p. 101).

The mass

The concept of the mass survives in our literature only in the first chapter of textbooks and introductory discussions of classes. A chronology of
theories of communication is usually presented as a story of progress, in
which earlier mistaken assumptions deriving from mass society theory
were overcome by the hard work of more recent researchers, who were
also more democratically inclined and showed greater cultural sensitivity
than their forebears. This story has a serious pedigree, perhaps first finding
print in Katz's and Lazarsfeld's *Personal Influence* (1955). The consensus opinion is that the concept of the mass is best left behind as empirically wrong and politically suspect. The result of the disparagement of the
mass concept and the abandonment of the literature in which it was

developed, however, is that the field is left less well equipped to deal realistically with communication phenomena on the scale of contemporary markets, nations, and world regions.

"Consensus and Mass Communication" is full of realistic ideas about the mass characteristics of modern society that are useful today. One concise and lucid section of the essay defines "mass" by a set of seven characteristics followed by a cogent discussion of their implications. The mass is defined by large numbers of dispersed members, socially heterogeneous, mutually anonymous, without organization, open to suggestions, and acting as relatively unattached individuals. Wirth does not present these characteristics as concrete empirical claims about the whole of anyone's life. They are analytical characteristics of aspects of people's lives in modern societies. When people experience relative anonymity in large, dispersed, heterogeneous groups, without organizational memberships or institutional traditions being invoked, then they can be expected to react as relatively unattached individuals. When large numbers of people do so, the behavior and opinions of the mass itself become a dynamic that can only be predicted in broad outline. The culture industries, as well as modern politics, show these characteristics. The "unknowable" audience (Ang, 1991; Peterson, 1994; Rothenbuhler, 1996), as well as uncertain electorates, are mass phenomena. The volatility of market performance for television shows, movies, and music is due to the "mass" characteristics of the audience. Broad as they may be, the predictable statistical patterns of the aggregate audience, independent of the decisions of individuals, also are mass phenomena. No one lives their entire life as an isolated, anonymous individual, just one among many interchangeable others in the aggregate. But some aspects of lives are lived that way, with implications that are crucial for the operations of modern communication systems, political systems, and national cultures.

Wirth proposes that democratic mass society faces a series of difficulties due to the attendant size and intricacy of mass social structures and the dynamic nature of equilibria in mass society; to the instability of interests and motives and the uncertainty of leadership; and the concentrations of power and authority and the complicated machineries of administration. This leads to a discussion of the dynamics of public opinion in a mass society.

Public opinion and control of the media

Consensus is a phenomenon of opinion, and if democracy depends on consensus, it therefore depends on processes of opinion. If group memberships,

traditions, ideologies, and so on provide stability to opinion, then phenomena in mass society – such as mass communication – that invoke
people as free-choosing individualists yield a much more changeable
dynamic in opinion processes. The goal of democratic mass society is,
therefore, simultaneously more dependent on opinion processes that
are less reliable. Control of the means of communication, leadership,
and the work of communication and culture producers is, therefore,
that much more important – and that much more the point of social
vulnerability.

Wirth's treatment of the mass and the mechanisms and dynamics of
public opinion reflects the accumulated wisdom of the Chicago school,
which pioneered the study of collective behavior in American sociology.
Park's German doctoral dissertation was on "The Crowd and the Public" (1972a); the *Introduction* co-authored with Burgess (1969) included
a chapter on collective behavior; and a number of Chicago students conducted studies of fads, fashions, social movements, and other aspects of
collective behavior. Park has even been credited with inventing the field
and defining its terms of analysis (Elsner, 1972; Kurtz, 1984, pp. 90–2).
In the older tradition represented by Le Bon (1977), collective behavior
was presumed to be irrational; crowds were bodies without brains, their
behavior symptoms of the breakdown of social control. Tarde (e.g. 1969)
added a conception of the public as a kind of dispersed crowd held
together by communication and opinion. Park (e.g. 1972a; Park and
Burgess, 1969) introduced thinking about the crowd and the public as
distinct but normal social forms. The crowd might think differently, but
it is not without thought; crowds might be characteristic of periods of
social change, but that in itself is not abnormal. The crowd is a form of
the public, and publics are capable of deliberation. From this, the modern study of audiences, movements, markets, fads, fashions, and public
opinion all followed. Wirth's presentation of the mass follows this tradition. The mass is a form of social organization that gives rise to particular dynamics of public opinion, with implications for democratic process
and order.

As opinion processes are less stable in the mass than when group or
institutional memberships are primary, and because of the size and complexity of structure of mass audiences, control of the means of communication becomes that much more important. Here Wirth addresses a topic
we tend to think was raised by few but Adorno (e.g. Horkheimer and
Adorno, 1972; see Peters, chapter 3 above) until decades later. "The fact
that the media of communication tend toward monopolistic control, as
is evidenced by the building up of industrial empires in this field of
enterprise, has serious implications for mass democracy" (Wirth, 1948,

p. 11). Wirth is concerned about the expression of minority opinions, interests, and tastes and with democratic processes under conditions of concentrated control of the media. As his analysis pins the survival of democratic societies to consensus and sees consensus as dependent on mass communication, control of the means of mass communication becomes crucially important.

> In a society where all men irrespective of race, creed, origin, and status claim and are to be granted an increasing share of participation in the common life and in the making of common decisions, the control of these media of mass communication constitutes a central problem. If it is consensus that makes an aggregate of men into a society, and if consensus is increasingly at the mercy of the functioning of the mass communication agencies as it is in the democratic world, then the control over these instrumentalities becomes one of the principle sources of political, economic, and social power. (Wirth, 1948, p. 12)

Consensus

Like "mass," "consensus" is also a term that has been abandoned in social analysis, and also, like mass, a term whose recovery would benefit the field. To at least as great an extent as mass, consensus was abandoned for its embarrassing associations, rather than for its particular conceptualizations or theoretical uses. "Consensus sociology" came to be the label applied to mainstream liberal sociology at a time when being mainstream and liberal was unattractive. Indeed there was, in the 1950s especially, some conceptual overreaching. As totalitarianism came into use as a conceptual category uniting Nazi Germany and other Fascist governments with the Soviet and Chinese Communist blocs, the liberal industrial societies of the West seemed obviously to be preferred – and to have only one opposite. The issue appeared to be how liberal society was better than totalitarian society, rather than how to improve the liberal one. Some theorists, then, offered theories and explanations of society that could be seen as little more than rationalizations for the status quo in America and Britain. Their theories appeared to presume that liberal societies were smoothly operating systems, characterized by agreement on the rules and fair scaling between participation and benefits. Characteristically, these theorists would appeal to value consensus as a key issue in the integration of modern societies. Individuals cohered into social systems because they had internalized the core values of the culture, and this implied agreement on fundamental values and beliefs integrated the society. Lukes (1977) provides a trenchant analysis of the problems with this thinking, and points the way around them.

Wirth's discussion of consensus is an entirely different creature from what later came to be known and rejected as consensus sociology. His "consensus" is not about agreement on values, but about the processes of communication that allow a society of diverse citizens to be governed liberally (similar to the proceduralist proposals of Habermas (e.g. 1981) and Sciulli (1985), though Wirth is not as conscious of, or as consistent in, that logic). He defines consensus as the social condition of wide-spread consent, which appears as a degree of tolerance, indifference, deference, delegation, and agreement which allows societies to continue to function in the face of differences of interest, competition, and con-flict. Such a definition could tip over into tautology and apology – the way things are muddled through taken as evidence of how they should be done – but neither the essay nor the larger context of Wirth's life and work provide reason to think that this was his intention. He worked his whole life as a social reformer. His discussion of consensus similarly emphasizes the activity of striving for social improvement.

Wirth's position was realist and political (cf. Reiss, 1964, esp. pp. xvii–xxii), in that it expected difference and disagreement as well as disinter-est, and aimed at ways to manage it under conditions of competition, conflict, and differential distributions of life chances, resources, author-ity, and power. Some of the more idealist statements of the pragmatist tradition on which Wirth's sociology is based actually preferred differ-ence and disagreement. Speaking of the group of pragmatists associated with the New School in the 1920s and 1930s, it was said that they "neither . . . expected or even looked forward to moral and ethical con-sensus. Debate and controversy seemed to them essential elements of a truly vital political community. . . . They enthusiastically endorsed political structures that encouraged dissent and tolerated a wide diversity of opinion" (Rutkoff and Scott, 1986, p. 77). If the pragmatist philosophers could prefer difference and disagreement, the pragmatist sociologist should certainly expect it. But rather than abandon the term "consensus," Wirth shifts its definition, reminding us of the role of consent in consensus and of the processes of communication that produce it.

> Consensus in mass democracies, therefore, is not so much agreement on all issues or even on the most essential substantive issues among all the members of society as it is the established habit of intercommunication, of discussion, debate, negotiation and compromise, and the toleration of her-esies, or even of indifference, up to the point of "clear and present danger" which threatens the life of the society itself. (Wirth, 1948, pp. 9–10)

Without such a conception of consensus – and other terms of liberal social theory that have been lost in the last 40 years – a working theory of non-totalitarian mass societies is very difficult to put together; that is why other proceduralist conceptions have been reintroduced by liberal and modernist thinkers such as Habermas. Otherwise the prevalence in social theory today of concepts derived from Marx, Engels, Lukács, Gramsci, and others addressed to feudal, early industrial, royalist, and Fascist societies yields a vocabulary with little ability to distinguish between the failings of democracy in America today, Mussolini's Italy, or the Englands of either Queen Victoria or Elizabeth II. We require a conceptual vocabulary tuned to the factual existence of liberal democracy in massively large nation-states; Wirth's conception of consensus can be one of those terms of analysis.

In the final section of the essay Wirth addresses problems of consensus in three specific areas: racial and cultural relations, industrial relations, and international relations. Note that in the language of the day, he is addressing race, class, and globalism. The only major item missing from the current agenda of cultural studies is sex and gender, reminding us once again how major a conceptual shake-up feminism has been.

Race and cultural pluralism

The topic of race can serve as a lever to open our understanding of Wirth's position on consensus and the role of communication in consensus processes. It provides another opportunity to show the connections of Wirth's work with the tradition of Chicago sociology and the larger context of pragmatist thinking. It also provides a perspective for understanding Wirth himself as the author.

Greater contact between racial and cultural groups is a characteristic of modern, mass societies. Urban concentrations of population, migration, communication, and the mobility of labor, capital, goods, services, and information put people of different backgrounds in more contact than their distinct group traditions may prepare them for. Relations between members of racial and other cultural groups, then, are key contingencies for democratic mass society. Wirth proposes that "the idea of cultural pluralism, which is another expression for the toleration of differences" (1948, p. 13), is the guide through this problem. Without extensive toleration of differences, there can be no consensus in mass society; without consensus, there can be no democracy. Given the unquestioned, high value Wirth places on democracy, the means of consensus across racial differences was of crucial importance to him. His concern with race and race relations began in his years as a student at Chicago in the late 1910s and continued until his last publications in the early 1950s. His dissertation, "The Ghetto," was a sociological study of the history of the Jewish enclave designed to aid understanding of the patterns of racial, ethnic, cultural, and economic segregation in modern cities. He wrote the article on "Segregation" for the 1930–4 *Encyclopedia of the Social Sciences*, and addressed race with increasing frequency toward the end of his career. In the post-World War II period, Wirth was a founder and director of the American Council on Race Relations and submitted a brief used in the *Shelley v. Kraemer* Supreme Court decision outlawing restrictive covenants. After his death in 1952, data he had compiled for the purpose were used in the Supreme Court decision in *Brown v. Board of Education* that eliminated "separate but equal" as a legal principle (Wirth Marvick, 1964).

No doubt Wirth's teachers at Chicago were important in introducing him to race as a sociological problem. The first studies of race at Chicago were by Thomas, *circa* 1904. Thomas met Park at a conference at Tuskegee in 1912, initiated collaborative research on race, and recruited Park to the faculty at Chicago. Park had followed his dissertation work in Germany by serving for seven years as Booker T. Washington's secretary. With Washington's encouragement he conducted research on the social conditions of American Negroes and was the ghost-writer for Washington's *The Man Farthest Down*. Park became a leader in the sociological study of race and in the mentoring of African-American sociologists, helping to make Chicago the center for both. After his retirement from Chicago, he joined the faculty at Fisk University, the oldest of the African-American universities (Bulmer, 1984; Hughes, 1968; Kurtz, 1984).

This environment, in which race was considered a sociological, not a biological, concept and one of the most important topics in the field, and in which African-American, Jewish, immigrant, and native white American students were all treated equally, likely resonated with Wirth's own biography. He was a Jewish immigrant from rural Germany, sent as a young teen to live with an uncle in Omaha, Nebraska, in the hopes of better education and future opportunities. A scholarship brought him to the University of Chicago for undergraduate studies. There he discovered a new world of possibilities, as different as could be from the world of his origins, a rural village of 900 people in which the Wirth family had lived in the same house for more than 400 years. Unlike many sociologists of his generation who wrote on community, Wirth never romanticized small town and rural life. If he was romantic about anything, it was the open possibilities of the modern city, where diversity was not just tolerated, but shaped the culture of the place. His daughter also reports that it was as a student at Chicago that Wirth developed an identification with American Negroes, and she says he raised his daughters with a "generalized minority ethnic identification" (Wirth Marvick, 1964, p. 337). He is reported to have said that reading DuBois' *The Souls of Black Folk* as a student was a moving experience with lasting impact. Given this personal background, then, Park's association with Washington, his research on race, and his mentoring of African-American, Jewish, and immigrant students at a time when such was not the norm, provided Wirth with a potent example.

For readers today Wirth's appeal to cultural pluralism as the key to race relations in mass societies requires a bit of interpretation, in light of his own work and a specific debate about American culture at that time. The pragmatist philosopher Horace Kallen (1956, 1998) presented the cultural pluralist position in that debate against both Eurocentric cultural elitists and the politically more dangerous Protestant white nativists who saw American culture as under attack from Blacks, Jews, and immigrants. For the pluralists, the health and vitality of modern culture grows from meaningful interaction across individual differences. "It is founded upon variation of racial groups and individual character; upon spontaneous differences of social heritage, institutional habit, mental attitude and emotional tone; upon the continuous, free and fruitful cross-fertilization of these by one another" (Kallen, 1998, p. 34). This is a democratic culture, dependent on democratic habits of mind, on the basis of which the pluralists expected democratic politics to grow. In this approach, then, social differences become resources (cf. Rothenbuhler, 2001).

Wirth's work as both sociologist and reformer shows these same liberal ideals. Communication across the individualities and differences of people and their cultures, races, religions, ethnicities, groups, and nations is the basis of democratic consensus in modern, massively large societies. But this is not because communication grows out of unity any more than because communication produces unity. Quite the contrary. The value of communication is that it makes a meaningful experience of differences, altering individualities in light of the other, making life together a product of those differences.

"Consensus and Mass Communication" is useful reading for its pluralist vision, its specific analyses, and the contact it provides with our intellectual past. Wirth's conceptions of the mass and consensus provide key analytic terms of significant use today. The pluralist vision underlying his turning consensus from a condition into a process, also leads to conceiving culture as a communicative activity, and turns social differences

from problems into resources. Finally, as a representative of the Chicago
school, his essay provides contact with a part of the history of the field
that has not received its due, even as it anticipated much of the current
agenda and could aid our work.[2]

Notes

1   My quotations and page number references are from the original publication
    of the Wirth essay in 1948 in *American Sociological Review*. It has also been
    widely reprinted, and may be more readily available from other sources. One
    source is the 1964 anthology of Wirth's articles *On Cities and Social Life*,
    edited by Albert Reiss, in the University of Chicago Press Heritage of Socio-
    logy Series. This is also available as a 1981 Midway Reprint from the same
    press.
2   I would like to thank John Peters and Tom McCourt for their useful sugges-
    tions on an earlier draft of this essay.

References

Ang, I. (1991) *Desperately Seeking the Audience*. London: Routledge.

Bulmer, M. (1984) *The Chicago School of Sociology: Institutionalization, Diversity, and the Rise of Sociological Research*. Chicago: University of Chicago Press.

Burgess, E. W. and Bogue, D. J. (eds) (1964) *Contributions to Urban Sociology*.
Chicago: University of Chicago Press.

Depew, D. J. and Peters, J. D. (2001) Community and Communication: The
Conceptual Background. In G. J. Shepherd and E. W. Rothenbuhler (eds),
Communication and Community, Mahwah, NJ: Erlbaum, 3–21.

Elsner, H. (1972) Introduction. In R. E. Park, *The Crowd and the Public
and Other Essays*, ed. H. E. Elsner, Chicago: University of Chicago Press,
pp. vii–xxv.

Habermas, J. (1981) *The Theory of Communicative Action*, ed. and tr.
T. McCarthy, 2 vols. Boston: Beacon; Cambridge: Polity, 1984, 1987.

Horkheimer, M. and Adorno, T. W. (1972) *Dialectic of Enlightenment*, tr.
J. Cumming. New York: Continuum. (Originally published in 1947.)

Hughes, H. M. (1968) Park, Robert E. In *International Encyclopedia of the
Social Sciences*, vol. 11, New York: Macmillan, 416–19.

Kallen, H. M. (1956) *Cultural Pluralism and the American Idea: An Essay in
Social Philosophy*. Philadelphia: University of Pennsylvania Press.

Kallen, H. M. (1998) *Culture and Democracy in the United States*. New Brunswick, NJ: Transaction. (Originally published in 1924.)

Katz, E. and Lazarsfeld, P. F. (1955) *Personal Influence: The Part Played by
People in the Flow of Mass Communications*. New York: Free Press.

Kurtz, L. R. (1984) *Evaluating Chicago Sociology: A Guide to the Literature with an Annotated Bibliography.* Chicago: University of Chicago Press.

Le Bon, G. (1977) *The Crowd: A Study of the Popular Mind.* New York: Penguin Press. (Originally published in 1895.)

Lukes, S. (1977) *Essays in Social Theory.* New York: Columbia University Press.

McKenzie, R. D. (1968) The Rise of Metropolitan Communities. In *On Human Ecology*, ed. A. H. Hawley, Chicago: University of Chicago Press, 244–305. (Originally published in 1933.)

Park, R. E. (1925a) The City: Suggestions for the Investigation of Human Behavior in the Urban Environment. In R. E. Park, E. W. Burgess, and R. D. McKenzie, *The City*, Chicago: University of Chicago Press, 1–46.

Park, R. E. (1925b) The Natural History of the Newspaper. In R. E. Park, E. W. Burgess, and R. D. McKenzie, *The City*, Chicago: University of Chicago Press, 80–98.

Park, R. E. (1929–30) Urbanization as Measured by Newspaper Circulation. *American Journal of Sociology*, 35, 60–79.

Park, R. E. (1972a) The Crowd and the Public. In *The Crowd and the Public and Other Essays*, ed. H. E. Elsner, Chicago: University of Chicago Press, 1–81. (Originally published in 1904.)

Park, R. E. (1972b): Reflections on Communication and Culture. In *The Crowd and the Public and Other Essays*, ed. H. E. Elsner, Chicago: University of Chicago Press, 98–116. (Originally published in 1938.)

Park, R. E. and Burgess, E. W. (1969) *Introduction to the Science of Sociology*, 3rd edn. Chicago: University of Chicago Press. (Originally published in 1921.)

Peterson, R. A. (1994) Measured Markets and Unknown Audiences: Case Studies from the Production and Consumption of Music. In J. S. Ettema and D. C. Whitney (eds), *Audiencemaking: How the Media Create the Audience*, Thousand Oaks, CA: Sage, 171–85.

Reiss, A. J. (1964) Introduction. In L. Wirth, *On Cities and Social Life*, ed. A. J. Reiss, Chicago: University of Chicago Press, pp. ix–xxx.

Rothenbuhler, E. W. (1996) Commercial Radio as Communication. *Journal of Communication*, 46 (Winter), 125–43.

Rothenbuhler, E. W. (2001) Revising Communication Research for Working on Community. In G. J. Shepherd and E. W. Rothenbuhler (eds), *Communication and Community*, Mahwah, NJ: Erlbaum, 159–79.

Rutkoff, P. M. and Scott, W. B. (1986) *New School: A History of the New School for Social Research.* New York: Free Press.

Sciulli, D. (1985) The Practical Groundwork of Critical Theory: Bringing Parsons to Habermas (and Vice Versa). In J. C. Alexander (ed.), *Neofunctionalism*, Beverly Hills, CA: Sage, 21–50.

Sheldon, E. B. (1968) Wirth, Louis. In *International Encyclopedia of the Social Sciences*, vol. 16, New York: Macmillan, 558–9.

Short, J. F. (ed.) (1971) *The Social Fabric of the Metropolis: Contributions of the Chicago School of Urban Sociology.* Chicago: University of Chicago Press.

Simmel, G. (1964) The Metropolis and Mental Life. In K. H. Wolff (ed. and tr.), *The Sociology of Georg Simmel*, New York: Free Press, 409–24. (Originally published in 1903.)

Tarde, G. (1969) The Public and the Crowd. In *On Communication and Social Influence*, ed. T. N. Clark, Chicago: University of Chicago Press, 277–94. (Originally published in 1901.)

Thomas, W. I. and Znaniecki, F. (1918) *The Polish Peasant in Europe and America*. Chicago: University of Chicago Press.

Whyte, W. F. (1955) *Street Corner Society*, 2nd edn. Chicago: University of Chicago Press.

Williams, R. (1983) *Culture and Society: 1780–1950*. New York: Columbia University Press. (Originally published in 1958.)

Wirth, L. (1948) Consensus and Mass Communication. *American Sociological Review*, 13, 1–15.

Wirth, L. (1964a) The Ghetto. In *On Cities and Social Life*, ed. A. J. Reiss, Chicago: University of Chicago Press, 84–98. (Originally published in 1927.)

Wirth, L. (1964b) *On Cities and Social Life*, ed. A. J. Reiss. Chicago: University of Chicago Press.

Wirth, L. (1964c) Urbanism as a Way of Life. In *On Cities and Social Life*, ed. A. J. Reiss, Chicago: University of Chicago Press, 60–83. (Originally published in 1938.)

Wirth Marvick, E. (1964) Biographical Memorandum on Louis Wirth. In L. Wirth, *On Cities and Social Life*, ed. A. J. Reiss, Chicago: University of Chicago Press, 333–40.

7

The Audience is a Crowd, the Crowd is a Public:
Latter-Day Thoughts on Lang and Lang's "MacArthur Day in Chicago"

Elihu Katz and Daniel Dayan

Tongue in cheek, and with apologies all around, this chapter is a soul-searching debate between two hardly disinterested co-authors over how much homage we owe to Gladys and Kurt Lang for having said in 1952 what we said only in 1992 about the television genre we call "media events." The paper is a reexamination of the Langs' "MacArthur Day in Chicago," the prize-winning essay originally entitled "The Unique Perspective of Television and its Effects: A Pilot Study," and first published in 1953 as the lead article in the *American Sociological Review*, just when television was rapidly diffusing.[1]

Our debate alludes to that thread of the philosophy of science which distinguishes between discoverers who did and did not realize the implications of what they had discovered (Patinkin, 1983). We consider whether the Langs "did" or "didn't," and while we present evidence on both sides, and sometimes differ between ourselves, we conclude, in the final analysis, that they "did," and, well, that they "didn't." Here is their story, and ours.

MacArthur Day as collective behavior

In 1951, when President Truman recalled General Douglas MacArthur for having overstepped his postwar authority in the Pacific, Kurt Lang and Gladys Engel Lang were graduate students of sociology at the University of Chicago, participating in Tamotsu Shibutani's seminar on crowd behavior. The news media followed the general's return very closely, and reported in detail on the widespread indignation over Truman's *chutzpa* and the enthusiastic welcome he was receiving. After a reception in San Francisco, MacArthur flew to Washington to address both Houses of Congress and went on to a "triumphal homecoming" in New York and, a week later, in Chicago.

The itinerary of the Chicago visit called for a festive welcome at the airport, a motorcade through the city, with a stop to dedicate a bridge in memory of the fallen at Bataan and Corregidor, and an evening rally at Soldier Field. Energized by the prospect of being able to make first-hand observations of the expected outpouring of agitated (perhaps enraged) well-wishers, the Langs and fellow students hastily designed a project of "firehouse research" (Hughes, 1970). Twenty-nine observers were trained and posted along the route of the march, after being debriefed about their own (nervous) expectations of the impending event.

Television scheduled three hours of live coverage, giving Chicagoans a first taste of the dilemma of having to choose between going out to an event and viewing it at home. Two observers were assigned to view the television coverage (videotape was not yet available). Nobody was assigned to observe the viewers at home. The Langs were focused on what would happen in the streets, and did not think to compare audiences at home and those on the streets. Later, however, as they began to reconceptualize the event, they set about analyzing the broadcast in order to infer some of the ways in which television must have been implicated, first, in "the 'landslide effect' of national indignation over MacArthur's abrupt dismissal" that constituted the prologue to the event, and then, in the live coverage of the event itself, which gave "the impression of enthusiastic support, bordering on 'mass hysteria'" (1953, p. 4).[2]

What the Langs saw

When the day was over, the researchers were surprised to learn that the *televised* event, not the "real" event, lived up to the excitement that had been anticipated. There were very large crowds – apparently the largest turnout since war's end – but these crowds were disappointed on the whole. At the airport, along the route of the motorcade, at the Bataan Bridge and at Soldier Field, would-be spectators were misinformed about the best vantage points, were left to wait and wait for the brief moment when the motorcade would pass by, and were jostled at the bridge ceremony, which they could neither see nor hear. They missed the pomp they had anticipated – no parade, no music, no patriotic gore – and there was very little tension. Some felt pride, they said, at being present at a historic event; some felt the thrill of the spectacle, however flawed; some had a glimpse of the general. Others began to perform themselves – for the TV cameras. Observers overheard remarks to the effect that it might have been better to stay home and watch the event on television.

Meanwhile, say the Langs, television was telling a better story, though not the whole of it. Let us review what they saw.

1   First, they were struck by the fact that television was giving life to an amorphous, episodic, somewhat dull event. They noted that the television narrator could provide continuity and that the cameras could play with "foreground and background." While the spectators were rubbing their hands and stomping their feet, television was producing drama.

2   They were surprised at how television distorted the "real" event. It portrayed the crowd as high-pitched and enthused; it exaggerated the size of the turnout and the extent to which the city had shut down to celebrate; it created the illusion of continuous cheering by combining the fragmented cheers of separate clusters of spectators. In their effort to understand, the Langs managed to infer and catalogue some of the major elements of media "selectivity," which guide us still today. These include (a) technological bias, whereby the production team selectively arranges the camera shots; (b) the bias of the commentary which provides verbal structure and meaning; (c) the rearrangement of the "real" world to match the timing and demands of the medium; and (d) the attempt to satisfy viewer expectations.

3   The Langs were distressed that television made no mention of the event's context. Even if spectators on the spot seemed uninterested in what had occasioned MacArthur's return, the Langs expected that a television news service would supply the missing information. They noticed that television limited its role to one of acclamation, and wondered whether the medium had been co-opted. They realized that television was catering to the celebratory register that public opinion had been led to expect, but also wondered whether the media weren't taking the hawkish side of the American debate over the Cold War. In other words, the Langs noted that television events might have political effects, wisely anticipating a situation in which the "imagery of momentary opinion" represented by live television "may goad [politicians] into action which . . . may objectively be detrimental" (cf. Liebes, 1998).

4   The Langs also speculated that the TV audience, sitting alone at home, might be particularly vulnerable to TV's uncritical message.

Spectators on the scene had recourse to each other; they could "test" reality by sensing and consulting their neighbors' thoughts and feelings. Television viewers had only themselves, and could be misled much more easily. Developed more fully in the 1968 version of their paper, this is an anticipation of the social psychology underlying "pluralistic ignorance," "spiral of silence," "bandwagon," and "brainwashing."

The Langs conclude that the event was poorly planned on the ground, and speculate that its schedule might have been more attuned to the dictates of the "air" than to the satisfaction of onlookers. This is an early insight into the ways in which the media privilege their viewers (and advertisers) at the expense of real-life spectators. Nowadays we take for granted that events are tailored and time-shifted to meet the requirements of the medium.

Within the limits of one early event in the history of television (Russo, 1983), the Langs saw very far. We certainly cannot fault them for having backed into the study of media events: we too began our work serendipitously, when we realized that the live broadcast of Anwar Sadat's visit to Jerusalem was of a piece with the moon landings and the Pope's visit to Poland, and was therefore better studied as a subtype of a genre of "media events" than as an example of "media diplomacy," as we had planned. Indeed, the Langs' later work includes studies of the Kennedy–Nixon debates, the Watergate scandal, the Dreyfus affair, and other mediated events, as well as a theory of reputation and renown (Lang and Lang, 1983, 1990) that led ultimately to the realization that a latent genre underlay all these public representations.

What the Langs didn't see

The Langs, however, did not see the genre of media events looming. They were first to identify many of its component elements, but they did not – could not, perhaps – recognize that the MacArthur broadcast was the harbinger of a new form of live television that would frame some of the most memorable moments of the second half of the twentieth century. For the Langs – at least in this essay – ceremonial media events are not yet clearly distinguished from the news, or from the then generic category "News and Special Event Features." "Unlike other television programs," they say, "news and special events features constitute part of that basic information about 'reality' which we require in order to act in concert with anonymous and like-minded persons in the political process" (1953, pp. 10–11). So far, so good. But where we differ, given the wisdom of hindsight, is in claiming that media events of this sort – openly constructed, clearly performative, and obeying specific sets of rules – are not tainted news events or shady practices of the sort that Boorstin (1964), some ten years later, would (also) describe as "pseudo events."[3]

Nor are they documentaries. They are a different genre of public affairs broadcasting, to which different rules apply. This is not just a quibble. The Langs accept the self-definition of "news and special events" as being bound by the classic norms of objective journalism, while we argue that the events genre in full bloom calls for a new theoretical perspective that asks different questions, makes different observations, and comes to different conclusions.

Our main difference with the Langs stems from their demand that television faithfully reproduce the "reality" they attribute to the crowd on the streets and to the politics of the Cold War. We ask: Is the street more "real?" If so, how do we access its "reality?" The Langs' observers represented the street as consisting of very large crowds – but the statistics of the transit system, the Langs discovered, diminished this claim. The observers represented the street as disappointed, based on tidbits of observation – but those who were formally interviewed by the same observers said that they were enthralled (as they said when interviewed on TV). There also seems to have been a different reality at the beginning, when enthusiasm was still high, and at the end, when the poor arrangements apparently dampened enthusiasm. As we know by now, street reality, too, needs to be represented (Peters, 1993).

A better answer, as far as the portrait of the street is concerned, is that television provided a *different* representation of reality. At each point the motorcade passed, there was loud cheering. Very interesting, too, is that there was cheering and miming when spectators saw the cameras. Television, then, both represented reality and changed the reality it was representing. In short, "reality" can be constructed in street fashion and in the fashion of ceremonial television, and the debate is no longer between reality and the lack of it, but between different constructions.

The Langs almost saw this – indeed, they themselves place "reality" in quotes – but they are hard put, as many of us are still, to grant equality to the reality of television and to accept the idea that genres signal the different ways in which reality will be processed. In fact, in describing the scene in the streets, the Langs do discern the ceremonial genre of "hero's welcome." While they do not elaborate on this point, they are aware that this is a particular type of crowd, quite different from a crowd that is "looking for trouble," though 37 percent of those interviewed in the streets expected trouble (1968, p. 41). Had this distinction been applied to broadcasting, the embryonic genre of ceremonial television would have been seen to stand apart from the genre of television news. In this case, television apparently performed a hero's welcome in its own way, using the street as raw material. That the genre borrows from fiction and from film, is true; but so does the writing of history (Bruner, 1998; Novick, 1998).

An ironic footnote is in order here. The spectators on the street had little interest in conflict; the fighting mood that was expected never materialized, according to the observers. If this is true, then in this matter at least, television faithfully represented the "reality" of the street. But the Langs expected that TV would do more, perhaps; that it would live up to its documentary mission.

While the Langs correctly perceive many of the ways in which ceremonial television "distorts" – or, in our terms, constructs – they would not be satisfied with our aesthetic explanation. They would not agree that the Truman–MacArthur conflict was being papered over for reasons of ceremony alone. From a media events perspective, the live broadcast of what we call "coronation" – or rites of passage of the great – precludes disruption. If the event is being protested, as was the royal wedding, or the Bush inaugural, the director will avoid tarnishing its reputation. There may be subtle hints of dissent, as when the archbishop of Canterbury refused to cooperate in labeling the royal wedding a fairy tale, or when the cameras at the Bush inauguration snatched close-ups of Al Gore to see if his face showed evidence of disapproval. But, on the whole, this type of media event is true to its "contract" with the organizers and with the audience.[4] It lives up to the expectations of both. The Langs suspect this, and say so, but disapprove.

The Langs do not want credit for ascribing this ceremonial role to television (even though that is what the paper is famous for). They prefer a political frame, not an aesthetic one. They believe that the broadcasters were rejecting not only the reality of the street, but also the authority of the President. In their introduction to the revised paper (1968, p. 36), the Langs cite Bent's (1927) thesis that a crusading press can whip up enough popular enthusiasm for a person or a cause to create a political bandwagon. They suspect that broadcasting was on the side of MacArthur's ardent Republican supporters, and was explicitly rejecting Truman's outrageous degradation of their hero, a theme echoed in Carey's (1998) analysis of the rejection of Justice Bork's Supreme Court candidacy.

Media events research also knows a thing or two about politics. While giving the ceremonial its due, it is continually aware of the political function of such events, where the establishment – not its rivals – is almost always the beneficiary. In a word, media events are hegemonic, almost without exception. They are collusions between officials (the Royal

Family, the International Olympics Committee, etc.), broadcasters, and audience, who enter into an implicit understanding that a certain event deserves ceremonial treatment. This understanding implies that the event will be treated reverentially, and that the hero will be duly crowned, married, or bid Godspeed.

The Langs' story is equally political, of course, but points to the possible collusion of broadcasters with counter-hegemonic forces. The very fact of the broadcast, they imply, celebrates the ousted general, and its enthusiastic content – compared with the reality outside – was designed to bring an ostensibly aroused public opinion to bear on the injustice that had been done. Maybe. But there is another, more likely reading, that coincides with our view that media events are (necessarily) biased in support of hegemony. We propose that President Truman may have been quite happy to help this old soldier fade away in the outstretched arms of popular acclaim, and in the aura of a broadcast "coronation." He may well have looked with favor on the interpretation of his action as a "golden handshake," giving the hero his due while blocking his further interference. He may have considered it a Turnerian "healing" ceremony.

Unfortunately the Langs do not provide the information we need to decide between these two possible versions of the story. Media events research needs to know much more about the "organizers" of the event. We are told only that the mayors of several cities, including the (Democratic) mayor of Chicago, invited MacArthur to visit upon his return (1968, p. 37). We are also told that a WGN employee proposed a number of symbolic salutes to coincide with the touchdown of the general's plane in the United States. But we are told little more about who the organizers really were. Was there a hidden hand overseeing the homecoming parade in the several cities? What was the interaction between organizers and broadcasters, if any? What pre-production planning and arrangements marked the event? Admittedly, this is a lot to ask of a group of graduate students who cooked up an original study at the last moment. Our only point, throughout this critique, is that genre research comes with a checklist – an accounting scheme, in Lazarsfeld's terms – to guide the analysis.

But if the production side of the MacArthur event was beyond the reach of the Langs and their fellows, surely the home celebration of the event should have occupied them. It did, but only after they began to glimpse that their research problem was undergoing transformation. They did not realize in time that the same ethnography that they were conducting in the streets could also be conducted in viewers' homes.[5] Had this happened, audience research would not have had to wait 50 years to find out how viewers view in their natural habitats. That the Langs did not think of this in time is not only because they were focused mainly on crowds, and only incidentally on TV. Even when they changed their focus to contrast the perspective of the crowd with "the unique perspective of television," it still could not have occurred to them – in the absence of a theory of media events – that viewers might "dress up" to view (Dayan and Katz, 1992, p. 125), that viewers would seek out others to share the experience with, that they might already be wise to the ceremonial encoding of such events.[6] The fact is, they did not know much about the situation of reception or the process of decoding. They had no direct knowledge of demeanor or effect, of the sort we have from Rothenbuhler (1988) on the Los Angeles Olympics, or Mindak and Hursch (1965) on the Kennedy funeral. Under the circumstances, all Lang and Lang could do was to *infer* the viewing experience from the content of the broadcast.

Note also that the two observers assigned to TV were saddled with a dual, somewhat contradictory role, which, for better and worse, is still the case today. At one and the same time, they were expected to try to live the experience of the homebound television viewers[7] and to report, in detail, as content analysts. This means that these observers were performing as (impressionistic) content analysts, while trying to observe their own cognitive and emotional reactions to what they were seeing. Subjective content analysis by audiences has interesting advantages, but it is different from "objective" analysis, and all the more difficult when coupled with introspection.

The MacArthur paper includes statistics about the language of narration, which must have been extracted from some kind of recording; these extracts illustrate the way in which the event was hyped and the thrill assigned by the narrators to the crowd in the streets. Not enough is made of the large amount of airtime that was supposed to hold viewers enthralled in the long absences of the principal from the screen. And there is little information in the paper about the behavior of the hero himself. Apart from a few observations on MacArthur's crumpled hat and coat (his trademarks), we are given very little idea of what he did (except follow the itinerary), and almost no idea of what he said. Were his remarks irrelevant or pointless? If so, how could he be perceived as dangerously charismatic? These questions are left unanswered.

The fate of the nearly canonic

The Langs' paper has had a bumpy ride in the interdisciplinary history of communication research, because it arose from the now neglected sociology of collective behavior (crowds, public opinion, fashion) and moved to the study of media effects just when sociology was abandoning the study of the media.[8] Effects fell into the hands of social psychologists, who were interested in the short run of persuasive campaigns, of uses and gratifications, of innovation diffusion. The Langs' effect, rather, is the imposition of a false consciousness of reality on the television viewer, who is led to believe that there was "overwhelming public sentiment in favor of the General" (1953, p. 11). With a force of its own, the Langs suggest, the TV audience might well have overwhelmed the more balanced reactions of the spectators on the spot. In this sense, the study comes closest to the "critical school" of media studies, whether from the left (Horkheimer and Adorno, 1972) or from the right (Noelle-Neumann, 1984), which sees the media as partners in a quasi-conspiracy to purvey a false sense of consensus by shutting out competing thoughts. This framing effect also figures in semiotic and textual theories, where the existence of an "apparatus" serves to position the viewer and focus his attention. But where critical theorists expect homogenization, even regimentation, the Langs flirt with the idea of "mass hysteria."

The Langs' thesis is also close to the ideas of Park, Cooley, Wirth (see Rothenbuhler, chapter 6 above), and other sociologists at the University of Chicago, who had earlier theorized the shared experience of the media – technology and content – as facilitators of national integration and enfranchisement, but minus the conspiratorial and deterministic bent of critical and technological theories. Indeed, Chicago's Herbert Blumer (1939) explicitly focused on the differences among audiences, crowds, and publics (as had Tarde [1898], 1969, before him); surprisingly, though near at hand, no reference is made to these categorizations.

With the reawakening of interest in sociological effects – albeit not in departments of sociology, but in schools of communication – the Langs have been rediscovered. Thus, "there is no doubt," writes Schlesinger,

> that the Langs' research had an impact on seminal studies of news production in the USA such as those of Herbert Gans, Edward Epstein and Gaye Tuchman. In the UK, the pioneering work of James Halloran, Philip Elliott and Graham Murdock on the 1968 anti-Vietnam demonstration in London, and then Elliott's brilliant study of the making of a television documentary series, also picked up on how the Langs had originally thought about the inferential structure of news. This influence also spilled over into Stuart Hall's research on news construction. In each of these cases the Langs' insight was combined with a range of other influences to produce the quite distinctive work of Anglo-American production studies. (private communication, 2000) [9]

The Langs also speak to the arrival of anthropology to the study of mass communication. They made a start toward employing ethnographic methods in the comparative study of situations of reception, although they did only half the job. Thus, their comparison of home and street, even if hypothetical, points up a major lesson for reception studies. The lesson is that reception does not simply consist of social semiotics or ethnosemiotics, or of the analysis of verbal accounts of meaning construction; reception is also a locus and a form of sociability. It is about the influence of the situation of contact (Freidson, 1953).

But the originality of the Langs' essay, in comparison with the many it has inspired, is to combine the study of the public sphere with that of public space. The Langs are perfectly aware that when the media became custodians of the public sphere, they surrendered the roles of observer and watchdog; they became judges of their own power. While the public sphere is theoretically restricted to the circulation of issues, the presence of the media in a public space raises Goffmanian questions about the meaning of cheers; about the difference between being there, being an onlooker, being committed. It raises Noelle-Neumann's (1984) question of when to speak, when to listen, and when to remain silent. More than their "firehouse" ethnography, it is the Langs' imaginative research design that has inspired so many researchers to look for the articulation between street and agenda, event and issue.

Mass hysteria?

Cognizant of all the credit the Langs deserve, we return to the major flaw in their work (and in ours): namely, the absence of serious study of the home reception of media events, beginning with MacArthur Day. The Langs have a separate record of the impressions of the two observers who were assigned to watch television. They also quote from an observer who happened on the discussion of the television transmission in a bar. Their most telling quote comes from one of the observers at Soldier Field, who noted that "the TV camera followed the General's car and caught that part of the crowd . . . that was cheering, giving the impression of a solid mass of wildly cheering people. It did not show the large sections of empty stands, nor did it show that people stopped cheering as soon as the car passed them" (1953, p. 10). But that's it, and the Langs know it's not enough. Most of their knowledge of TV's effect comes from "newspaper coverage emphasizing the overwhelming enthusiasm, [and] from informal interviews, even months later, showing that the event was still being interpreted as a display of 'mass hysteria'" (1953, p. 11n.).

Of course, the Langs do not believe that there was mass hysteria – not initially, when news of Truman's "disruptive" decision to fire the general (Turner, 1974) was published, certainly not in the Chicago streets, and not in the homes of viewers of the event. What they believe is that this image originated in the press, in its perception of "the national indignation at MacArthur's abrupt dismissal and the impression of enthusiastic support, bordering on 'mass hysteria'" (1953, p. 4), and was reiterated on television in its willfully misleading report of the temper of the crowd in the streets. And that the whole may be part of a right-wing machination.

The brilliance of the Langs' paper is in showing how this process works. As sociologists of public opinion, as well as of collective behavior, they are *not* claiming that each member of the television audience was directly infected by the reported hysteria of the crowd. They say, rather, that

> the most important single media effect . . . was the dissemination of an image of overwhelming public sentiment in favor of the General. This effect gathered force as it was incorporated into political strategy, picked up by other media, entered into gossip, and thus came to overshadow immediate reality as it might have been recorded by an observer on the scene. We have labeled this the 'landslide effect' because in view of a particular public welcoming ceremony the imputed unanimity gathered tremendous force. This 'landslide effect' can, in large measure, be attributed to television. (1953, p. 11)

As already noted, the Langs are here invoking "pluralistic ignorance" and the "third person effect" (Davison, 1987), where it is enough for everybody to believe that everybody else is "hysterical." But, despite the elegant explanation provided, should we agree that the media are at all capable of fomenting "mass hysteria"? Cantril et al. (1939) and McLuhan (1964) thought so about radio, and Daniel Schorr (1976) thinks so about television. In the history of media events, however, there is no solid evidence that television coverage induces hysteria. Hysteria, if that's the right word, comes from assembled crowds, not from television viewers. To overthrow Milosevic or the president of the Philippines, Serbs and Filipinos took to the streets. The Czech revolution took place in Wenceslas Square (although some viewers perhaps joined the demonstrators outside). There were significant outbursts of emotion at the funerals of Kennedy, Rabin, and Princess Diana – but not from those who mourned on television.

Yet there are a few counterexamples. The live broadcast of Ayatollah Khomeini's return to Iran, which was suddenly interrupted, did lead to a hysterical outpouring into the streets. Broadcasting of certain terrorist events, though hardly ceremonial in form, often degenerates into urban unrest (Liebes, 1998). Another exception that comes to mind is the rush of football fans to honk their cars and splash in fountains after the televised victory of a home team. Admittedly, this behavior is contagious and mobilizes non-fans as well, but such "mass hysteria" – even if it had been true of the crowd – is extremely unlikely to have spiraled up from the televised broadcast of MacArthur Day. Exceptions do exist – but they are rare. Hysteria, whatever it means, is part of the "experience of being there," not of "the experience of *not* being there."

The Langs are on safer ground when they argue that collective memory of the event will call up the televised ceremony more than the "real" event. This is true not only because so many more view such events on television than attend them in person, but because the television treatment of "media events" is *designed* to be memorable.

The hypothesis that the audience is a crowd, and the crowd is a public

Equal in importance to their canonic study of how a lukewarm reception in the streets is transformed into a memorable media event is the Langs' insightful observation that the crowd may have been more deliberative than the television audience. Translated into the language of hypothesis – after all, this is billed as a pilot study – the Langs seem to be suggesting that, at the onset of the television era, the crowd may have become a public, and the audience may have become a crowd.

As far as the crowd is concerned – even this welcoming crowd – the Langs expected "trouble." Classic theories of crowd allude to the possibility, of course. But the Langs found otherwise. Their "crowd" – the hundreds of thousands who turned out to greet the general – seems deliberative. Its members chat with each other, exchange impressions, allow for ambivalence. They leave the scene more sober than when they came. The Langs might have done better, it seems to us, had they avoided the word "crowd" in their paper, after observing that the spectators on the route of the march had consulted each other and read each other's reactions. In this sense, they were more like a public than a crowd. The Langs' report surprises because their theory of crowds led them to expect otherwise.

The Langs' television audience, on the other hand, is both atomized and vulnerable – the essence of the mass society – brainwashed by a monolithic paean of praise in a situation that does not allow for any kind of reality check (cf. Gerbner and Gross, 1976). It is from this comparison that the Langs permit themselves to hint – perhaps unbeknown even to themselves – that television might be creating a crowd in the sense of fixating its audience on one single object, possibly obliterating all context and opposing views, while the crowd, by comparison, was acting like a rational public. Or, in their own words:

> Whereas a participant was able to make direct inferences about the crowd as a whole, being in constant touch with those around him, *the television viewer was in the center of the entire crowd.* Yet, unlike the participant, he was completely at the mercy of the instrument of his perceptions. He could not test his impressions – could not shove back the shover, inspect bystanders' views, or attempt in any way to affect the ongoing activity. To the participant, on the other hand, the direction of the crowd activity as a whole, regardless of its final goal, still appeared as the interplay of certain peculiarly personal and human forces. Political sentiment, wherever encountered, could thus be evaluated and discounted. Antagonistic views could be attributed to insufficient personal powers of persuasion rather than seen as subjugation to the impersonal dynamics of mass hysteria. The television viewer had little opportunity to recognize this personal dimension in the crowd. What was mediated over the screen was, above all, the general trend and the direction of the event, which consequently assumed the proportion of an impersonal force, no longer subject to influence.
>
> This view of the "overwhelming" effect of public moods and the impersonal logic of public events is hypothesized as a characteristic of the perspective resulting from the general structure of the picture and the context of television viewing. (1953, p. 11)

This specter leads naturally to the last element needed to turn an audience into a crowd: the invitation to action. Here the Langs take an important methodological step, by proposing that the effect of television should be studied cumulatively, not person by person. This explains their otherwise enigmatic preface, which urges sociologists to consider how the millions of television viewers – all of one mind – can (superorganically?) overwhelm a rational public to create a tyrannical intolerance that may direct fury against anyone who might dare defile the glory of the hero. This fear of a technology-based Fascism calls for criticism – as we and others have attempted to point out. But right or wrong, it is also worthy of respect as a serious challenge to theorists of "limited effects," whom the Langs have so steadfastly opposed for 50 years.

Notes

1   While the original was published in 1953, the Langs presented an elaborated version as chapter 11 of their *Politics and Television* (1968), alluding also to more recent theoretical concerns such as agenda setting and the spiral of

silence. Here we take note of certain differences between the two texts. The book is being reprinted in 2001 by Transaction Publishers.

2 "Mass hysteria" here refers to the Langs' inference about how television (mis)reported what was happening in the street. Later we raise the question of whether the Langs also believed this "hysteria" to be contagious, such that the TV viewers would ("also") become emotionally aroused. Katz thinks that the Langs do suggest this, at least in the original paper; Dayan disagrees. In any event, the later version (Lang and Lang, 1968, pp. 36–61) retreats from this theme.

3 Boorstin (1964) would discredit any ceremonial performance, including televised press conferences, as "pseudo," going far beyond the Langs' displeasure with the media's fictionalizing of the "real" event.

4 The idea that genres are a sort of "contract" between producers and audience is discussed by Cawelti (1976). In the case of media events, the contract is expanded to include the organizers of the event, in addition to broadcasters and audience (Dayan and Katz, 1992, p. 56). The extent to which the MacArthur audience could have insight into this as yet unwritten contract is at issue here, of course. We are probably overstating the likelihood of this insight.

5 Gladys Lang did interview viewers of the 1952 nominating conventions, but there is no report on the focus of these interviews (Lang and Lang, 1968, ch. 4).

6 Our chapter 10 in Dayan and Katz, 1992, brings together a variety of data on viewing experiences, but the archive is still not rich enough. Nor have we ourselves done the empirical work that needs to be done on the ethnography of home reception of media events. We also need to remind ourselves from time to time that television was very new in 1951, so the Langs have a better excuse than we have had in the 40 years since.

7 Given the importance of the locus of the TV set, it is clear that the two TV observers could hardly empathize with home viewers.

8 To be fair, there simply isn't a lot of communications research history. The Langs' paper is one of only four papers found worthy of reprinting in both editions of Schramm's definitive books of readings (Schramm, 1952; Schramm and Roberts, 1970).

9 Philip Schlesinger was kind enough to write elaborate comments on an earlier draft of this paper.

References

Bent, S. (1927) *Ballyhoo: The Voice of the Press*. New York: Boni and Liveright.
Blumer, H. (1939) Collective Behavior. In R. E. Park (ed.), *An Outline of the Principles of Sociology*, New York: Barnes and Noble, 221–80.
Boorstin, D. J. (1964) *The Image: A Guide to Pseudo-Events in America*. New York: Harper & Row.

Bruner, J. (1998) What is a Narrative Fact? *Annals of the American Academy of Political and Social Science*, 560 (November), 17–27.

Cantril, H., Herzog, H., and Gaudet, H. (1939) *The Invasion from Mars*. Princeton: Princeton University Press.

Carey, J. W. (1998) Political Ritual on Television: Episodes in the History of Shame, Degradation and Excommunication. In T. Liebes and J. Curran (eds), *Media, Ritual and Identity*, London: Routledge, 42–70.

Cawelti, J. (1976) *Adventure, Mystery, Romance: Formula Stories as Art and Popular Culture*. Chicago: University of Chicago Press.

Davison, W. P. (1987) The Third-Person Effect in Communication. *Public Opinion Quarterly*, 41, 1–15.

Dayan, D. and Katz, E. (1992) *Media Events: The Live Broadcasting of History*. Cambridge, MA: Harvard University Press.

Freidson, E. (1953) The Relation of the Social Situation of Contact to the Media in Mass Communication. *Public Opinion Quarterly*, 17, 230–8.

Gerbner, G. and Gross, L. (1976) Living with Television: The Violence Profile. *Journal of Communication*, 26 (2), 173–99.

Horkheimer, M. and Adorno, T. W. (1972) *Dialectic of Enlightenment*, tr. John Cumming. New York: Continuum.

Hughes, E. C. (1970) Teaching as Fieldwork. *American Sociologist*, 5, 13–18.

Lang, G. E. and Lang, K. (1983) *The Battle for Public Opinion*. New York: Columbia University Press.

Lang, K. and Lang, G. E. (1953) The Unique Perspective of Television and its Effects: A Pilot Study. *American Sociological Review*, 18, 3–12.

Lang, K. and Lang, G. E. (1968) *Politics and Television*. Chicago: Quadrangle Books.

Lang, K. and Lang, G. E. (1990) *Etched in Memory: The Building and Survival of Aesthetic Reputation*. Chapel Hill: University of North Carolina Press.

Liebes, T. (1998) Television's Disaster Marathons: A Danger for Democratic Processes. In T. Liebes and J. Curran (eds), *Media Ritual and Identity*, London: Routledge, 71–84.

McLuhan, M. (1964) *Understanding Media: The Extensions of Man*. New York: McGraw-Hill.

Mindak, W. H. and Hursch, G. D. (1965) Television's Functions on the Assassination Weekend. In B. S. Greenberg and E. B. Parker (eds), *The Kennedy Assassination and the American Public: Social Communication in Crisis*, Stanford, CA: Stanford University Press, 130–41.

Noelle-Neumann, E. (1984) *The Spiral of Silence: Public Opinion – Our Social Skin*. Chicago: University of Chicago Press.

Novick, P. (1998) The Death of the Ethics of Historical Practice (and Why I Am Not Mourning). *Annals of the American Academy of Political and Social Science*, 560 (November), 28–42.

Patinkin, D. (1983) Multiple Discoveries and the Central Message. *American Journal of Sociology*, 89, 306–23.

Peters, J. D. (1993) Distrust of Representation: Habermas on the Public Sphere. *Media, Culture and Society*, 15, 541–71.

Rothenbuhler, E. (1988) The Living Room Celebration of the Olympic Games. *Journal of Communication*, 38, 61–81.

Russo, M. (1983) CBS and the American Political Experience: A History of the CBS News and Special Events and Election Units, 1952–1968. Ph.D. dissertation, New York University, and Ann Arbor: University Microfilms.

Schorr, D. (1976) Reality of "Network." *Rolling Stone*, December 16.

Schramm, W. (ed.) (1952) *Process and Effects of Mass Communication*. Urbana: University of Illinois Press.

Schramm, W. and Roberts, D. (eds) (1970) *Process and Effects of Mass Communication*, 2nd edn. Urbana: University of Illinois Press.

Tarde, G. ([1898] 1969) Opinion and Conversation. In T. N. Clark (ed.), *Gabriel Tarde on Communication and Social Influence*, Chicago: University of Chicago Press, 130–41.

Turner, V. W. (1974) *Dramas, Fields and Metaphors*. Ithaca, NY: Cornell University Press.

8

Towards the Virtual Encounter: Horton's and Wohl's "Mass Communication and Para-Social Interaction"

Don Handelman

It ain't exactly real,
or it's real, but it ain't exactly there.
Leonard Cohen, "Democracy"

The question of how the television viewer relates to the screen is no small matter, now that two full generations have grown up with television in the Western world. In using the word "relates," I am not referring to the content of programming or to how the viewer interprets this. In question is whether television as a medium, in McLuhan's terms, has interactive qualities in relation to a viewer who, I will suggest, is interactive within himself. At issue, then, is the capacity of the medium *qua* medium to be interactive with the viewer. My sense is that this interactivity depends on *intra*-activity – that is, activity *within* that selfsame viewer. To relate to issues of this kind requires thinking, on the one hand, about the TV screen as a medium of communication, and on the other, about the organization of selfness within the viewer, and whether this interiority can be conceptualized as social. How may this meeting between viewer and screen be conceptualized, as they face one another?

In their article, "Mass Communication and Para-social Interaction," Donald Horton and Richard Wohl (1956) seem to have been the first sociologists to address the qualities of communication between viewers and performers (whom they called "personae") on the TV screen. It is especially on this account that their thought deserves discussion. Horton and Wohl called this communication between viewers and personae *interaction*, but qualified this with the prefix *para*. The term *para* denotes a closeness of position: a correspondence of parts, a situation on the other side – but also wrongness and irregularity. In Horton and Wohl's usage, para-social interaction seems to denote a closeness, a correspondence to face-to-face interaction; yet at the same time a wrongness, an incompletion, an irregularity in the conduct of interaction. In social science usage, *para* refers to mimetic and derivative, rather than foundational, qualities. The para imitates its foundation-for-form, yet incompletely. Something, some crucial quality, is missing. In these terms, para-social interaction is less real, less authentic, than face-to-face interaction.

This distinction between social and para-social interaction was in keeping with the symbolic interactionist thought that was prominent in Chicago school sociology at the time, and with its Meadian premise that personal identity was predicated on the individual's capacity to be social by taking the role of the other and responding accordingly. The paramount reality of everyday life and living, as understood by symbolic interactionists, hinged on this premise.[1] In these terms, faced with the images on the TV screen, the viewer could not fully take the role of the other, just as the TV persona could not do this with viewers – hence the deficiencies that Horton and Wohl attributed to the para-social.[2]

In this section and the following I discuss the Horton and Wohl argument on para-social interaction. Following this, I criticize their approach along two avenues: that of the viewer and that of the TV screen. In terms of the viewer, I argue that his inner being, his selfness, is highly social in and of himself, rather than being a unitary existential quality. In terms of the TV screen, I follow McLuhan in arguing that the medium of TV invites interaction that is hardly *para* in its orientations and capacities. In conclusion, I suggest in a preliminary way that viewer–TV screen interaction can be conceptualized in terms of a *virtual encounter*. Such terms would add emergent structural, processual, and relational qualities to this kind of meeting between viewer and screen.[3]

In their essay Horton and Wohl refer to American radio and television shows of the early 1950s; my comments here will be restricted to television. As noted, their concept of para-social interaction refers to an imitation of paramount reality and its authentic interactivity.[4] Parasocial interaction imitates conversational give-and-take between the television persona and the unseen spectators. The persona accomplishes this by insinuating the absent viewers into his talk, thereby simulating conversation between himself and them. The audience of unseen viewers is thought, in turn, to make the appropriate interactional response, thereby sustaining the fiction that the persona is speaking with them and enabling him to continue his conversational routine. The television programs paid especial attention are talk-and-variety shows hosted by performers like Dave Garroway and Steve Allen, perhaps the precursors of today's talk show hosts.

The situation on the other side

The situation on the other side is that of the viewer who is not seen by the persona but is assumed to be watching the telecast. Horton and Wohl argue that there is para-social interaction between persona and viewer, and that this approximates interaction within primary groups (that is, within families). They maintain that such interaction has compensatory functions, especially for viewers whose inter-facial capabilities are limited by health and age. The para-social, then, is a product of machine prosthetics for human beings, of prosthetic interaction for persons who are disabled or deficient in some way.

In this regard, the Horton and Wohl argument is unabashedly functionalist, since, like all arguments for the existence of para-communicative modes, it is predicated on communicational supplements that are partial or deficient in their own right, yet contribute to and complement the fullness of a paramount reality. Bachelard's (1964) comment that "man is a creation of desire, not a creation of need" (p. 16) is apt here. However, the Horton and Wohl argument is based on bald need, in the functionalist sense, rather than on fascination and desire. Our fascination with electronic media continues to be more mysterious than transparent. By taking a functionalist tack, the argument established a conceptual design for comprehending television viewing that was similar to how Chicago school interactionists comprehended the framing, negotiation, and intimacy of everyday social relationships, the pathological deviations from these, and social deviance in general. Horton and Wohl's innovation was the application of this perspective to television viewing.

Horton and Wohl did not consider the effect on the viewer of the TV screen as a medium; nor did they conceptualize what I will call the "interior sociality" of the television viewer. They simply transposed, without modification or qualification, an interactionist perspective onto contacts between viewer and screen. The interactionist model had foundational status, so contacts between human being and inhuman machine were seen as less than fully human, rather than as a different but equally real form of communication. Whether there is a foundational reality and sociality in human life is not a question that should be taken for granted. The interior of the human being may be intensely social, while realities may be simulacra of one another in Baudrillard's (1983) terms, such that realities generate realities, with none of them having foundational status as the mold in which all others are cast. In this regard, rather than positing the separate existence of the social (with its implications of being the "truly real") and the para-social (with its implications of being less than real), there are instead a variety of socialities constituted through different logics and modalities. These socialities are in asymmetrical and problematic relationships amongst themselves. Thus, the interior sociality of the self, the exterior sociality of the world, and the sociality generated between TV viewer and TV screen are likely to be ongoing transformations of one another, of the realities they generate through these transformations.

With regard to the interior sociality of the self – the most problematic, conceptually, of the domains raised here – consider the following experiment. As I grow silence outside and around my self, I become aware of a simple phenomenon that I have always experienced yet rarely paid evident attention to: within myself I talk to myself in ongoing and continuous ways. I discover that I hear (or, more accurately, feel or sense) voices, at times one and at times many, within myself – that is, within my selfness. Often I am a monologue, sometimes a dialogue, and sometimes a conversation of more voices. At times these voices address one another as "I" and "you," but at other times "I" and "I" seems more the case as they agree, contest, interpolate, laugh at, comment on, and cry through one another. They may flow together into a single voice or split into different voices resonating through a range of registers of self-engagement. I am not saying that this interiority of selfness is psychologistic (or social-psychologistic) in its organization just because it is within the individual. Rather, I am saying that this interiority is *social in relation to itself*. Its self-organization as social within itself gives to selfness a degree of autonomy as a world unto itself on the micro-scale of human existence.

The interior sociality of selfness has particular relevance to television viewing, given Marshall McLuhan's claims about the "cool" nature of the television medium, and arguments for the existential identification of visual perception with the sense of touch. Before returning to these relationships, I will recount the main points of the Horton and Wohl argument in greater depth. I suggest that their conception of the para-social underestimates the interior sociality and creativity of the individual viewer, and that this interior sociality may be active as the individual watches television. Rather than the para-social lacking qualities of the social, it is another form of sociality, as is the interior sociality of selfness.

Para-social interaction: the Horton–Wohl argument
in more detail

According to Horton and Wohl, the personae have the capacity, through the designs of their shows, to achieve intimacy with crowds of strangers, each of whom feels she knows the persona the way she knows her chosen friends. In this regard, the persona offers a continuing relationship, in the Weberian sense of expecting future meetings whose very anticipation becomes a crucial parameter of the relationship. The viewer is implicated imaginatively in the persona's performance, but the viewer herself does *not* imagine this enactment. The persona creates the illusion or imitation of intimacy with great care, since the relationship is one-sided in the extreme. He or she does this by maintaining patter, a flow of small talk, giving the impression that he or she is responding to, and sustaining, the input of an invisible interlocutor – for example, by continually referring to and addressing the home audience as a party to the telecast. The persona creates the viewer in the image of his style.

Unlike friends and coevals of the viewer, the persona is typified according to standard formulae suited to his character and performance. Through this typification the persona becomes a locus of stability in the changing world, a character with predictable empathy and problem-solving capacities. Horton and Wohl conceive of the viewer as a passive being: there are no challenges to her selfness or to her ability to take on the reciprocal niche assigned to her in the persona's performance. Though she maintains control over the *content* of her participation, the niche of response (which has something of the deterministic format of a question/answer sequence) is opened and controlled by the persona.

The spectators at home must accept the conditions of the viewer's role offered by the program, in order, in the authors' words, "to enter" themselves into the performance. Horton and Wohl maintain, I think correctly, that "merely witnessing a program is not evidence that a spectator has played the required part . . . the experience does not end with the program itself" (p. 221). The experience of the program is evaluated by the "self" (their term). The implication is that the self is the psychological or social-psychological being, rather than the selfness of interior sociality. I will return to this point further on.

Horton and Wohl put great store in the values of the para-social role for TV viewers. They make four points in this respect. First, they state unequivocally that the enactment of a para-social role may constitute the exploration of new role possibilities. I would call this the potential opening up of creativity in the viewer, and link this quality to the interior sociality of selfness. Second, in a strongly homeostatic tilt, the para-social is understood as complementary to daily life, such that everyday premises and understandings of interaction and sociability are demonstrated and affirmed. This is especially significant as a prosthetic attachment for those isolated socially, for the socially inept, for the aged and invalid, the timid and rejected. Their social pathologies are compensated for by the artifice of sociality supplied by the TV screen. Third, there is no functional discontinuity between everyday life and para-social experience, since the viewer takes on roles at home that socially complement the persona in the television studio. Para-social relationships feed back into peoples' lives (the authors use the phrase "play back into"), and these relationships are again analogous to social interaction within mundane primary groups. In other words, the para-social prosthesis enables viewers to simulate, to a degree, the existence of a primary group in their everyday lives. Fourth, despite the functional complementarity of the para-social prosthesis for the everyday lives of viewers, the para-social relationship is pathological when it substitutes for autonomous social participation, existing in defiance of the singularity of objective reality. In other words, the sole paramount reality is that which exists among persons – among their social exteriors, as it were – and is the foundation of all other socialities and mimetic para-socialities.

Cool medium, haptic gaze, and the interior sociality of selfness

Marshall McLuhan's understanding of the TV screen as a "cool" medium encourages the premise that the viewer must be active within her self when watching television, and that viewing has (in his terms) tactual qualities which integrate perspective, content, and vision. With regard to the viewer, there are scholars who discuss the gaze in terms of its potentially haptic qualities: the tactual aspects of vision that, in my terms, enable the viewer, in a sense, to enter the screen. As noted, I will suggest in conclusion that this joining of viewer and screen has the qualities of a virtual encounter, a positioning that gives human beings a greater fullness to create and to exist in multiple realities than does the idea of the prosthetic para-social.

A phenomenology of the screen is needed in order to discuss the quality of contact between viewer and TV. What sort of phenomenon is a TV screen? How is it apprehended and experienced? At one extreme are the views of critics like Paul Virilio (1997), who draws on the imagery of the futuristic "citizen-terminal," the imagined being who is connected to numerous electronic prostheses, wired to control his environment but also controlled by it, the catastrophic being who is unable to move, locked into and wholly dependent for his existence on remote control scanners (p. 20). At the other extreme is the individual with personal agency, the imagining being. To no small degree, television transfers the agency of perception to the individual viewer. This brings the significance of the quality of the viewer's gaze into focus. Here McLuhan's distinction between "hot" and "cold" media of communication is apposite.

The hot medium "extends one single sense in 'high definition.' High definition is the state of being well filled with data" (McLuhan, 1994, p. 23). Because of the completeness of this data, audience members have little of their own to fill in. Hot media, therefore, are relatively low in participation (though, I would add, they may encourage high degrees of reflexivity). Film and radio are hot media. Television, however, is a cool medium: one that leaves a good deal to fill in, and is therefore high in participation (p. 31). McLuhan, writing in the early 1960s, stated that, "with TV, the viewer is the screen" (p. 313). Unlike film, the TV image is visually low in information. The TV screen offers a few million dots per second to the viewer, who assimilates only a few dozen, in any given instant, from which to make an image. Unconsciously, the TV viewer configures the dots like a pointillist painter, so that the image is an ever-changing mosaic mesh of spots of light. To connect the dots, the viewer becomes involved in the *depths* of the image. According to McLuhan, the TV image "requires each instant that we 'close' the spaces in the mesh by a convulsive sensuous participation that is profoundly kinetic and *tactile*, because *tactility* is the interplay of the senses, rather than the isolated contact of skin and object" (p. 314; my emphasis). In other words, the tactile is an index of the bringing together of all the senses, the touching of the senses by one another, the interaction and intertwining of the senses. The TV image is synesthetic, encouraging imagination and creative responsiveness, perhaps as a complex gestalt of information (p. 317).

McLuhan stresses that television is "above all, an extension of the sense of touch, which involves maximal interplay of all the senses" (p. 333). Yet, like touch, the tactual TV image is discontinuous and non-lineal: "To the sense of touch, all things are suddenly counter, original, spare, strange" (p. 334). We use our eye, McLuhan claims, "as we use our hand in seeking to create an inclusive image, made up of many moments, phases, and aspects of the person or thing" (p. 334).

McLuhan's focus on the screen, which evokes the touching qualities of the gaze, has parallels from the perspective of the viewer. Emmanuel Levinas (1987) likens sensibility – the movement and organization of feelings towards exteriority – first and foremost to touch. To approach exteriority is touching, yet it is not reducible to a (reflexive) experience of such proximity. The act, the practice, of contact is touch and touching – that is, full of feeling. In terms relevant to McLuhan, one could say that the viewer who "touches" the dots of the screen, connecting them, engages in an embodied practice that is already framing his own anticipation. "The visible," writes Levinas "caresses the eye. One sees and one hears like one touches" (p. 118). Proximity in and of itself has effects on being that intentionality (that is, conscious cognition) cannot account for. The effects of proximity are sensible (and sensuous) – they are restless, moving, complicit, passing (p. 121). Through McLuhan and Levinas, one can gain a sense of how the viewer relates to the screen. The TV screen joins the viewer in an intimacy of sensibility, the viewer touching and entering the screen with his gaze, the screen opening to, and acting in, the viewer. In these regards, contra Horton and Wohl, the viewer constitutes the image no less than it is constituted for him.[5]

Are there gazes that are potentially more creative for the individual, in contrast to other ways of seeing? Focusing further on the gaze may suggest more about the viewer's capacity to penetrate the screen. Given the agency of the viewer's gaze, as well as the electronic composition of the screen, she not only sees but probably *imagines*, to a degree, what she sees. Though television attracts and shapes the gaze, *how* one looks may be a crucial factor in whether the gaze mostly reflects images (a position closer to taking on a role niche in the TV program, as Horton and Wohl might have put it) or also rearranges the play of images on the screen, thereby composing realities within the viewer.

One approach to considering how the viewer touches the screen is to distinguish among gazes that may be termed *optic*, *haptic*, and *virtual*. These distinctions are not absolute, but refer more to emphases on qualities of looking. The *optic* gaze indexes what we usually call "seeing." It outlines surface shapes and forms. The optic gaze shows us that the TV screen appears to be a concrete, dimensional surface of representation. The *haptic* gaze, on the other hand, perceives surface as texture. It is tactually sensible, touching and feeling the textures of another surface and penetrating its contours. Sensually, the haptic gaze creates depth where none had existed. In relation to the TV screen, such depth is likely related to the viewer's completion (indeed, the making) of the image.

When gaze is optic it is more superficial, brushing surfaces. When it is haptic, it "penetrates in depth, finding its pleasure in texture and grain" (Gandelman, 1991, p. 5). According to Taussig (1993), the tactile capacity of the haptic gaze indexes "the unstoppable merging of the object of perception with the body of the perceiver and not just with the mind's eye" (p. 25). Thus Walter Benjamin (1968) compared Dadaist art to "an instrument of ballistics. It hit the spectator like a bullet . . . thus acquiring a tactile quality" (p. 238). To reiterate, haptic gaze is an active creator of reality, moving into and occupying such space.

Haptic gaze seems to border on, and at times become, gaze that may be called *virtual*. If the haptic gaze creates the depths of reality, then the virtual gaze is that of the imaginary, a gaze that opens to one's existential horizons. The viewer dreams or, more accurately, daydreams through virtual gaze. Virtual gaze takes the viewer to the edge of possibility. It is seductive, in Baudrillard's sense of the term. In the instance of the TV viewer, virtual gaze is likely to be self-seductive, since the recursive loop that comes into being between the viewer and that in which she participates creates the play of images of which she is a part.

It is the virtual gaze of the TV viewer in interaction with the screen that challenges the literate ego consciousness engendered by book culture. Romanyshyn (1993) argues that the TV viewer, awake, is also dreaming, because television blurs or eclipses a host of boundaries between reason and madness, fact and fiction. "Watching television . . . exposes the ego to the bizarre experience of being awake in one's dreams. Or, watching television is akin to interpreting dreams, making sense of them, while dreaming" (p. 353). The viewer is awake, yet dreaming, as the interaction between viewer and screen collapses values of lineal rationality, contextual coherence, narrative continuity, and infinite progress (p. 345). Television consciousness works especially on the emotional body, as does dreaming: the viewer is "immersed in a landscape that is more mythical than it is logical, and invited into action that is more ritual in texture than moral in outlook" (p. 358).

The haptic touching of the television screen by the viewer opens into the fluidity of virtual possibility, into a condition of playfulness (Sutton-Smith, 1997), into the capacity of reimagining one's selfness. The malleability of playful possibility opens to the viewer the capability of altering the ongoing telecast in relation to herself. Baudrillard (1990) comments that "seduction represents mastery over the symbolic universe . . . the capacity immanent to seduction [is] to deny things their truth" (p. 8). The virtual gaze dreaming the imaginary is seductive, because the imaginary enables the existence of the symbolic universe, and with it the landscape of dreaming. The virtual self-seduction of the TV viewer opens her to the play of the imaginary – of her own existential imaginary – in which distinctions between truth and falsehood, the authentic and the inauthentic, and many more, are bent back on one another, whorled, whirled through one another, and erased.

Television viewing may encourage the kind of creativity that we associate with dreaming. Here the television image ceases to be representational, and the viewer is no longer a linear reflection of anything. The viewer becomes an agent in the creation of reality, even though this agency is microcosmic and is situated primarily within the social interiority of the viewer. The viewer is an active agent engaged in recreating herself through such experiences, largely without the intervention and mediation of other persons (Handelman, 2000, 2001). Moreover, within her selfness the viewer is in a condition of interaction among her interior voices. Through the emergence of this interior interaction she creates (and re-creates) for herself the television persona, as it were, on the other side of the screen.

Horton and Wohl claim they are concerned with what "actually happens" in the home audience of TV viewers, insisting that viewers are not passive recipients of telecasts. Nonetheless, the authors are conventional and normative in their understanding of social interaction, in that they posit a paramount social reality that is complete in itself, thereby reducing other realities to the ontological status of the less-than-complete, the *para*. According to their position, if other realities occupy the person, then the presence of these realities is pathological. The relatedness of viewer and TV screen has no reality in any full sense. At best, the telecast makes available the *illusion* of social roles or slots into which the viewer inserts himself in para-social fashion. Given the illusory reality of viewer/TV relatedness, according to Horton and Wohl, there are no challenges to the selfness of the viewer. Moreover, the entire burden of creating a plausible imitation of intimacy is shouldered by the persona and by the show of which he is the pivot. The agency of the viewer is limited to adopting social roles whose molds are preformed; but, as noted, if she is overly adoptive of such roles, her behavior is pathological. Despite their disclaimers, the TV viewer of Horton and Wohl is more a Schutzian puppet than a virtual explorer of the imaginary.

The social in the psyche: towards the virtual encounter in viewing television

In one of his lesser-known works, Erving Goffman (1961) argued that every face-to-face meeting between persons constituted an "encounter," a temporary reordering and repatterning of selected elements of a social order (of whatever scale) that are permitted entry to, and expression within, the encounter. He described the encounter as follows: "A locally realized world . . . [that] cuts the participants off from many externally based matters that might have been given relevance, but allows a few of these externally based matters to enter the interaction world as an official part of it" (p. 31). Goffman put forward four criteria to identify an encounter of co-presence: a single visual and/or cognitive focus of attention; a heightened, mutual relevance of acts, with the act as the observable component of social action; an eye-to-eye ecological huddle that maximizes each participant's opportunity to perceive how other participants monitor his behavior; and an openness to verbal communication. He argued further that the encounter should be conceptualized in terms of rules that constitute its structure during its existence. The rules of irrelevance specify what should and should not be paid attention to; the realized resources are the local identities and roles that participants are able to use; and the transformation rules describe the fate of any element that is selected to become part of the internal order of the encounter (pp. 19–29).

Here Goffman lays out a schema for analyzing face-to-face interaction as a morphological, relatively static form of organization. In my own work (Handelman, 1977, pp. 94–133) I point to three consequences of Goffman's theory that are significant if one relates the encounter more processually to ongoing social order. First, given that every occasion of face-to-face interaction creates an encounter, then the encounter is a form of social organization, micro in scale, temporary and transient, since it exists only for the duration of the face-to-face occasion. To interact is to create social organization. Second, every encounter is an evolving micro-form of organization – that is, its form and its consequences are both *emergent*, and such emergence is often open-ended and unpredictable. The emerging form taken by the encounter shapes, and is shaped by, the ongoing interaction that emerges within it. Form and process emerge from one another. Third, a series of encounters between the same persons, or among overlapping sets of persons, function as feedback loops in the emergence of any social relationship in which they are constituents.[6] Encounters, themselves phenomena of emergence, are integral to the emergence and reproduction of micro-social order, which has its own relationships with macro-social order. In terms that are prominent today, there are powerful elements of autopoiesis, of self-organization, in the structuring of emergence (and the emergent structuring) of a given encounter, and so, too, through a series of encounters.

Horton and Wohl premise the interaction between viewer and TV screen as a functional substitute for face-to-face interaction, which becomes pathological and dysfunctional when the viewer becomes really attached to, and involved in, the substitution. The idea of pathology depends on a premise of normality within a paramount reality. Thus, Horton and Wohl begin their argument with a discussion of normal interaction within a paramount reality constituted, to a high degree, through face-to-face interaction. By definition, then, TV viewing must be less-than-normal, hence from the outset a deviant or abnormal form of interaction. The para-social cannot be interactive, since neither viewer nor persona actually respond to one another.

By contrast, in my formulation, the theory of encounters begins with the premise that the human being is interactive in all domains of being, no less so when this interaction is intra-active and when it is virtual. The theory of encounters does not begin with a paramount reality that specifies what is normal and what is abnormal interaction. Rather, it premises the existence of the encounter on contact. The contact between viewer and TV screen is interactive, as the former actively participates in the constitution of the image and responds to this within himself, intra-actively. Suitably modified, the theory of encounters would perceive the meeting between viewer and TV screen as a *virtual encounter*, one that triggers interaction among the voices that constitute the selfness of the viewer.

In this confluence, the qualities of the screen image and the haptic and virtual gazes of the viewer join together to create a virtual space of interaction that is also intra-active within the viewer. In McLuhan's terms, the medium indeed becames an extension of selfness, activating reflexivity within the virtual space of the imagination.[7] As the viewer enters the screen, the screen enters the viewer. The virtual encounter constitutes itself with the fullness of a phenomenal world that the viewer contains and is contained by. Hypothetically, like the face-to-face encounter, the virtual encounter between viewer and TV screen is a ruled, dynamic form of organization, but one that joins together the images of the screen and the intra-active interior of the viewer. However, we do not know whether such ruledness in viewing and relating is that of the micro-order of the individual, or whether there are also complex interrelationships between the individual and the broader social order that affect his own micro-ordering in relation to viewing. Thus, whether the rules of the virtual encounter should be conceived in terms of the theory of encounters outlined above, or whether a new epistemology of encounter is needed, requires further thought.

This perspective is not solipsistic. Neither is it deterministic. The viewer does not simply disappear deeper and deeper into an inevitable hermeneutic of self-interpretation while watching television. As I pointed out, we talk to ourselves continually during our waking hours. We often engage in an interior discourse, perhaps at times a dialogue, within our selves. This interior discourse is intensely and intimately social, even though it emerges wholly within our own interiorities. The social, like the tactual, does not begin at the interface of body and environment. It is embedded in the psyche – more accurately, perhaps, *embodied* in the psyche – such that interior interaction within the individual is a transform of interaction among individuals, and vice versa.

One signal difference between interior and face-to-face interaction is, of course, that interior discourse is among "parts," or voices, of the individual. As the viewer encounters the screen in their mutual virtual space, so too do the images of the screen and the interior voices of the viewer. Yet these interiorities are, more generally, the conditions of virtual realities. If our perceptions of the interactivity of virtual encounters and other forms of virtuality are to be enhanced and appreciated, then ways need to be found to do this. The writing was already on the wall (or, rather, the image was already within the viewer) with the appearance of television. Still, logocentric perspectives dominated, and confronting the powerful presence of virtual realities was elided. Now, either one must find ways to relate theoretically and empirically to virtual realities, or much that happens through these media will not exist for students of communication. Horton and Wohl brought the social qualities of the interaction of viewer and screen to our attention. Theorizing this interaction through a phenomenological sense of virtuality may give us insight into the deep processes that organize our incessant contacts with the television screen.

Notes

Epigraph: words and music by Leonard Cohen. By kind permission © 1993, Sony/ATV Music Publishing.

1   The direct influence of George Herbert Mead, the apical ancestor of symbolic interactionism, is minimal in the Horton and Wohl text (1956, p. 218), though the text echoes the zeitgeist of Garfinkel's ethnomethods.

2   Nonetheless, one could argue that both the viewer at home and the TV personae performing live in the television studios were taking on roles that accorded with what Mead called the "generalized other," only these may not have been the same generalized others. So here was one of the more hidden needs for polls and ratings, to try to synchronize just what manner of others viewers and personae were generalizing.

3   Ideas of virtual space had been around for some time, in physics and in the philosophy of aesthetics (see Langer, 1953, pp. 69–103).

4   The Horton and Wohl article was published during a period when various so-called *para* aspects of social interaction – primarily non-verbal face-to-face interaction – were being paid serious attention by scholars. In 1941, Daniel Efron published *Gesture, Race and Culture*, his pioneering comparative study of the body movements of Jewish and Italian men in New York City. During the 1950s the study of para-communication (or para-linguistic communication), as non-verbal interaction often came to be called, was thought

to be at the cutting edge of discovering the linguistically styled lawfulness of all human interaction. Since language was seen as constitutive of paramount reality, all non-verbal modes of communication were complementary for this linguistic reality, and their ruled character was modeled on the linguistic. Birdwhistell (1952, 1970) and Scheflen (1965) were developing the study of kinesics, in order to identify systemic ruledness for languages of non-verbal communication. So, too, proxemics (see Watson, 1970), personal space (Sommer, 1969), and tacesics (Kauffman, 1972) were being conceptualized. In terms of symbolic interactionism, Goffman (1959, 1967) and Strauss (1959) were major contributors to the theorizing of interaction between self and other. By the mid-1970s, the study of para-communication had retreated into sociolinguistics, and the search for languages of non-verbal communication was regarded pretty much as a dead end.

5   I note, in passing, how the TV screen privileges the gaze of the viewer. In the Elizabethan theater, for example, there was only a single seat with perfect perspective. This was where the monarch sat (Orgel, 1975, pp. 10–11). So, too, the "Baroque 'stage' consists of the foot of an imaginary visual pyramid, perceived from the position of the king" (Bartels, 1993, p. 58). Watching TV, the viewer has the apical perspective of a Renaissance monarch.

6   I adapted Goffman's conception of encounter to theorize face-to-face interaction in small-scale work settings. There I distinguished in a preliminary way between four forms of encounter: abortive, oscillating, oppositional, and consensual, arguing that a predominance of any one or any combination of these forms was consequential for the shaping of future encounters among the same persons.

7   My use of reflexivity refers to the awareness of the viewer in relation to herself, in the sense of turning selfness back on its self, "so as to cause it to engage in more complex behavior" (Hayles, 1996, p. 16).

References

Bachelard, G. (1964) *The Psychoanalysis of Fire*. Boston: Beacon Press.
Bartels, K. (1993) The Box of Digital Images: The World as Computer Theater. *Diogenes*, 163, 45–70.
Baudrillard, J. (1983) *Simulations*. New York: Semiotext(e).
Baudrillard, J. (1990) *Seduction*. New York: St Martin's Press.
Benjamin, W. (1968) *Illuminations*, tr. with Introduction by Hannah Arendt. New York: Harcourt, Brace.
Birdwhistell, R. (1952) *Introduction to Kinesics*. Washington, DC: National Service Institute.
Birdwhistell, R. (1970) *Kinesics and Context*. Philadelphia: University of Pennsylvania Press.
Efron, D. ([1941] 1972) *Gesture, Race and Culture*. The Hague: Mouton.
Gandelman, C. (1991) *Reading Pictures, Viewing Texts*. Bloomington: Indiana University Press.

Goffman, E. (1959) *The Presentation of Self in Everyday Life*. New York: Doubleday Anchor.

Goffman, E. (1961) *Encounters: Two Studies in the Sociology of Interaction*. Indianapolis: Bobbs-Merrill.

Goffman, E. (1967) *Interaction Ritual: Essays on Face-to-Face Behavior*. New York: Doubleday Anchor.

Handelman, D. (1977) *Work and Play among the Aged: Interaction, Replication and Emergence in a Jerusalem Setting*. Assen: Van Gorcum.

Handelman, D. (2000) Into the Television Screen: The Individual as a Locus of Creativity? In G. Thomas (ed.), *Religiose Funktionen des Fernsehens?*, Wiesbaden: Westdeutscher Verlag, 247–58. (In German.)

Handelman, D. (2001) The Interior Sociality of Self-Transformation. In D. Shulman and G. Stroumsa (eds), *Undoing the Person: Self-Transformation in the History of Religions*, New York: Oxford University Press, 236–53.

Hayles, N. C. (1996) Boundary Disputes: Homeostasis, Reflexivity, and the Foundations of Cybernetics. In R. Markley (ed.), *Virtual Realities and their Discontents*, Baltimore: Johns Hopkins University Press, 11–37.

Horton, D. and Wohl, R. (1956) Mass Communication and Para-social Interaction: Observations on Intimacy at a Distance. *Psychiatry*, 19 (3), 215–29.

Kauffman, L. E. (1972) Tacesics, the Study of Touch: A Model for Proxemic Analysis. *Semiotica*, 4, 149–61.

Langer, S. K. (1953) *Feeling and Form: A Theory of Art*. London: Routledge & Kegan Paul.

Levinas, E. (1987) Language and Proximity. In *Collected Philosophical Papers*, Dordrecht: Martinus Nijhoff, 109–26.

McLuhan, M. (1994) *Understanding Media: The Extensions of Man*. Cambridge, MA: MIT Press. (Originally published in 1964, New York: McGraw Hill.)

Orgel, S. (1975) *The Illusion of Power: Political Theater in the English Renaissance*. Berkeley: University of California Press.

Romanyshyn, R. D. (1993) The Despotic Eye and its Shadow: Media Image in the Age of Literacy. In D. M. Levin (ed.), *Modernity and the Hegemony of Vision*, Berkeley: University of California Press, 339–60.

Scheflen, A. (1965) *Stream and Structure of Communicational Behavior*. Philadelphia: Eastern Psychiatric Institute.

Sommer, R. (1969) *Personal Space*. Englewood Cliffs, NJ: Prentice-Hall.

Strauss, A. (1959) *Mirrors and Masks*. Glencoe, IL: Free Press.

Sutton-Smith, B. (1997) *The Ambiguity of Play*. Cambridge, MA: Harvard University Press.

Taussig, M. (1993) *Mimesis and Alterity: A Particular History of the Senses*. New York: Routledge.

Virilio, P. (1997) *Open Sky*. London: Verso.

Watson, O. M. (1970) *Proxemic Behavior*. The Hague: Mouton.

PART IV
The Toronto School

———

Introduction

Marshall McLuhan entered media studies through a side door and stormed onto center stage. A scholar trained in English literature, he shifted from an initial interest in media content to put all his weight on form (of which his Cambridge mentors might approve) and on technology. By "the medium is the message," the best known of his aphorisms, he meant that the dominant medium of each age uniquely constrains the ways in which our brains process information, which, in turn, shapes our personalities and our social systems. The linearity of print, for example, induces causal thinking, unfeeling individualism, and social arrangements such as assembly lines. Unlike mainstream researchers who consider the abstractness of print more involving than the literalness of television, McLuhan claimed that the unambiguous ("hot") medium of print imposed a barrage of alien messages from outside ourselves, and was therefore less engaging than the "cool" medium of television, which actively invites meaning making by involving us in piecing the pixels together.

McLuhan was a great hit among executives of the culture industry, and attracted considerable attention from humanists (though not from social scientists), who initially warmed to his poetic provocations and then cooled down. His renown has also had ups and downs – and ups. In the process, Toronto became known as the center for the study of the social effects of media technologies.

Harold Innis, the economist, also entered through a side door, but his interest in the economics of nation building pointed him to the role of media technologies, and to close affiliation with McLuhan, more as mentor than collaborator. Innis classified the media in terms of space and time, distinguishing portable media – the key to centralized control in space – from monumental media, such as pyramids, which assure continuity over time. While Innis's technological theories are less deterministic than McLuhan's, allowing for more societal control, their classificatory scheme runs into some of the same sorts of troubles. As Blondheim explains, Innis's labeling of speech as a time-concurring medium is a subject for debate.

McLuhan concurs that word of mouth is a medium of "heart," favoring the communication of practical wisdom across generations, hence tradition and religion. Print, on the other hand – an extension of the eye for McLuhan – is a medium of "mind," favoring the communication of specialized knowledge across space, hence nationalism and empire. McLuhan's "global village" is a prophecy that sees the revival of oral culture in television and a welcome liberation from the tribalism of radio and the imperialism of print. McLuhan was not in love with television, however; he only hated it less than print.

Other students of technological effects – Eisenstein and Ong, in particular – have expressed their indebtedness to the inspiration of the Toronto school, while distancing themselves from its methodologies.

9

Harold Adams Innis and his Bias of Communication

Menahem Blondheim

The idea of canon has a dialectic to it, of precisely the kind that fascinated Harold Adams Innis. This dialectic follows one of Innis's theoretical staples – a Hegelian triad.[1] Canonic texts were originally a revelation, often a revolution. They came to be revered, even ritualized; and they remain referential, and therefore relevant. The tension in this triad of revolution, reverence, and relevance stems, fundamentally, from the polarity of the absolute and the relative, or, as Innis would have put it, the rigid and the flexible. The original novelty represented by the emergence of the work that would later be canonized at a certain point in historical time, and its inevitable contingence on the circumstances surrounding its emergence, conflicts with the notion of the work carrying an absolute truth, a message good for all time. In turn, this notion of absolute authority is threatened by subsequent, unanticipated references and new applications of the work, if it is to remain relevant, validating the canon's fundamental flexibility and mutability. Innis might have put this latter tension, or at least an important aspect of it, in terms of the problematics of oligopoly or monopoly of knowledge. Societies secure and buttress breakthroughs in knowledge or in tools for its generation, diffusion, and preservation, by granting them a privileged position. Yet this pampering inevitably carries the specter of stagnation, of fossilizing the revelation, destroying the necessary responsiveness and flexibility of knowledge in society.[2]

These tensions immanent in the concept of canon may be illustrated by the most dominant one known to Western culture, possibly the formative specimen of canon in that culture – the Bible.[3] Here, the dialectic of canon was inevitably worked out in theological terms. Theologians, over the ages, had no real difficulty with the apparent contradiction between the eternity of what they ritualized as divine texts and their appearance at a particular point in history. It was not that historical developments conditioned the Scriptures; rather, the Creator had the Scriptures in his game plan all along, including their launching into history at a specific juncture. The theological task of reconciling the eternal truth of the Bible and its inevitable adaptation to changing circumstances proved much more difficult. To the rescue came the twin ideas of typology and accommodation: the Creator's blueprint of the world pregnant with all its future applications and the Creator accommodating the creative powers of subsequent apostles of the canonized message.[4] The canonic work thus carries within it an adaptive mechanism, an applications generator that, if properly operated, could provide for legitimate adaptation to changing circumstances and sensibilities.[5]

None took the liberty of adapting ancient and supposedly divine texts to the present more luxuriously than North American Protestants. They found their errand into the wilderness of an unknown continent to represent the ultimate interpretation, and therefore also an original meaning, of the ancient biblical canon; and paradoxically, the older the Testament, the more relevant it was to the New World experience (Bercovitch, 1967; Davis, 1972). This hermeneutic liberty was exercised by way of at best creative, more commonly tortured, misreadings of the canonic text. These American Protestants would later endorse, most naturally, a performative text – the Constitution – into which was consciously built an adaptive mechanism that made it "a machine that would go of itself." Subsequent generations, the devout among the founders understood, would do to the Constitution what they had done to the Scriptures (Bercovitch, 1978, pp. 132–52; Kammen, 1994, pp. 116–24, 219–31).

North American Baptists, whose clergy was among the vocations the young Innis was made to consider (Creighton, 1981, p. 18; Neill, 1972, p. 10), were among the most daring denominations in modernist readings of the classical Scriptures, and one of the most mindful of constitutional transformation and reframing (McDonald, 1985, p. 73; Isaac, 1982, pp. 317–22).[6] An older, "mildly agnostic" Innis, making reference in one of his last great texts to an entirely different canonic work of Western culture, would find this ostensible contradiction between the eternity and flexibility of canon to be elemental. In acknowledging the tremendous influence of Plato's work, he referred, most naturally, to the compound of "inconclusiveness and immortality" (Innis, 1972, p. 57; 1951, p. 10). Moreover, according to Innis, it was precisely this play of the absolute and the relative, the "immortal inconclusiveness" of Plato's legacy, which enabled it to "dominate the history of the West."

Thinking about Innis's work in terms of canon can imply an exercise in reflexivity. Since Innis's focus is the nature of knowledge and its role in society, a consideration of his own work in terms of its history and impact suggests applying it to itself.[7] In doing so, it would be proper to consider the three vertices of the triad of canon: revolution, reverence, and relevance. However, in Innis's case it may be best to invert the order and first consider relevance, in the sense of the flexibility of his work, its inconclusiveness, and its potential for renewal. This is followed by an assessment of reverence – an evaluation of the place of his work in contemporary thinking about communication. While indications of reverence will be proposed impressionistically, a short survey will critically consider features of Innis's works that have been crystallized and widely referenced in communication studies.[8] Then, a consideration of the extent to which his thinking about communication was revolutionary, or even novel, is attempted. Such an assessment necessarily draws on the sources and origins of his communication scholarship. Finally, I return to one aspect of relevance, and consider if and how Innis's perspective has sufficient power of renewal to be applied to emerging perplexities and dilemmas as our communication environment undergoes thorough change. This triangular investigation of Innis as canonical will focus on one of his best-known texts, "The Bias of Communication," originally a paper presented at the University of Michigan in 1949, then an essay that gave its name to a collection of Innis's studies of communication, published by the University of Toronto Press shortly before his death, half a century ago (1951, pp. 33–60).

Relevance: "The Bias of Communication" and its readers

If, as Innis implied, inconclusiveness is fundamental to canonicity, his own work would surely qualify: inconclusiveness is one of its hallmarks. One conspicuous way in which Innis cultivated flexibility was his unique style in communicating his ideas. Indeed, "The Bias of Communication" may appear as a bag of tricks that Innis played on his fellow scholars by way of his choice of sources, his method of organizing and analyzing them, and his mode of presentation. In "The Bias," as in his other communication texts, Innis's ideas are supposed to emerge, somehow, from a survey of communication in history, and lots of it. These works are essentially a parade of historical facts and experiences, marched, over and over again, in lectures, articles, and monographs about communication. This recurring parade proceeds, as in "The Bias," along a chronological axis, though lapses and errors occur quite frequently. As if viewing the parade from a grandstand, Innis occasionally seizes on a fact or a relationship to make an editorial point. He apparently had no intention of changing this scholarly strategy and plan of composition as his research into communication progressed. His "History of Communication," a 1,000-page manuscript left among his papers, is an impressive, if disorganized, collection of fragments of historical information in more or less chronological order, from an eclectic array of sources. It follows the same pattern of a historical play-by-play, interlaced with expert analysis.[9]

Innis culled the data presented in his survey from a mammoth reservoir of some 2,000 titles which he set out to read when entering upon his communication project. This dizzying array of sources covers all periods of human history, in many parts of the world.[10] Notwithstanding this promiscuous variety, there is a striking common denominator in the sources Innis referred to in "The Bias" and in his other communication writings. In sharp contrast to the sources used in his studies of Canadian economic history, practically all of them were secondary works, rather than primary sources. Thus, the historical experiences that are the topical focus of "The Bias" are filtered twice: first by secondary sources, then by Innis's own analytic treatment of them.

Innis's analytical interventions in "The Bias" tend to be short and condensed, frequently opaque, and occasionally cryptic; to use Greek imagery, they range from the laconic to the delphic. All too often they resemble entries in "The Idea File," a compilation of research notes and occasional insights which Innis wrote in an unpolished, scholarly shorthand for his own files.[11] These textual deficiencies are commonly brushed aside as a demonstration of bad writing, as though Innis had a composition problem ("his wretched writing style," or his "infuriating gnomic style," to quote Cohen's (1993) evaluation). Innis the writer, however, was certainly capable of producing a smooth narrative and well-structured, clear arguments. In *The History of the Canadian Pacific Railroad* (1971) – originally his dissertation at the University of Chicago – and *The Fur Trade in Canada* (1930a), as well as other titles in political economy and economic history, his information and analysis are well organized and quite readable.[12] Although hardly a page-turner, *Peter Pond, Fur Trader and Adventurer* (1930b) even makes for fairly compelling reading. What is described as a composition problem emerged only when Innis focused his scholarly efforts on understanding communication.

Given the problem of style, it is only after engaging in a deliberate, word-by-word, deciphering process that the reader encounters the real problems of "The Bias" – above all, the problem of coherence. One aspect of the problem is that Innis's specific comments and analyses cannot easily be constructed into a complete, fully developed argument or theory; they do not even appear to present a distinct point of view. But more immediately troubling are patent inconsistencies in the text, from non-sequiturs in the reasoning to glaring contradictions between interpretations, between data, and between data and interpretation.[13] These conflicts do not merely concern matters of detail. As will be demonstrated, they can pertain even to the most pivotal arguments that Innis proposed.

Two major explanations have been proposed for this set of textual problems; appropriately, they are contradictory – even mirror images of each other. One takes the old-man-in-a-hurry approach, based to a large extent on the influence of Donald Creighton's (1957) standard biography of Innis. According to this argument, Innis entered into the study of communication in his later years, in bad health and burdened by numerous academic and public responsibilities. By the time he was composing "The Bias," he had emerged as a central power broker at the University of Toronto, and more generally in Canadian academia. Further afield, he had become a prominent authority in shaping Canadian national economic policy. As Royal Commissioner, he discharged the extensive responsibilites that went with his commission with considerable diligence. More generally, he had to act his emerging part as celebrated symbol of Canadian letters.

Studying the field of communication, Innis accomplished a great scholarly breakthrough, which he thought was of the highest civic importance and urgency. But he was simply too burdened by his weighty public responsibilities to be bothered with fine-tuning the scholarly and literary details of his discovery, and settled instead for a hasty sketch of his ideas without fully working them out. Innis's haste and the difficult circumstances in which he studied communications were responsible for the shortcomings of "The Bias" and his other communication works, their lack of coherence, and even their inner contradictions.

Based on this approach, scholar James Carey, with all his appreciation of Innis, proposed the Gordian knot solution to the problem of inconsistency and contradiction. Canon does not necessarily imply sanctity, nor does reverence require prostration; accordingly, Carey recommended simply overlooking contradictions and inconsistencies in the text. "It is best to avoid excessive piety before Innis's work," he opined, "Innis's books are not sacred texts to be exegetically struggled with" (1981, p. 78). Marshall McLuhan, in his introduction (1951) to *The Bias of Communication* – essentially a critical hagiography of his colleague the "hick Baptist," who was "the real freak" – demonstrated a variant of this same approach. Pointing out what he considered glaring misperceptions in the text he was introducing, McLuhan proposed that readers keep a critical distance and take Innis's statements as challenge and inspiration. The master, after all, did not always sufficiently think through all his statements and arguments.

The second, and much more compelling, explanation to the problem presents the Innis who composed "The Bias" as the mirror image of an old man in a hurry. In this theory, Innis is the patient sage, the consummate artist-scholar deliberately devising a revolutionary literary medium for communicating his revolutionary ideas about communication and knowledge. In fact, in forging his unique mode of presenting scholarship, Innis was applying one of the most profound insights to emerge from his odyssey into the history of communication: the crucial importance of orality and dialectic as they affected the interaction, exchange, and change of ideas. For culture to remain vital, Innis found, varying opinions and different sides to arguments must be co-present. Script, then print (together with the related modernist idea of science), had banished dialogue, and ultimately dialectic, from Western civilization. Their restoration, Innis thought, was imperative. By cultivating contradictions, by juxtaposing data and ideas that were not necessarily compatible, he was emulating the oral form of reasoning, learning, and knowing. Innis was thus demonstrating how traditional dialectic could be rediscovered and exercised, just as he was saying how important it was to do this (Theall, 1981, pp. 228–30; Stamps, 1995, pp. 90–6).

Neither of these contrasting approaches to the problem of coherence in "The Bias" is fully convincing, however. Notwithstanding its elegance, the validity of the "oral text" or "constellational mode of writing" approach (Stamps, 1995, p. 67) is highly questionable on points of strategy, structure, and personal temperament. Western literature emerged from an oral past, and traditional societies that cherished it found textual contrivances for sustaining dialectic in the ages of script and print. After all, even a yelling and kicking Plato was delivered into the orbit of the written word without losing his inconclusiveness. No one was better informed about these strategies than Innis. He could have adopted a historically successful model.[14] Moreover, the text of "The Bias" does not appear to successfully structure a complex dialectic. Innis's individual statements are closed and rather "cold"; contradictions are not made explicit and are not negotiated; they commonly emerge only by comparing different texts and are not jettisoned in the same context.

Finally, if an "oral text" was what he was attempting, Innis would have told us so. Judging from the portrait of Innis that emerges from biographical accounts, it would be unlike him to pull a subversive punch on his readers. Innis the child, the father, and the social man did enjoy playing a practical joke, yet nowhere is he described as manipulative (Cooper, 1977). Moreover, he was extremely sensitive to his readers' expectations: in the opening of "The Bias," as well as in other lectures and articles, Innis strains, at the expense of elegance, to clarify exactly what he is about to do and how. He emerges from his texts and from reminiscences as too concerned about the fate of Western civilization, too serious about scholarship, and too respectful of his audiences to cynically turn their expectations against them.

Biography, however, should not be taken too far in trying to explain the nature of Innis's text, which appears to be precisely what the alternative approach attempts to do. The impression of a harassed, then critically ill, Innis, desperately trying to win one for the West by his communication studies, sacrificing consistency and coherence in his haste, simply does not emerge from the text of "The Bias" or from his other writings on communication. The evidence he cites is too rich, the references are too many and too meticulously crafted to indicate a hasty, pressured composition. The mammoth bibliography he assembled upon entering on the study of communication, the monumental dimensions and ambitious nature of the manuscript of "A History of Communication," suggest a most deliberate scholarly process.

Innis apparently found it necessary to drastically change his plan of composition and mode of writing upon moving from economic history to the history of communication. As we shall see, it was not only that the style appropriate for tracing the history of communication was very different from the ways one traced a cargo of codfish or described a trekking beaver. Innis's mode of scholarship, even his purpose in presenting the history of communication, represented a sharp break from the approach of his economic history scholarship. It thus dictated a radically different mode of composition and a unique strategy for communicating scholarship.

Whether valid or not, and however contradictory, both previous approaches to the problem of contradiction and inconsistency in "The Bias" are highly relevant to the question of canon. For both agree that Innis's unique mode of composition and the nature of his text result in inconclusiveness. Whether he left his work open intentionally or unintentionally, by default or design, his apostles had great responsibility – and great liberty – to adapt and re-create his work by their own sensibilities and imaginations, circumstances and concerns.[15]

This was not the case in Innis's earlier work on Canadian economic history. Far from it: his project of comprehensively documenting and analyzing the extraction of the major Canadian export staples and the process of bringing them to market were, and still are, considered definitive.

But, precisely because they are definitive, they are limited, in the sense captured by Harold Bloom: "the book goes on the shelf and we go elsewhere." "The Bias," like Innis's other studies of communication, inconclusive but intriguing, begs development and extension, as if anticipating its subsequent re-creators. Innis left room, in a deep sense, for modification, for unforeseen applications of his typologies, and for accommodation to wildly different circumstances. It is not surprising, therefore, that those who picked up the gauntlet developed creative works of their own in response to Innis, rather than pious incantations of the master's work. Yet, for all their novelty, these later attempts at understanding communication emphatically, and almost ritualistically, attributed their new departures to Innis's legacy. Thus Marshall McLuhan (1951) suggested that his own work could be seen as a mere footnote added to Innis (p. ix), and James Carey (1975) phrased his own influential intervention as "a gentle extension" of Innis (p. 30).[16]

But even in these attributions, McLuhan and Carey seem to be taking a page, or rather a footnote, from Innis's own book. In the opening paragraph of "The Bias," Innis positioned his thinking about communication and culture in relation to Alfred Louis Kroeber's *Configurations of Cultural Growth*. "I do not propose to do more," averred Innis, "than *to add a footnote* to [Kroeber's] comments and in this to discuss the possible significance of communication to the rise and decline of cultural traits" (p. 33). It may also be noted that in this preamble Innis was quoting the title of a programmatic essay by Chicago sociologist Charles Horton Cooley, titled "The Significance of Communication." In turn, Carey titled his own collection of essays *Communication as Culture* (1992), possibly echoing Innis's agenda of uncovering "the significance of communication to the rise and decline of cultural traits." Even Carey's "gentle extension" apologia was preempted by Innis. In *Empire and Communication* (1972) Innis modestly described his work as "an extension of the work of Graham Wallas and of E. J. Urwick" (p. 9). This dynastic succession of footnotes, extensions, and possibly titles, illustrates the ritualistic dimension of canon as an authoritative chain to which one links oneself, but at the same time the merely referential, unbinding nature of that link. The reverence of canon is conditioned on its potential renewal and relevance, for it is a useful revelation only if it can beget revelations.

As noted, the reader of "The Bias" is engaged by the problem of coherence on two levels: first he is alerted to the problem by confronting the contradictions and inconsistencies that emerge from a close reading of the text. Seeking a dialectic that would clarify these specifics, he is challenged by the more general problem of the tremendous scope, but fragmentary nature, of the historical evidence and of the chaotic nature of the observations and arguments in "The Bias," their tendency to go "backwards and forwards and sideways all at the same time." He must ask whether a real, coherent theory or point of view may be found, whether there really is a demiurge somewhere. Then the reader discovers that he himself must be that demiurge.

For Innis leads his followers to the edge of chaos; once there, they discover that it may be a very productive place. The edge of chaos, but not quite chaos itself, is where "the fullest range of productive inter-actions and exchanges" are effected, and where people may operate "at their most robust and efficient level." It is where Koestler's "sudden interlocking of two previously unrelated skills or matrices of thought" occurs. And it is there that the reader may discover the prescribed anti-dote to chaos – coherence as an overall pattern in the conflicting, contra-dictory, or even unrelated facts and events that border on chaos (Lissack and Roos, 1999).

And indeed, many who undertook the challenge of an active reading of "The Bias" found that it yielded a unique experience. They likened the reading of Innis to exposure to modern works of visual art: the more generous likened it to observing a mosaic or a work of pointillism; the more critical invoked the Rorschach ink blot. In either case, the work represents a challenge or stimulus, and the viewer must create his own gestalt in response to it. In this sense Innis's work is inconclusive, but also referential. By allowing, even making, readers develop ideas rel-evant to their own time and place in response to his own, his texts are uniquely accommodating.

The dimensions of coherence gleaned by those who expose themselves to "The Bias" and journey with Innis to the chaotic universe of com-munication history are what we may expect to find in the standardized versions of communication theory as they incorporate Innis's ideas about communication in the broader tapestry of thinking about communica-tion. The tentative – possibly even illusive – coherence gleaned by his readers, combined with their appreciation of the exciting challenge he posed, must have contributed to the appreciation, and even reverence, of Innis.

Reverence: the canonized Innis

The inclusion of a chapter on "The Bias" in the present volume is one indication that Innis's work may be considered part of whatever canon communication studies may have. Summaries of his ideas appear in most standard textbooks on communication – a criterion that Innis himself had proposed as a measure of the crystallization and embeddedness of particular ideas and ideologies.[17] His canonicity is further confirmed by the rapid accumulation of books and articles, theses and dissertations, devoted to his work, by citation indexes and course syllabi, by search-engine hits, and most probably by the balance sheets of the University of Toronto Press, which has managed to achieve a near-monopoly of re-print editions of Innis's books. His work may thus safely be considered a continuing source of reference.

The Innis of our contemporary textbooks and college courses, of footnotes to scholarly works and entries in encyclopedias, emerges as refreshingly coherent. The canonized version of Innis, rather than being contradictory and open-ended, yields a comprehensive theory of communication. Even more striking, perhaps, is the uniformity of these summaries and references, and how handily his approach is com-partmentalized in the broader landscape of communication theory. The process through which Innis was canonized – the streamlining of his ideas into a coherent whole and its positioning alongside other formative works in the process of mapping the field – is worthy of an independent study. Such a study would most probably suggest that the complexity of Innis's work made for its radical reduction and ultimate uniformity. Many, it would appear, settled for a received, and necessarily watered-down, synthesis of Innis, rather than attempting to grapple with the complexities of the genuine article (Westfall, 1981, p. 38; Stamps, 1995, p. xiv). More generously, and deploying one of the most characteristic dialectics emerging from "The Bias," it may well be that precisely the work's overwhelming openness compelled the creation of a clear, well-defined intellectual icon of it, if it was to be inducted into a communica-tion canon.

Be that as it may, the canonized icon of Innis includes a number of consensual components. The first concerns Innis's methodological approach, and points out the fundamental historicity of his scholarship and theory. His ideas about communication emerge from, and are sus-tained by, the study of communication in history and the history of communication. It is further held that in his historical approach, tech-nology, to an important extent, drives history. And indeed, a second element of the canonized Innis is his focus on the medium – a technolo-gical artifact – in analyzing processes of communication and their social significance.[18] The particular technological attributes of a medium or a mix of media prevalent in a given society condition the practice of com-munication in that society, the institutions and socio-cultural arrange-ments associated with those practices, and through them more general social arrangements. Given this emphasis on media in determining the institutions and systems of social communication, the label of "techno-logical determinism" is commonly applied to Innis's approach.[19] Thus, in one of the most respected standard textbooks in mass communica-tion theory, the section discussing Innis is titled "Technological (Media) Determinism." The textbook, echoing Innis in "The Bias," posits that

> the most complete and influential variant of media determinism is prob-ably that of the Canadian economic historian, Harold Innis . . . especially as elaborated by Marshall McLuhan. Innis attributed the characteristic features of successive ancient civilizations to be prevailing and dominant modes of communication, each of which will have its own "bias" in terms of societal form. (McQuail, 1994, pp. 97–8)

Marshall McLuhan (1951), in introducing *The Bias of Communication* – an introduction toned as a ceremonial induction of Innis into a com-munication theory hall of fame – enunciated these two cornerstones of the ritualized Innis, historicism and technological determinism, in a single sentence: "He had discovered a means of using historical situations as a lab in which to test the character of technology in the shaping of cultures" (p. xi).

A third, and one of the most broadly applied elements of Innis's legacy, was his notion of monopoly of knowledge.[20] By transplanting the eco-nomic concept of monopoly to the field of communications – to know-ledge artifacts and skills – Innis elegantly buttressed his media determinism. When certain media or knowledge products dominate society's commun-ication environment, the peculiar dynamics of oligopoly make for ampli-fying and perpetuating the hold of those media or bodies of knowledge, block the emergence of alternatives, and ultimately enhance the effects of the monopolistic media and skills on society and on its political, social, and cultural profile.

Finally, Innis is held to have proposed an extremely effective criterion for organizing and analyzing the plethora of communication media that bowed in and out in the course of history, affecting communication systems, societies, and their culture in the process. This criterion is the time–space divide, as applied to the performance of media and their underlying technologies. In this view, some media are more effective in delivering knowledge over time – from past to present and from present to future – whereas other media are more effective in delivering know-ledge across space. The divergence of orality and literacy serves as the fundamental model, as well as the historical origin, of the time-media/space-media polarity.

The proposition that individual media, and ultimately media mixes, diverge on a time–space axis has been solidly entrenched in the canonized version of Innis. Following Innis's lead, subsequent scholars crystallized elaborate series of variables: social, political, economic, religious, legal, administrative, managerial, and others as well, that parallel the time–space polarity. They made these variables intersect in exquisite sets of coherent and congruent overall portraits of societies and their biases. Not least among the factors converging in the conflicting time and space sets were the nature of knowledge and knowing, even states of consciousness (Christian, 1977; Stevenson, 1994, 115–16).[21] And indeed, on this central point Innis is unusually clear. In the first paragraph of "The Bias," he suggests that any medium of communication

> has an important influence on the dissemination of knowledge over space and over time. . . . According to its characteristics [it] may be better suited to the dissemination of knowledge over time than over space, particularly if the medium is heavy and durable and not suited to transportation, or to the dissemination of knowledge over space than over time, particularly if the medium is light and easily transported. (Innis, 1951, p. 33)

There is a considerable consensus on the validity and usefulness of this basic observation. In fact, there appears to be only one conspicuous dissenting voice that challenges the relation of the media durability–ephemerality continuum to the time–space divide. In discussing the *metabolé* of the Old Kingdom in Egypt into the Middle Kingdom, this scholar states:

> A decline of centralized bureaucratic power and a shift from an emphasis on control over space reflected in the pyramid to a decentralized bureaucratic power with an emphasis on continuity and religion [namely time] to be seen in the spread of writing and the use of papyrus . . . weakened control over space.

This argument appears to stand on its head Innis's proposition that durable media such as the pyramids are associated with a time bias, and light, short-lived media such as papyri, with a space bias. The argument was made by none other than Innis himself, in "The Problem of Space" (1951, p. 95).

One could take this glaring contradiction to be a blooper by an enthusiastic, overworked, aging man trying breathlessly to communicate a great discovery. Conversely, it may be seen as the gambit of a whimsical pedagogue planting a conspicuous misstatement to tantalize and vitalize his audience. But a distinct possibility is that Innis actually meant what he wrote, and that his meaning can be arrived at by struggling over it exegetically. In doing so, it may be well to first consider a preliminary, and much more fundamental, challenge to the time- and space-media theorem. The source of the problem is the nature of orality itself. As noted, a central insight that Innis had developed, conspicuously presented in "The Bias," traceable throughout *Empire and Communication* (1972), and elaborated on in "Minerva's Owl" (1951, pp. 3–32) and "A Plea for Time" (1951, pp. 61–91), concerned the social implications of orality as opposed to script. Orality, according to Innis, is not space-binding, but time-binding. Now, the space side of the equation appears to work well enough. After all, there are severe physical limitations on the reach of the human voice in space, and the corruption of oral knowledge as it is relayed from place to place and from person to person makes the oral medium ineffective in binding space. However, the fact that orality is not effective in binding space does not necessarily yield a fit between the oral medium and time on the durability of messages. In fact, the opposite would seem to be true: the oral medium is anything but heavy and durable as are pyramids, stele, or clay tablets. Innis, however, clearly considered orality to be the model, the cornerstone, of time-biased communications.

The answer to this conundrum appears to be built into human adjustment to the peculiar limitations of the medium. Given the fleeting, ephemeral, evanescent nature of oral knowledge, it can be preserved only through internalizing and repeating the message time and again – to oneself but, more effectively, to others. Thus, if orally transmitted knowledge is to exist at all, it is received from a predecessor, internalized, and made part of living consciousness. It is in this sense that orality is time-binding: it creates a concern with preserving useful knowledge from the past, demands continuity, and requires keeping that knowledge, and through it the past, alive. For knowledge of and from the past to exist in an environment lacking durable media, it must exist through continuity, and, as living knowledge, it binds the present to the past. Thus, precisely the limitations on the durability of oral knowledge bind and bias an oral society to its past.

Armed with this dialectic module, which appears time and again in his reasoning, the conflict between the Innis of "The Bias" and the Innis of "The Problem of Space" can be resolved quite simply. In line with the structure of orality's time-binding dynamic, Innis is telling us that if a socio-political system is shaped to be effective in its control over, say, space, its problem becomes time; it is threatened by discontinuity in time. Once it becomes conscious of this deficiency and its dangers, it will invest considerable effort in developing time-binding media: it will develop a concern, or bias, toward time. By the same token, a socio-cultural system with effective time-binding media in place may become concerned about its space-binding powers and necessarily focus on them. More generally, a bias, if recognized, will generate a counter-bias as a corrective, in the cause of equilibrium.

Innis presented this dynamic of inverted determinism most straightforwardly in "The Bias," a page after having pointed out the basic polarity of media of time and media of space. In describing the rise of the early monarchy in Egypt, he suggests that the "success of the monarchy in acquiring control over Egypt in terms of space necessitated a concern with the problem of continuity or time." This concern translated into mummification and the construction of the pyramids, "as a device for emphasizing control over time" (p. 34). Similarly, after recovering from the Hyksos occupation in the middle of the second millennium and building an empire over a vast expanse, it was precisely the "solution to the problem of space" that "compelled the king to attempt a solution of problems of continuity" (p. 35).

Even the contradiction that McLuhan pointed out so prominently in his introduction to *The Bias* (alluded to above) presents no real problem if we assume that Innis was using his inverted determinism interpretive staple. McLuhan was troubled by Innis's statement, in "Industrialism and Cultural Values" (1951, pp. 132–41), that the Greeks' adoption of an alphabet and its improvement by adding vowels was a victory for the ear over the eye – indeed a strange thing to say when it is the eyes that see and read vowels. However, studying the text that expounds the same idea in "The Bias," we find that Innis presented the case of the oral and the written in Greek society after adjustment to the dynamics of inverted determinism. He was suggesting that the adoption of an improved alphabet enabled the Greeks to refocus on the oral tradition and on time. In conformity with the inverted determinism rationale, once the Greeks had an effective space-binding medium in place, they could safely set out to rebalance their media environment by conserving their original time bias, with its inevitable emphasis on sound and the ear.

While Innis applies this dialectic frequently and does not elaborate on it, its shaping and origin were far from casual. Rather, this turn of thought appears to represent a deliberate response to the classic problem of the dynamic relation of opposites. Innis, following a dominant strand in Western thought at the time, considered time and space to be opposites. Their relation was therefore particularly complex, since opposites essentially involve each other both as concepts and as real phenomena. Moreover, as many held, and as some – possibly Innis too – attributed to Hegel, opposites tend, particularly at their extremes, to pass over into each other, thus confirming the fundamental Platonic notion that change represents the transition from one opposite to another. By pointing out the polarity of time and space, Innis upholds the prospect – even the inevitability – of the change of one bias into the other.

Innis clearly believed that an equilibrium between a time bias and a space bias was possible, and had in fact been achieved in certain places and epochs in history, most notably Athens in the classical period and Byzantium in the early Middle Ages. He viewed the Western world of his times as being in a state of extreme imbalance, tending almost exclusively in the direction of space. Since a correction was inevitable, with extremes passing into each other, the more severe the imbalance, the more radical the process of change would be. A pessimist, he feared the ultimate consequences of the inevitable radical correction to Western civilization.

It is in the context of this inverted determinism dialectic that Innis's concern with monopoly of knowledge assumes its greatest significance. Media are essentially an apparatus that provides for the interface of mind and matter – a technical resource that sustains the lifeworld of ideas. By achieving a monopoly, a certain communication apparatus may become the sole provider of the physical infrastructure for communications, and thus dominate the nature of knowledge and its diffusion. Since this monopoly of matter serves the mind, however, it can perpetuate and fixate not only itself, but also the concerns of society, shaping them in its own image and solidifying the status quo. The dynamics of oligopoly operate even more directly when, beyond the technical resources that sustain it, knowledge itself is monopolized. All the more so when the party in possession of this knowledge is compact and effectively organized. Either way, the most dangerous aspect of monopoly of knowledge is in barring mental and ideological change. By virtue of their uncontested power, monopolies of knowledge and consciousness may blind individuals and societies even to the mere fact of imbalance between time and space media, let alone to its dangers and to the feasibility of alternatives. The consequent fixation on either trajectory – of time or of space – precludes correction and readjustment. It makes the inverted deterministic thrust towards balance impossible.[22]

Yet, if this understanding of Innis's theory of dynamic equilibrium of time and space concerns is valid, it undermines one of the most prevalent assumptions about his approach: namely, that he is a technological determinist. A technological deterministic approach is usually construed to include three elements. First, that technology, as the bastard offspring of pure science – itself the source of novel ideas presumably developed independently of social expectations – is an autonomous force. Second, that, given social equilibrium, technology is the primary source of change in the human condition. And third, that, given social equilibrium, changes launched by new technology are prone to have major effects that reverberate throughout society and transform it.[23]

Innis himself, in the first paragraph of both the first and the second pages of "The Bias," appears to claim the questionable distinction of being a technological determinist. "A medium of communication," he writes, "has an important influence on the dissemination of knowledge . . . and it becomes necessary to study its characteristics in order to appraise its influence in its cultural setting" (p. 33). Such an examination of the characteristics of a technological medium may indeed yield dramatic results:

> The use of a medium of communication over a long period will to some extent determine the character of knowledge to be communicated and suggest that its pervasive influence will eventually create a civilization in which life and flexibility will become exceedingly difficult to maintain and that the advantages of a new medium will become such as to lead to the emergence of a new civilization. (p. 34)

The character of this new civilization may in turn be determined by the nature of its media, and so turns the wheel.

Inverted determinism, however, could prevent such a sorry state of affairs, and also redeem Innis from the onus of being a technological determinist. If Innis maintains that societies are capable of balancing their time–space act through encouraging and appropriating communication technologies that would counter the monopolizing tendencies of entrenched media, and ultimately their freezing into an unadaptive, inflexible state, he is not much of a technological determinist. Rather, he emerges as a through-and-through social constructivist, holding that technological change is engineered and affected by society's strategies and choices.[24] It is society that decides how much literacy it wants to mix into its orality, whether it wants to journey in space or in time, whether it prefers Xerox machines or Pravdas, satellite feeds of Seinfeld or sermons preached in a local mosque, synagogue, or church. Media determinism, as disinfected by the prospect of inverted determinism, posits that the social dog wags its technological tail, rather than being wagged by it.

Nor is communication technology, however introduced into society, the primary source of change for Innis. In the parade of historical datum after historical datum marched over the pages of "The Bias," the origins of social change vary considerably. It may be the pattern of the Nile's flooding, foreign invasion, military victory or defeat, the invention of new gods and new ideas, or numerous other novelties that both reflect and affect change in societies. Technology as the source of social change is the exception, not the rule. In only one feature of Innis's portrayal of the dynamics of change can one hear an echo of technological determinism. As noted, a technological deterministic approach expects the introduction of new technologies to a homeostatic society to yield effects of the greatest magnitude. For even if it is society that drives technology, even if technology is deployed only to react to change enacted by other factors, communication technologies, once selected and deployed by society, may have powerful and significant consequences. In this respect, at least, Innis would fit the bill of a communication technology determinist.

But there is a small footnote to be added at this point, possibly a gentle extension or shift in emphasis. When Innis parades human history, he indeed pays considerable attention to communication technologies, and points out the explosive changes they were capable of bringing about, even if as agents, rather than sources of change. However, he places the accent in the communication technology determinant emphatically on the communication, not the technology, side of the compound. In other words, Innis was a *communication* determinist. He considered processes of communication and the institutions associated with them to have tremendous effects on the nature of societies and on the course of their history.

Revolution: "The Bias" and communication determinism

If canonicity implies a revolutionary revelation, Innis's discovery was communication determinism. He uncovered "the significance of communication" – the fact that civilizations are "profoundly influenced by communication and that marked changes in communication have had important implications" (1951, p. 3). The economic historians found that communication, rather than money, makes the world go around. And since Innis believed that communication history was the key to world history, he went on to read the history of the world as a history of communication, just as a younger Innis wrote national history as a history of political economy. Thus, in a sense, his great revelation in communication theory was that there could be such a thing, and his revolution as a communication theorist was being one.[25] As noted, upon embarking on his exploration of communications, Innis assembled an imposing bibliography of potentially relevant works. A generous selection from that bibliography found its way, in the form of quotations and references, into "The Bias" and the other essays comprising *The Bias of*

Communication. Not one of the works cited therein includes the word "communication" or "media" in its title or subtitle. It was in isolating communication as an aspect of history and culture, and further positing its development as a key to unlocking the vicissitudes of mind, matter, and their interface, that Innis's work was revolutionary.

Given the bias of social and academic life in the late twentieth and early twenty-first century, Innis's revelation of the "significance of communication" may appear commonplace. As communication developed into a legitimate field of academic inquiry, featuring university departments and professional associations, scholarly periodicals and textbooks, the proposition of thinking about communication as a distinct field of social experience, one which could, moreover, serve as a key to understanding other fields, realized and to an extent depleted itself. Further, the latter part of the last century was historically unique in its sharp focusing of change in everyday life on a single aspect of experience: communication. Its characteristic rhetoric celebrated a "communication revolution" that was supposed to usher in an "Information Age." Thus, the professional bias of contemporary communication scholars, and the bias of the period they live in, seems to make Innis's discovery a trivial truism rather than a breakthrough.

Innis presented his discovery at the beginning of "The Bias." As noted, he usually commenced his articles by succinctly exposing their purpose as part of an overall agenda, and "The Bias," originally presented as a paper at the University of Michigan in 1949, was no exception. In its opening paragraph Innis put his cause in the form of a proposition:

> The appearance of a wide range of cultural phenomena at different periods in the history of Western civilization has been described by Professor A. L. Kroeber in *Configuration of Cultural Growth*. He makes comments at various points to explain the relative strength or weakness of cultural elements, but refrains from extended discussion. I do not propose to do more than add a footnote to these comments and in this to discuss the possible significance of communication to the rise and decline of cultural traits.

It is indeed in relation to Kroeber's argument that the revolutionary nature of Innis's suggestion emerges. Kroeber, like other prominent scholars of the World Wars era, focused on civilizations as his unit of analysis (Sanderson, 1995). Kroeber's project was first to establish, then to account for, the pattern of simultaneous, rapid advances in the major branches of cultural endeavor in the rise of civilizations. He categorized the key branches of cultural development as philosophy, science, literature, fine arts, and the performing arts. Innis, in humbly "adding a footnote"

to Kroeber's project, was proposing much more than adding communication as a sixth item on the list; he was proposing communication as a
meta-category that would not only co-change as part of the pattern of
congruent acceleration of cultural development but, to an important
extent, condition the entire process. In this context, "footnote" should
be construed expansively. It was not meant in the diminutive sense of
tagging on a secondary idea or fact. Rather, it meant taking a further
step, piggy-backing on the validity of Kroeber's findings and subsuming
them.[26]

In aligning himself with Kroeber, Innis was doing more than eco-
nomizing on scholarly energy by taking a ride on a giant's shoulders. He
was also indicating a dramatic shift in his outlook and method, even in
his scholarly identity. Kroeber, in his *Configurations,* was venturing into
history from anthropology, expecting that history might validate his grand
hypothesis about the structures of cultural development. Innis found
himself at a similar methodological juncture as Kroeber, but he reached
it by taking the opposite tack – from history to general theory. In taking
this path, Innis was once again acting on his notion of a Hegelian idea.
Hegel differentiated several levels of historical inquiry, spanning the
"original" history of the primary source, through "reflective" history,
which represents attempts by later historians to record and make sense
of the past (inevitably in terms of their own experiences), and finally,
"philosophical history," which is an interpretation of history yielding a
general understanding of human development. Philosophical history,
according to Hegel, uses the findings of reflective history in its quest for
a general understanding of the world. Most importantly, he saw histories of specific fields such as art or religion, which take a "universal point
of view," as a bridge between reflective and philosophical history. Innis,
in his ecumenical study of communication, was consciously crossing over
from the reflective to the philosophical, from history to theory.

Innis's redefinition of himself as a philosopher of history has important implications for understanding his legacy, not least the textual problems of "The Bias." One such problem, pointed out above, is the radical
and otherwise inexplicable shift in his sources, from the use of primary
materials when studying Canadian economic history to the practically
exclusive use of secondary sources in his studies of communication.
Assuming that on this, as on other issues, Innis was following Hegel,
his choice of sources is fully understandable. Since Hegel taught that the
universal history of an isolated field is philosophical history, and since he
prescribed reflective histories as the material for writing philosophical
history, Innis's change of methodology on entering on the ecumenical
study of communication is accounted for. The mode of presentation

characteristic of his communication studies, described above as a historic play-by-play interlaced with analytic comments, reflects a self-conscious adaptation of form and structure to the rationale and method of philosophical history. Facts of history are paraded chronologically, one by one, and Innis, the philosopher in the grandstand, contributes comments on them as they relate to his philosophical focus: the dynamics of communication and culture.

Similarly, Innis's self-perception as a philosopher of history puts a new face on the problem of internal contradictions in his work: the source of contradictions as well as their toleration. Many explicit contradictions in "The Bias," and even the systematic ones in *Empire and Communication*, reflected disagreements between Innis's sources. Since it was no longer his task to establish an accurate historical record and ascertain the facts, these conflicts could only be documented and acknowledged, not resolved. Moreover, both sides of the contradiction were pertinent to the main thrust of "The Bias," since all possibilities ultimately demonstrated the "significance of communication." On points of interpretation, too, the new Innis could afford great leeway: his varying, even conflicting interpretations of the effects and consequences of communication technologies were essentially equivalent, since his purpose was to demonstrate that they did indeed have effects, and significant ones.

Revolution: the origins of "The Bias"

The origins of Innis's discovery and the process through which he came to realize the "significance of communication" to human development are surprisingly vague. One way of approaching the problem is through a close scrutiny of the internal evolution of Innis's works, tracing the theme of communication within them. This approach assumes that Innis developed his revolutionary perspective *sui generis*, through a complex process of intellectual growth. An alternative approach is to scan the intellectual horizon of his times, seeking external influences. A particular focus on the University of Chicago is especially important in such a canvass, given the ferment in social thinking there during Innis's time, and the interest of its luminaries in problems of communication. Innis's affiliation with the University of Chicago, first as student and then as a prospective teacher, make a Chicago connection particularly plausible.

In pursuing the first approach, the question of continuity from the early Innis of Canadian staples to the later Innis of world communications becomes important.[27] The radical shift in the nature of his research upon moving from economic history to communication history – his move from history proper to philosophy of history – would appear to support the notion of discontinuity. Yet the fundamental hypothesis of Innis's philosophy of history – "the significance of communication" – appears to span both phases of his scholarly career, representing a stable core. The inverted determinism dialectic may present itself as a key to bridging these two phases of his scholarship.

Communication was on Innis's mind from the earliest stages of his scholarly career. His first major work, a reflective history of the Canadian Pacific Railroad (CPR), was essentially a study of a medium of communication at a particular time and place. A two-volume critical source-book of documents in Canadian economic history, which Innis prepared together with A. R. M. Lower, is particularly revealing of this early focus on communications. The first volume, which was mainly Lower's production, treats communication issues sparingly and sporadically. The second volume, which was mainly Innis's handiwork, was divided into four sections, each covering a region of Canada. In each of these sections the very first subsection, and one of the most substantial, was devoted to "Transportation and Communication" (Innis and Lower, 1929, 1933). Clearly, Innis recognized the significance of communication, in this case as a key to economic history, from early on.

The place of communication in Innis's staple studies is less obvious, but at least as important. In one of its broader meanings, the staple theory represented a critical response to Frederick Jackson Turner's frontier thesis.[28] According to Turner, the frontier, a fact of space, had a major transformative influence on the dimension of time, making for dramatic discontinuities in the received, traditional heritage of individual, community, and society. Innis, however, was more impressed by how European and, later, eastern American institutions shaped a response to the challenge of the frontier. In his inverted deterministic perspective, the distance and isolation of the frontier, precisely by representing potential wedges of discontinuity and separation, generated a reactive response toward connection and continuity.[29] By establishing and perfecting effective means of transportation and communication, a veteran mercantilist system could expand westward, from Europe over the Atlantic, and on across the new continent all the way to the Pacific. The social desire to overcome space was realized through the establishment of a grand, space-binding economic and social system founded on powerful media of transportation and communication. The potentially deterministic influence of the frontier generated a response which was the staple economy.

Innis's direct and unequivocal response to Turner's revolutionary 1893 essay, "The Significance of the Frontier in American History," was thus "the significance of communication" in North American history. Ultimately this outlook broadened in space and time to become an ecumenical panorama of institutions as creatures of communication, yielding a unique and original theory of the role of communication in the development of civilizations, showcased in "The Bias of Communication." This understanding of historical development as anchored in changing processes of communication was very much Innis's own, the product of a career-long investigation into the flow of goods and ideas.

This does not, however, preclude external influences. A most probable source of such influences was the "Chicago school." Prior to Innis's discovery of communication determinism, John Dewey and Robert Park, Herbert Mead and Charles Horton Cooley had developed a body of theory which took processes of communication to be a significant source and instrument of social organization. As noted, "The Significance of Communication," a short programmatic essay by Cooley, pre-dated and pre-phrased Innis's proposition in "The Bias" that communication may serve as a key to understanding social and cultural development.[30]

Cooley had an expansive grasp of communication. He took it to include all expressions of, and exposure to, human meaning, and thus saw it as the cause and effect of human consciousness. Like Innis, he found media significant, and believed that meaning – the cause and effect of consciousness – was channeled by the media. The son of an eminent railroad scholar, Cooley, like Innis, had studied the railroad as a key to understanding North American economic development.[31] Furthermore, Cooley had identified four fundamental factors determining the nature of communication processes, which together foregrounded the dimensions of time and space. These were, alongside expressiveness, permanence ("the overcoming of time"), swiftness ("the overcoming of space"), and diffusion (a space-oriented measure of the size of the audience). Here, then, were time and space as fundamental variables of the communication matrix.

At this juncture, with both Cooley and Innis understanding communications as bridges in time and space, their paths parted. Cooley was locked onto the idea of progress as the sweeping, inevitable course of human history; he considered it an accelerated conquest of human happiness evolving in time and spreading in space. This was also the course of the evolution of communication: no contradiction hindered the parallel, onward march of "swiftness," "diffusion," and "permanence"; indeed, Cooley found no fault with the globalizing, unifying thrust of communication over space. Even if he had understood that there was a trade-off between space and time, it probably would not have dampened his enthusiasm for the advent of powerful, rapid new media of space.

Progress, in its future-orientedness, had nothing to gain from time – from memory, continuity, and history.

Innis disagreed sharply. He found that the expanding reach and accelerating swiftness of media came at the expense of "permanence," and ultimately of stability. Given the trade-off between time and space media, unbalanced progress was inevitably regressive. Most generally, Innis didn't buy into the Whig interpretation of human history and the utopian world anticipated by the idealist progressives. His historicism compelled him to consider the decline and fall of civilizations as well as their rise, and his pessimism, to consider potential dangers in the evolution of media. His credo was balance rather than progress, and his agenda, its deliberate restoration. His was an orientation toward historical consciousness, tradition, and memory, rather than a future-orientedness. Innis's analysis of communication and social and political organization thus evolved along the same lines as, but reached conclusions that were diametrically opposed to, those of Chicago's enthusiastic progressives. To the extent that he was a disciple of Chicago's communication-minded scholars, Innis was an apostate, a new light spreading a new and revolutionary message. He preached the gospel of history and time, of looking back as a way of marching forward.

Renewal: "The Bias," the present, futures

The relevance of canon has two dimensions: the text's continuing power to engage, and its continuing power to explain. Innis's work has proved successful mostly on the first account, less so on the second. As we have seen, "The Bias" and his other communication texts have been found stimulating and inspiring: their inconclusiveness and flexibility left room for – even invited – creative misreadings, extensions, and elaboration. They have been particularly relevant to thinking on media technology, on the problem of the monopoly of knowledge (as ultimately subsumed by critical theory), and to the linking of communication phenomena to a wider field of social, political, and cultural variables. By contrast, Innis's work has failed, on the whole, to serve as a foundation for understanding later-day, real-world developments, as media and their institutional environments changed and the broader social, political, and cultural landscape changed with them.

But even where Innis's work has proved relevant in inspiring subsequent thinking about communication and culture, an important aspect of his legacy has been neglected. In textbook extensions – gentle or otherwise, in scholarly footnotes – small or extensive, in courses and their syllabi, the implications of Innis's historical approach have not been followed up meaningfully. Innis's historicity had two complementary planks. One was basing a philosophy or theory of communication on historical evidence, using history as the great laboratory to generate and test ideas about communication. The other was understanding communication as a key to interpreting history. Neither of these prospects generated much methodological interest or practical emulation.

As it appears, Innis made these propositions both much too late and much too early. They came too late for both communication studies and historical studies: by the time the full power of his dual proposition could be appreciated, communication was rapidly developing as an academic discipline well within the sphere of the behavioral social sciences, keeping a safe distance from historical and humanistic studies. Within historical studies the age of the grand synthesis, of historical works of ecumenical scope, had passed. Clio moved into an era of sharp reflectivity, of in-depth, detailed scrutiny of specialized phenomena on a narrowing temporal, spatial, and topical scale. More generally, as both of these disciplinary dynamics unfolded, solid walls separating the behavioral social sciences from the humanities were rapidly building up, decisively severing history and communication. The interdisciplinary buzz of the 1970s and 1980s accented disciplinary boundaries. It was essentially a call for a flag of truce that would allow safe conduct and exchanges between the separate domains, thereby underscoring their distinctiveness rather than an overall unity.

Innis's attempt at an integrative history and communication perspective was also premature, coming too early in the development of either of the two disciplines. History was not yet prepared to provide evidence that would sustain a philosophical history of communication, and Innis did not have enough, or good enough, historical data to substantiate his theoretical thrust. Paradoxically, the enormity of the heap of reflective histories he assembled as historical fodder for theorizing about communication illustrated the paucity of knowledge on communication in history, rather than its abundance. Previous generations of historians had not been aware of "the significance of communication," and had not isolated communication as a meaningful aspect – let alone a focus – of their inquiries. With little by way of authoritative works to go on, Innis had to quarry an abundance of historical works to find pertinent facts and insights about communication. Scavenging secondary histories for passing references to media, and extracting them from a wild variety of contexts representing a great variety of approaches, led to data that were inconsistent; often, his facts conflicted with each other and, inevitably, so did their interpretations. The frequent contradictions, non-sequiturs, and elements of incoherence so prominent in and between Innis's texts were to an important extent a reflection of the deficiencies of his historical data.

Given the shaky outcome of Innis's ambition to establish theory on the basis of history, other scholars and subsequent theorists of communication could reasonably conclude that history did not provide a firm basis on which to establish theory. Nor were Innis's theories a sufficient basis for orienting historical research. Here, too, Innis was too early. His philosophy was not coherent enough to launch specific hypotheses for historical investigation; it was too crude to frame an overall agenda that would guide historical research in the direction of communication.

This does not mean, however, that Innis's historicism was necessarily an abortive exercise or that his approach is doomed to oblivion. On the contrary, historicity may ultimately represent one of Innis's most useful and inspiring messages. As historians have become more aware of communication as a significant factor in their lives, communication has emerged as a topical focus of an ever-increasing number of responsible, specialized studies based on primary sources. This research, over the past decade, has yielded a body of works which may effectively be applied to writing ecumenical histories of communication, and which may serve as sound bases for generating and testing communication theory.

Communication theory, in turn, is no longer as crude and as speculative as when Innis and his contemporaries were taking their first steps in establishing it. It can conceivably serve to orient historical research, and ultimately to provide for a better understanding of human history. These prospects for serious studies of the history of communication and of communication in history are emerging just as academia is entering on a post-interdisciplinary thrust, razing walls separating disciplines, rather than building bridges for crossing them as in its interdisciplinary phase. Innis's pioneering effort in this vein may yet serve as an inspiration and a model for such a project, and represent a formative, or even a founding, text of a history and communication canon.

As noted, Innis has proved only marginally relevant to the understanding of our contemporary communication environment, and in this sense the canonicity of his work is compromised. Few, if any, observers resort to his ideas or make reference to his texts in attempting to interpret the rapid and radical changes in the communication environment over the past half-century. Surprisingly, perhaps, the neglect of the historical dimension of Innis's work – its orientation to the past – may help account for its limited usefulness in groping with the present and future. History, after all, is the study of change, and Innis, a historian, carefully and methodically merged dynamic mechanisms with the structural and systemic thrust of his theory. The play of determinism and inverted determinism was the central dynamic element of his approach, and, as we have seen, it tended to be downplayed, or even eliminated, in the process of streamlining the canonic icon of Innis in communication theory.

Part of the responsibility for the unfortunate freezing of Innis's ideas into a static mold must be shouldered by Innis himself. Ever curious, and ever aware of biases, he perhaps underestimated his own bias as a man of affairs in presenting his scholarly theory. He surely was not sufficiently aware of the effects that his blending of scholarship and ephemeral commentary would have on the biases of his readers. Innis, the scholar, taught us that media deliver a message that society and individuals could and would answer. At best they would react to an overemphasis, even a monopoly, of time by deliberately shifting their emphasis to space, and would highlight time if space threatened to monopolize society's horizon. Optionally, peripheral players not dominated by the monopolistic tendencies at society's center would reintroduce the suppressed, opposite tendency. At worst, severely imbalanced entities would become dysfunctional, and only a drastic correction, usually by unfriendly outside forces, would restore a balance.

A scholar deeply involved in the here and now, and a pessimist, Innis observed with foreboding that what he labeled a space bias seemed to be threatening his society's well-being. A monopoly was driving Western civilization generally, and Canada in particular, into a dead end of infinite space. Innis had emphatically declined his Chicago predecessors' Whig interpretation of communication development, their belief that technical and institutional advances in communication inevitably made for improvements in social conditions. Granted, more effective communications would have great effects, but they could just as easily be for the worse as for the better. Innis the public man feared the worst, and sounded an alarm.

Not that Innis was sounding a false alarm. At the time he was thinking through the biases of time and space, Western society was indeed marching to the frontiers of space – space in the expansive, composite sense that Innis had construed. In mid-century the Cold War was the stage on which two enormous empires played out their antagonistic game, supported by an ever-expanding cast of players merging into two globe-wide blocs. Experimental science was celebrating unparalleled triumphs, grounding the military might of the superpowers and the economic power of business enterprises ballooning into global scope. As physical space was capturing imaginations that would ultimately launch man to the moon, an entertainment and culture industry was diverting minds the world over from complexity and dialectic, from concern with religion,

tradition, and history, to a celebration of present-mindedness and consumerism. Giant corporate conglomerates footed the bill for the amusement extravaganza, realizing windfall profits in the process. Within a
few decades it was only one empire – as Innis would have predicted, the
American one – stretching its influence over the entire globe, setting a
new political and economic order, imprinting the world with a common
price and a common value system to the beat of a globalizing amusement industry. Taken together, these processes were bringing about what
one Hegelian historian called "The End of History," or, as Innis would
have put it, an end of time.

Yet Innis the theorist, if not Innis the pessimistic public man, would
expect a reaction to set in, a resurgence of the time set. The dynamic
elements of his theory allowed for the liberating prospects of emergence,
correction, and rebalancing. His theory held that individuals and societies had the dignity of liberty and power to determine their course, shape
their environment, and – by rearranging their media ecology – drive
history. As we know with the benefit of hindsight, that is precisely
what happened. Paralleling the globalization trend, there has emerged a
counter-movement, in numerous places and taking a variety of cultural
expressions. Past-oriented loyalties have flowered into a new emphasis
on ethnicity and a demand for multiculturalism and multilingualism.
There emerged a revival of interest in, and commitment to, religion and
mysticism, all underscoring a revived concern with time. A new, inward-
looking subjectivity has come to hold the modernist notion of objective
science irrelevant. In line with the emergence of these time-biased concerns, fundamentalism and tribalism have begun fragmenting political
and administrative units into their barest and most basic elements, in a
quest oriented toward tradition, history, time.

Innis's concerns about the state of world and Canadian politics,
economics, and ideologies were inseparable from his analysis of the
development of communication technologies. Indeed, his pessimism
was understandable, given the shape of the media environment of his
times. Throughout his lifetime, media developed in a single direction –
spaceward. Following the script–print model, the new media of his
times made it possible to engage ever more people, less intimately, and
with greater authority. The telephone had been the last technological
improvement applied to oral, two-way communications, and it had
arrived three generations before "The Bias" was written. But after the
telephone, the progress of media was the progress of scale, scope, and synchronicity, with fewer doing the talking, ever more people listening, and
no one questioning, answering, or talking back. First the mass-circulating
national magazines and the grand newspaper chains emerged. Then

wireless, originally a two-way medium, was converted to broadcast radio; and by the time Innis was writing his communications essays, television was on its way to becoming a major fact of Western life. With the arrival of television, the mix of available media reached an unprecedented degree of imbalance on the time–space axis, tending decisively to the space pole. Single, uncontested messages were reaching unprecedented numbers of people, over an ever-expanding space, in real time. To invert McLuhan, the lecture superseded dialogue.

As Innis's theory of inverted determinism, of correction and rebalance, predicted, it was the turn of the time trajectory to take off, inverting the dominant trend. And indeed, before long, the history of communications changed its course, in a reaction that was inevitable by the logic of the theory. On the heels of the steep upsurge in the space trajectory of media development, an opposite trajectory of media of time was emerging. Founded on the same powerful technologies that served the twentieth century's media of space, alternative media that structurally paralleled orality and time were coming to the rescue. The audio cassette and VCR, voice mail and electronic mail, the answering machine and the personal computer, were working against breathless synchronicity. Technical improvements enabling a dramatic increase in bandwidth and channels for voice, video, and data transmission paved the way for narrowcasting, fragmenting mass – even global – audiences into compact communities (Teheranian, 1979; Mowlana, 1986; Blondheim and Caplan, 1993). Satellite-mediated video conferences, computer-mediated chats and discussion groups, and ultimately interactive TV emerged to counter the one-way plan of broadcast media. In short, just as one thrust of media development was enabling a uniform, synchronous, global information environment, an opposite thrust was enhancing time-oriented communication plans (Blondheim, 1995). Innis would have been particularly amused by how what is possibly the most centralizing, space-minded bureaucracy of modern society – the national security establishment – would invert the centralized, hierarchic structure of its communication network through space and seek a decentralized, non-hierarchic, periphery-focused communications medium that would mature into the Internet: an inverted deterministic move if ever there was one.

But the *fin-de-siècle* experience presents a further challenge to thinking about communication, society, and culture. It focuses on the relationship between the two sets of developments just described – change in the social and political organization cluster, and change in the media proliferation cluster. For there appears to be a striking parallel between the duality of globalization and fragmentation in social organization, on the one hand, and the duality of global media developing in tandem with "little media" of small-scale, non-synchronous, multidirectional inter-action, on the other. In juxtaposing these recent changes in the forms of social, political, and cultural organization, on the one hand, with the changing composition of our contemporary media map, on the other, the problem of causality, of the nature and direction of mutual influences, forcefully presents itself. In addressing this problem, Innis's primary revelation in "The Bias of Communication" would be eminently relevant. His finding for "the significance of communication" and his communication deterministic approach present themselves as major reference points for creative thinking about causality in the co-changing of media and society in our times.

Notes

1 For short but significant references to Innis's incorporation of Hegelian models and concerns see Theall, 1981, pp. 225–34; and Stamps, 1995, p. 68.
2 This aspect of monopoly of knowledge is best developed in Innis, 1949.
3 The literature on the formation and nature of the biblical canon is vast. Useful introductions include Herbert Edward Ryle, *The Canon of the Old Testament: An Essay on the Gradual Growth and Formation of the Hebrew Canon of Scripture* (London: Macmillan and Co., 1909); essays in George W. Coats and Burke O. Long, *Canon and Authority* (Philadelphia: Fortress Press, 1973); Sid Lehman, *Canonization of Hebrew Scripture: The Talmudic and Midrashic Evidence* (New Haven: Connecticut Academy of Arts and Sciences, 1991). But see, for the Jewish concept of biblical canon, a perspective diverging from the one proposed here: Jacob Neusner, *Canon and Connection: Intertextuality in Judaism* (Lanham, MD: University Press of America, 1987).
4 Gershom Scholem elegantly explains this approach in the context of Jewish thinking about sacred texts in *The Messianic Idea in Judaism* (New York: Schocken Books, 1995), pp. 284–91. See also Harold Bloom, *Kabbalah and Criticism* (New York: Seabury Press, 1975), pp. 32–5, 71–89; Amos Funkenstein, *Perceptions of Jewish History* (Berkeley: University of California Press, 1993), pp. 88–121; and recently, Y. D. Silman, *The Voice Heard at Sinai: Once or Ongoing?* (Jerusalem: Magnes Press, 1999), pp. 11–15, 89–116 (Hebrew).
5 Thus, Coats and Long suggest that "biblical authority" can be seen as "a kind of power which is created, legitimated, and actualized in a complex interaction among the believer, his sacred book, and others in his social situation" (1973, p. ix).
6 This inclination became evident early on: the Baptists were prime movers in the framing of the Bill of Rights, yet they were fully resigned to first ratifying the Constitution *sans* the Bill, and only then amending it (McDonald, 1985, p. 73; Isaac, 1982, pp. 317–22).

7 A recent student of Innis indeed considered the main thrust of his later work, that focusing on communication, as a response to the problem of reconciling the absolute and the relative in human knowledge. Innis's interest was in the clash of the claim of modernity that human knowledge is capable of establishing objective, absolute, and eternal truth, and the vision of human knowledge as inevitably subjective and relative, transient and inconclusive (Stamps, 1995, ch. 4).

8 Here canon will be considered in an expansive sense, relating not to a specific text or texts, but to a set of ideas, or an approach, a sense developed by Even-Zohar (1990).

9 Innis, "A History of Communication," located in the Innis collection, University of Toronto Archives, Thomas Fisher Library, University of Toronto; available on microfilm.

10 Based on Watson, 1981.

11 The idea file is available in print: Christian, 1980.

12 A possible exception is the final chapter of 1930a; cf. Creighton, 1957.

13 The most obvious example of this pattern of contradiction emerges from comparing the text of Innis's *Empire and Communication* (1972) to a layer of annotations he provided for the text. The notes quite frequently suggest the exact opposite of the thrust of the text.

14 The Talmud, the essential text of Judaism as we now know it, represents one such accessible model. On the orality of the Talmudic text see Menahem Blondheim, Shoshana Blum-Kulka and Gonen Hacohen, "Traditions of Disputes," forthcoming in the *Journal of Pragmatics*; and my review of Marvin J. Heller, *Printing the Talmud*, in *Papers of the Bibliographical Society of America*, 94 (3) (2000), pp. 437–40.

15 See, e.g., Heyer, 1972, p. 258: "[Innis's] work is perhaps more incomplete than that of any other major scholar. . . . However, within Innis's incomplete researches are viable directions that can be freshly followed." Heyer holds that this inconclusiveness was deliberate, and "prevented him from achieving intellectual stasis" (p. 250).

16 Carey's other influential "interpretations and extensions" of Innis include "Harold Adams Innis and Marshall McLuhan" (1968) and "Culture, Geography and Communications" (1981). A revised version of the latter was published as "Space, Time and Communications" (1992). See also Carey, with J. J. Quirk, "The Mythos of the Electronic Revolution" (1992).

17 Innis discusses textbooks in numerous works, e.g.: "The Teaching of Economic History in Canada" (1958, p. 3); Idea File, p. 268. Given his concern over the role of textbooks, his own compositions in the genre are of great interest. Two models emerge: lightly treated collections of primary sources, as in Innis and Lower (1929, 1933), and highly synthetic works such as his contribution to *Engineering and Society: With Special Reference to Canada*, Part II, with J. H. Dales (Toronto, 1946) – essentially a textbook for engineers. See also Neill, 1972, pp. 27–8.

18 There is considerable disagreement on whether speech may be considered a technology; the varying opinions depend on the definition of technology

(see, e.g., Beniger, 1986; Ong, 1982). However, even if not a technology, orality may surely be seen as a baseline for evaluating all other media which are necessarily based on technology. For this reason, orality is highly relevant to a technological analysis.

19 Arthur Kroker's discussion of Innis's emphasis on technology sidesteps the question of determinism and considers Innis's focus on technology as a heuristic device. See Kroker, 1984, pp. 87–122.

20 A short, representative discussion of monopoly of knowledge oriented to students is Marshall Soules, "Harold Adams Innis: The Bias of Communication and Monopoly of Power."

21 Carey's construction of these time and space sets is particularly illuminating; see n. 16.

22 Innis found such imbalances to be of particular concern to the national state, which is founded on identities forged over time and dependent on historical consciousness, and on a definition of a coherent and exclusive geographical space. A balanced combination of the two elements is therefore crucial for the well-being of the modern state. For a short consideration of nationalism in the context of time and space biases, see Stevenson, 1994, pp. 116–17. Such balance is particularly important in the case of Canadian nationalism, given its relative recency and enormous expanse. Discussions of Canadian nationalism in relation to communication have been strongly influenced by Deutsch (1966). See, e.g., Fortner, 1900, pp. 24–31.

23 A useful source for a variety of perspectives on the construction of technological determinism and social constructivism is Smith and Marx, 1996.

24 William Westfall (1981, p. 43) has suggested that Innis, always intrigued by theological questions, applied the tension between free will and God's plan of history to the concept of bias. This present tension between determinism and inverted determinism would surely represent a tension congruent with the theological archetype.

25 "There is good reason to regard Innis as the first writer to create a distinct field of inquiry using the social and economic consequence of developments in communication as subject matter" (Heyer, 1972, p. 250).

26 Innis employs a similar usage in the opening of *The Press: A Neglected Factor in the Economic History of the Twentieth Century* (1949): "I am aware that I am only presenting a footnote on the work of Graham Wallas." There, too, Innis's footnote was a radical extension of Wallas's work.

27 This issue is the subject of extensive debate. Creighton (1981) presents perhaps the most extreme position of discontinuity. Interestingly, attempts at interpreting the shift in Innis's work from staple economics to communications in effect highlight the chasm between the two phases of his scholarly career (e.g., Berger, 1976; and, to an extent, Pal, 1977, who emphasizes Innis's thinking about scholarship and academia as the contingency for the shift between the two). One of the most insightful discussions of the shift, but also of the thematic links between the two phases, is given by Watson (1977); Neill (1972) provides a broad basis for the continuity perspective. Parker (1981) demonstrates the relevance of the staple studies to the political

economy of communications, and in "Harold Innis: Staples, Communications, and the Economics of Capacity, Overhead Costs, Rigidity, and Bias" (1985) points out the implications of Innis's findings in his communication studies to fundamental problems of economic theory.

28   Carey has perceptively pointed out relationships between Innis's thinking on communication and Turner's frontier thesis. See, e.g., Carey, 1981, pp. 80–4, and his other discussions of Innis (n. 16 above). The literature on the frontier thesis is vast. Good introductions include Billington, 1973; Bogue, 1998; and the essays in Taylor, 1972.

29   This theme may be traced to Innis's study of the Canadian Pacific Railroad. There too he might have been indirectly engaging Turner; see, e.g., 1971, p. 287.

30   Authorities on Innis differ in their evaluation of the influence of these Chicago predecessors on his thinking and scholarship. While McLuhan thought of Innis's work as an extension of the Chicago tradition, and went as far as considering Innis "the most eminent of the Chicago group headed by Robert Park," Carey found only a limited carry-over from Chicago to Toronto. Other scholars take intermediate positions between the poles of a dominant and a marginal Chicago influence (Stamps, 1995, pp. 51–6; Neill, 1972, pp. 25–34).

31   For a short and authoritative summary of Cooley's ideas see Peters, 1999, pp. 184–8.

References

Beniger, J. R. (1986) *The Control Revolution*. Cambridge, MA: Harvard University Press.

Bercovitch, S. (1967) Typology in Puritan New England: The Williams Cotton Controversy Reassessed. *American Quarterly*, 19, 166–91.

Bercovitch, S. (1978) *The American Jeremiad*. Madison: University of Wisconsin Press.

Berger, C. (1976) *The Writing of Canadian History: Aspects of English-Canadian Historical Writing, 1900–1970*. New York: Oxford University Press.

Billington, R. A. (1973) *Frederick Jackson Turner: Historian, Scholar, Teacher*. New York: Oxford University Press.

Blondheim, M. (1995) Knowledge, Communication and Society in the Superhighway Age. *Meida Vesafranut*, 21, 19–26.

Blondheim, M. and Caplan, K. (1993) The Evil Broadcasters: Communications and Cassettes in Ultra-Orthodox Jewish Society. *Qesher*, 14, 51–68.

Bogue, A. G. (1998) *Frederick Jackson Turner: Strange Roads Going Down*. Norman: University of Oklahoma Press.

Carey, J. W. (1968) Harold Adams Innis and Marshall McLuhan. In R. Rosenthal (ed.), *McLuhan Pro & Con*, Baltimore: Penguin Books, 270–308.

Carey, J. W. (1975) Canadian Communication Theory: Extensions and Interpretations of Harold Innis. In G. J. Robinson and D. F. Theall (eds), *Studies in*

Canadian Communications, Montreal: Programme in Communication, McGill University, 27–58.

Carey, J. W. (1981) Culture, Geography, and Communications: The Work of Harold Innis in an American Context. In W. H. Melody, L. Slater, and P. Heyer (eds), *Culture, Communication, and Dependency: The Tradition of H. A. Innis*, Norwood, NJ: Ablex, 73–91.

Carey, J. W. (1992) Space, Time and Communications: A Tribute to Harold Innis. In *Communication as Culture: Essays in Media and Society*, New York: Routledge, 142–72.

Carey, J. W. and Quirk, J. J. (1992) The Mythos of the Electronic Revolution. In J. W. Carey, *Communication as Culture*, New York: Routledge, 113–41.

Christian, W. (1977) The Inquisition of Nationalism. *Journal of Canadian Studies*, 12 (5), 62–72.

Christian, W. (ed.) (1980) *The Idea File of Harold Adams Innis*. Toronto: University of Toronto Press.

Cohen, H. (1993) Review of Dependency/Space/Policy: A Dialogue with Harold A. Innis, ed. I. Angus and B. Shoesmith. Perth: Center for Research in Culture and Communication. http://www.cjc-online.ca/~cjc/BackIssues/22.1/dorland.r.html.

Cooley, C. H. (1998) The Significance of Communication. In H-J. Schubert (ed.), *On Self and Social Organization*, Chicago: University of Chicago Press, 100–9.

Cooper, T. (1977) The Unknown Innis. *Journal of Canadian Studies*, 12, 111–18.

Creighton, D. (1957) *Harold Adams Innis: Portrait of a Scholar*. Toronto: University of Toronto Press.

Creighton, D. (1981) Harold Adams Innis – An Appraisal. In W. H. Melody et al., *Culture, Communication, and Dependency: The Tradition of H. A. Innis*, Norwood, NJ: Ablex, 13–25.

Davis, T. M. (1972) The Traditions of Puritan Typology. In S. Bercovitch (ed.), *Typology and Early American Literature*, Amherst: University of Massachusetts Press, 11–45.

Deutsch, K. (1966) *Nationalism and Social Communication*. Cambridge, MA: Harvard University Press.

Even-Zohar, I. (1990) Polysystem Studies. *Poetics Today*, 11, 15–26.

Fortner, R. S. (1979) The Canadian Search for Identity, 1846–1914: Communication in an Imperial Context. *Canadian Journal of Communication*, 6, 24–31.

Heyer, P. (1972) Innis and the History of Communication: Antecedents, Parallels, and Unsuspected Biases. In Melody et al., *Culture, Communication, and Dependency*, 247–59.

Innis, H. A. (1930a) *The Fur Trade in Canada: An Introduction to Canadian Economic History*. New Haven: Yale University Press.

Innis, H. A. (1930b) *Peter Pond, Fur Trader and Adventurer*. Toronto: Irwin and Gordon.

Innis, H. A. (1949) *The Press: A Neglected Factor in the Economic History of the Twentieth Century*. London and New York: Oxford University Press.

Innis, H. A. (1951) *The Bias of Communication*. Toronto: University of Toronto Press.

Innis, H. A. (1958) The Teaching of Economic History in Canada. In *Essays in Canadian Economic History*. Toronto: University of Toronto Press.

Innis, H. A. (1971) *A History of the Canadian Pacific Railway*. Toronto: University of Toronto Press.

Innis, H. A. (1972) *Empire and Communication*. Toronto: University of Toronto Press.

Innis, H. A. and Dales, J. H. (1946) *Engineering and Society: With Special Reference to Canada*, Part II. Toronto: University of Toronto Press.

Innis, H. A. and Lower, A. R. M. (1929, 1933) *Selected Documents in Canadian Economic History*, vols 1 and 2. Toronto: University of Toronto Press.

Isaac, R. (1982) *The Transformation of Virginia, 1740–1790*. Chapel Hill: University of North Carolina Press.

Kammen, M. (1994) *A Machine that Would Go of Itself: The Constitution in American Culture*. New York: St Martin's Press.

Kroeber, A. L. (1994) *Configurations of Cultural Growth*. Berkeley: University of California Press.

Kroker, A. (1984) *Technology and the Canadian Mind: Innis, McLuhan, Grant*. New York: St Martin's Press.

Lissack, M. and Roos, J. (1999) *The Next Common Sense: Mastering Corporate Complexity through Coherence*. London: Nicholas Brealey.

McDonald, F. (1985) *Novus Ordo Seclorum: Intellectual Origins of the Constitution*. Lawrence, KS: University Press of Kansas.

McLuhan, M. (1951) Introduction. In H. A. Innis, *The Bias of Communication*, Toronto: University of Toronto Press, vii–xvi.

McQuail, D. (1994) *Mass Communication Theory: An Introduction*. London: Sage Publications.

Mowlana, H. (1986) *Global Information and World Communication: New Frontiers in International Relations*. New York: Longmans.

Neill, R. (1972) *A New Theory of Value: The Canadian Economics of H. A. Innis*. Toronto: University of Toronto Press.

Ong, W. J. (1982) *Orality and Literacy: The Technologizing of the Word*. London: Methuen.

Pal, L. A. (1977) Scholarship and the Later Innis. *Journal of Canadian Studies*, 12 (5), 33–44.

Parker, I. (1981) A Theoretical Aspect of Canadian Political Economy, in Melody et al., *Culture Communication, and Dependency*, 127–43.

Parker, I. (1985) Harold Innis: Staples, Communications, and the Economics of Capacity, Overhead Costs, Rigidity, and Bias. In *Explorations in Canadian Economic History: Essays in Honor of Irene M. Spry*, Ottawa: University of Ottawa Press, 73–93.

Peters, J. D. (1999) *Speaking into the Air: A History of the Idea of Communication*. Chicago: University of Chicago Press.

Sanderson, S. K. (ed.) (1995) *Civilizations and World Systems: Studying World-Historical Change*. London: Altimira.

Smith, M. R. and Marx, L. (1996) *Does Technology Drive History? The Dilemma of Technological Determinism*. Cambridge, MA: MIT Press.

Soules, M. Harold Adams Innis: The Bias of Communication and Monopoly of Power. http://www.mala.bc.ca/~soules/media212/Innis/Innis.htm.

Stamps, J. (1995) *Unthinking Modernity: Innis, McLuhan, and the Frankfurt School*. Montreal: McGill–Queen's University Press.

Stevenson, N. (1994) *Understanding Media Cultures: Social Theory and Mass Communication*. London: Sage.

Taylor, G. R. (ed.) (1972) *The Turner Thesis*. Boston: Heathe.

Teheranian, M. (1979) Iran: Communication, Alienation, Revolution. *Intermedia*, 7 (2), 6–12.

Theall, D. F. (1981) Explorations in Communications since Innis. In W. H. Melody et al., *Culture, Communication, and Dependency: The Tradition of H. A. Innis*, Norwood, NJ: Ablex, 225–34. Also in Stamps, 1995, pp. 90–6.

Watson, A. J. (1977) Harold Innis and Classical Scholarship. *Journal of Canadian Studies*, 12 (5), 45–61.

Watson, A. J. (1981) Marginal Man: Harold Innis' Communication Works in Context. Ph.D. dissertation, University of Toronto, 1981, as summarized in Stamps, 1995, p. 68.

Westfall, W. (1981) The Ambivalent Verdict: Harold Innis and Canadian History. In W. H. Melody et al., *Culture, Communication, and Dependency: The Tradition of H. A. Innis*, Norwood, NJ: Ablex, 37–52.

10
Canonic Anti-Text: Marshall McLuhan's *Understanding Media*

Joshua Meyrowitz

In the early 1960s, Herbert Marshall McLuhan argued that print culture was becoming "obsolescent" in the face of the widespread use of television and other electronic media. In his view, the ways of thinking and feeling and of organizing society that were encouraged by printed texts were on the decline. McLuhan would have found it rather ironic, therefore, to have his *Understanding Media* nominated as a canonic *text*. Yet, despite this seeming paradox, despite many of the difficulties with and limits of McLuhan's writings, and despite the vicious attacks that many noted scholars and literary critics have made against McLuhan, I will argue that McLuhan's work should be viewed as an essential text – or, perhaps more properly, an essential anti-text – of media studies.

McLuhan's rejection of text-based analysis

To McLuhan, text-based thinking meant taking a "fixed point of view" and searching for a fixed "truth"; being concerned with linear, logical sequence; emphasizing the mechanical over the organic; separating action from reaction and thought from emotion; focusing on what is happening at the "center" of the society, while ignoring activity at the "margins"; carefully categorizing and classifying objects, animals, people, and ideas; working toward a discrete niche for every thing (and every body), so that all would be in their designated places.

McLuhan, who was trained in the study of literature, recognized himself as a product of print culture. And in his private world of conversation and letters, he often expressed a personal preference for print ways of being over electronic modes of thought and experience. Yet, despite his deep attachment to print culture, McLuhan worked very hard in his public writings to fail the typical standards for printed texts. *And he largely succeeded in his failure.*

McLuhan strove for an organic, rather than a mechanical, form of argument. Even his two best and most "bookish" books, *The Gutenberg Galaxy* (1962) and *Understanding Media* ([1964] 1994), have no indexes, no notes to identify sources, and only skeletal tables of contents. Although *Understanding Media* (unlike *The Gutenberg Galaxy*) is divided into chapters, the chapters do not clearly build on each other into some larger ideational structure or conclusion. McLuhan's writing style is elliptical rather than linear; he runs from the beginning of one argument to the middle or end of another argument, only to return later to finish (partly) the first argument. Many sections of his books read more like transcripts of extemporaneous speaking than traditional scholarly texts.

"Probes" versus scientific claims   McLuhan frustrated scholars who wanted to know exactly what could occur that would falsify his theses (in keeping with Karl Popper's ([1935] 1959) notion that "falsifiability" distinguishes scientific theory from mere belief). McLuhan explicitly rejected the fixed point of view and logical sequence of scholarly argument, and suggested that his theoretical claims were not meant to be testable theories, but merely "mosaics" or "probes" that provided insights – even when one conclusion seemingly contradicted another. This stance struck many traditional scholars as a lack of willingness on McLuhan's part to be accountable for his scholarly claims, a way for him to dodge consideration of disconfirming examples and competing theories.

Declaring versus persuading   McLuhan's style of argument worked against making converts to his way of thinking. He usually did not try to *persuade* readers; rather, he simply *declared* his view that a medium has an impact apart from its messages, while often belittling other perspectives. For example, he stated, "Our conventional response to all media, namely that it is how they are used that counts, is the numb stance of the technological idiot" (p. 18).[1] And he likened those who studied media messages to the family watchdog distracted from what is really happening by focusing on the content of the raw meat brought in by a burglar. "Hot" statements such as these did not foster the cool participation and dialogue that might have led to a wider embrace of McLuhan's thinking and perhaps encouraged McLuhan himself to acknowledge that other ways of analyzing media – yes, even content studies! – have merit.

Fuzzy terminology   McLuhan rarely followed the traditional scholarly strategy of stripping words of their multiple meanings and defining a term precisely to mean one specific thing. Instead, he attempted to use the textured oral language of puns and poetry to make the arguments of science. He did not create new terminology to describe what he was observing and arguing. Instead, he drew on familiar words ("hot" and "cool," "open" and "closed," "exploding" and "imploding," "visual" and "tactile," etc.) and stretched their meanings to apply to his unfamiliar notions. And he rarely described explicitly *how* he was using his terms. The results were understandably mixed, with the most acceptance coming from those who already shared his perspective, those who quickly understood and agreed with his ideas, or those who accepted his pop pronouncements without much thought. Scholars and cultural critics who were invested in other ways of thinking and research about media and society could easily dismiss McLuhan's arguments because of the *way* he presented them.

Lack of methodological "maps"   Unlike many scholarly mentors, McLuhan did not encourage others to follow him. In addition to presenting incomplete arguments with often confusing terminology, he did not lay out a clear methodological map. Instead, he simply gave out a battle cry and pointed in a general direction. He told us to explore the nature of technologies, not their specific uses. He told us to look at changes in the balance of the senses and the structure of the human environment, not at narrow effects of media messages (such as persuasion or imitation). But he did not tell us how one goes about studying what he described as a "shifting sensorium," or what types of behavioral change to look for. How, for example, does one study people who now "live mythically and integrally" because of electronic media? As I have argued elsewhere, McLuhan would have been wise to study some of the structural aspects of face-to-face communication and of social roles in order to find less mystical principles that could be adapted to analyzing how changes in media could alter everyday behavior and social reality (Meyrowitz, 1985).

Absolutist claims   The absolutist form of McLuhan's sentences makes them compelling to read, but also exposes them to refutation by even the slightest qualifying argument or evidence. Have electronic media really "abolished" both time and space, as he declares at the beginning of *Understanding Media?* Or have time and space merely been "demoted" to determinants of a smaller proportion of human interaction? Writing of Tocqueville, McLuhan makes the improbable claim that "he *alone* understood the grammar of typography" (p. 15; emphasis added). Criticizing Wilbur Schramm's *Television in the Lives of Our Children*, McLuhan writes that since Schramm focused on television content, "he had *nothing* to report" (p. 19; emphasis added). And, he claims, human failure to understand the impact of new media has been "total" (p. 20). One can hear in these phrases the spoken words of a compelling lecturer (or stand-up comic), but *written* scholarship typically contains careful qualification and more detailed arguments and evidence to guide and persuade the reader. McLuhan's direct, declaratory, and conclusive tone opens his claims to complete embrace or complete rejection, but makes them difficult to apply or explore further.

Lack of a scholarly domain   McLuhan's writings on media fail to meet the traditional standards of scholarly texts in other ways. He did not give sustained attention to anything resembling a typical scholarly domain. In part, this lack of central focus resulted from the fact that, in analyzing cultural changes, McLuhan paid more attention to the margins than the center, the shifting relationships between the two, and the interplay of cultural elements rarely analyzed in relation to each other. Moreover, McLuhan saw his writings as illustrating a "changeover to an interrelation in knowledge, where before the separate subjects of the curriculum had stood apart from each other" (p. 35). This fractionating of knowledge was, in his view, the result of the "explosive" power of print. And the dissolution of disciplinary boundaries was a consequence of the "implosive" power of electronic media.

McLuhan's writing style is implosive. He does not isolate topics or extend a single line of reasoning. His thoughts are not arranged in any clear sequence; there is no overarching structure. Within a single article or chapter, sometimes even within a single paragraph or sentence, his ideas range widely and – from the perspective of a print-based logic – wildly. He has left us with hundreds of intriguing, but underdeveloped, theories that attempt to grapple with seemingly everything, from manuscripts to massages, teeth to typewriters, automobiles to alienation, nuclear families to nuclear bombs. In covering so much territory, McLuhan's writing inevitably suffered from what traditional scholars in each area would see as serious omissions and errors. And it is true that McLuhan was sometimes sloppy with his facts and with historical sequence. Yet, if one follows McLuhan's call to defocus each element and step back to view the overall mosaic, some clear and intriguing patterns emerge.

History à *la* McLuhan

Although McLuhan presented his world view in non-linear form, it is possible to arrange his elements into a more traditional narrative. He divided history into three major periods, each shaped by a dominant communication form: oral, writing/printing, and electronic. According to McLuhan, each era is characterized by its own interplay of the senses, and therefore by its own forms of thinking and communicating.

Oral culture   Oral societies live in an "ear culture" of simultaneity, circularity, and immersion. Hearing is multidirectional, fluid, and constant (the ear cannot be turned off in the way one can avert or shut one's eyes). Since the primary form of communication is speech, the oral world is "unified" both informationally and sensorily. There are not great differences in what different people know and communicate about. And people in oral societies have a mythic, "in-depth" experience, where all the senses live in relative balance. Multiple daily experiences and interactions involve sight, sound, taste, touch, and smell woven together. The oral tribal world is a "closed society" of high interdependence and lack of individuality.

Literate culture   The development of writing with the phonetic alphabet – especially the explosive extension of writing through print – breaks through the tribal balance, gives oral peoples "an eye for an ear," makes the sense of sight dominant, and distances people from sound, touch, and direct response. Unlike the other sense organs, the eye can experience the world from a great distance and with detachment. Such detachment is encouraged by the use of semantically meaningless symbols that represent sounds to produce words and sentences and paragraphs. Unlike earlier ideographic symbols, phonetic writing bears no resemblance to the physical world experienced through multiple senses. It takes many sequentially written words (themselves composed of sequentially organized arbitrary symbols) to describe what can be understood in an instant through the tone and gesture of oral interaction. With the spread of phonetic literacy, the oral world, which fostered shared experiences for those in the same space, divides into separate experiences for those who read and those who do not. The literate world splinters further into different experiences for people who read different types and levels of texts.

  The spread of individual writing and silent reading encourages the development of introspection, individuality, "rationality," and abstract thinking. The shared experience of the tribe and the experiential cohesion of the extended family diminish. With the coding and decoding of lines of one alphabetic symbol after another, the oral world of circles and cycles – with its repeating seasons, chants, and rituals – yields, over time, to a world of straight lines: assembly lines, single story lines, "rational" lines of thinking, belief in linear progress. Organic "acoustic space" is replaced by "visual space" that is divided into uniform and sequential areas. This new sense of space encourages the development of an artificial perspective, which shows a scene from a fixed viewpoint. With printing, large territories can be subjected to homogenized practices (nationalism, standardized laws, fixed pricing, standardized measures of intelligence, and so forth). From the circular world of sounds, with its round huts and round villages, people move over time toward houses with straight walls on relatively straight streets in grid-like cities. The world of simultaneity shifts toward one-thing-at-a-time, one-thing-after-another experiences. Magical thinking bows to linear cause-and-effect analysis. In short, the structures of the physical, social, and mental worlds of literate cultures come to resemble the linear patterns of letters on the pages of printed texts.

Electronic culture Electronic media bypass the lines of print and cause an overlap in experiences that resembles the directness, speed, and simultaneity of oral interaction. Humans are "retribalized." Electronic media return us to village-like oral encounters, but on a global scale. With electronic media, print-fostered divisions fade in significance, and everyone is involved in everyone else's business. Empathic responses extend beyond local geography. The widespread use of radio, television, and computers leads to a decline in all those cultural structures fostered by the spread of printing, including one-thing-at-a-time logic, disciplinary boundaries, print-supported hierarchies, and delegated authority. Instead, there is a "revulsion against imposed patterns," and people hunger for "wholeness" and "depth of awareness" (p. 5).

Major principles

Supporting McLuhan's view of history are several key principles.

"The medium is the message." In his most famous pun, McLuhan tried to highlight and move beyond the narrow message focus of most media criticism and research. Instead of echoing the typical concerns with persuasion and imitation, he argued that the *form* in which people communicate – the medium itself – has influence far beyond the choice of specific

"content." Indeed, the nature of the medium shapes what "content" works best through it. Further, the acts of encoding and decoding within a medium mold the perceptual processes of users. And, more broadly, McLuhan believed that the widespread use of any artifact – whether or not it is clearly a medium of communication – sends a "message" to the whole culture by shaping human thinking, behavior, and interaction into a particular pattern. These influences occur regardless of the specific "purpose" to which the artifact is put. McLuhan argued, for example, that the railroad fostered the development of "new kinds of cities and new kinds of work and leisure," regardless of "whether the railway functioned in a tropical or a northern environment, and . . . quite independent of the freight or content of the railway medium" (p. 8). In the same way, McLuhan analyzed the development of "print culture" and "electronic culture," apart from the particular contents of books or TV programs. I use the singular "medium theory" to label this approach to studying the particular characteristics of each medium, or each *type* of media (Meyrowitz, 1985, p. 16).

This form of analysis is rarely controversial in other fields. Although a barefoot peasant might prefer to have a pair of shoes rather than a hammer, regardless of whether they are hand-made or mass-produced, an economic historian might note that a shift from manual to mass production of goods affects many aspects of a society, including the proportion of the population that is barefoot. Similarly, McLuhan himself expressed a personal preference for some TV shows over others (*Playboy* [1969] 1995), but also recognized that "television culture" was more than the sum of its programs. Many of his critics, however, had a hard time letting go of their message focus, perhaps because many of them were the craftsmen (in this case, the writers) whose work was being co-opted by the new forms of production, such as television, that McLuhan was analyzing dispassionately. The result was often hostile or mocking rejections of McLuhan's level of analysis. As *New Yorker* media critic Michael J. Arlen smugly commented, "It's hard to forget that the first thing that boring old Gutenberg printed was the Bible and the first thing television gave us was Uncle Miltie – and, on present evidence, there doesn't seem to be any very pressing basis for tossing out the first because of the second" (1968, p. 85).

"Media as extensions"   One way that a medium (or any technology) is a message, in McLuhan's view, is that it extends a human sense or process. The wheel extends the foot, the microphone extends the ear, and so forth. The widespread use of a medium thereby alters the ratio of the use of the human senses. Ironically, in McLuhan's view, the more

extreme the effect of such extensions, the less aware humans are of the impact, because the shock to the system is muted by "auto-amputation" of the extended sense, a process akin to the human response to extreme stress (pp. 42–4). McLuhan probed and provoked in a conscious effort to awaken the culture from its "Narcissus narcosis" (p. 41); that is, he tried to make us aware that the technologies we perceive as being separate from us are in fact "put out" by us, extensions and reflections of ourselves that are also changing us.

"Hot" versus "cool" media   Struggling for a way to explain how the sensory characteristics of a medium have an impact apart from the particular messages, McLuhan examined how "highly defined" is a medium's extension of a sense. Radio is "hot," in his view, because it extends sound in high definition. One could, for example, mistake a radio voice in the next room for a real person in the house. A television image is "cool," however, because of the fuzziness of the image. (The US system from 1948 until the high-definition system of the twenty-first century has had only 525 horizontal scan lines of information, regardless of the size of the screen.) A 35-millimeter movie image is hotter than a TV image, because, although one would be unlikely to mistake it for a real person or object, the visual resolution is much higher than that of a TV image. Similarly, McLuhan would argue that the new high-definition television (HDTV), which dramatically increases the resolution of the image, will actually be a new, "hotter" medium, not simply "better television."

McLuhan claimed that, to be effective in a medium, the style of communicating has to match the hotness or coolness of the medium. He argued, for example, that a rehearsal of a symphony orchestra, including mistakes and false starts, makes for a more interesting television program than a polished performance by the same orchestra (p. 31). The opposite would be true on radio. Similarly, he argued that both Hitler and FDR had intense styles suited to radio, and that both would have been less effective presenting their hot, abstract messages in a television close-up. By contrast, the cooler, less filled-in styles of Kennedy (and later, Reagan and Clinton) and talk show host Jack Paar (and descendants Johnny Carson, Jay Leno, David Letterman, et al.) better matched the coolness of television. McLuhan also argued that highly defined "hot" media tended to create more passive consumers of the message, whereas "cool" media encouraged the audience to "fill in" the missing information. Thus, he saw TV as more "participatory" than radio, in the same way that a seminar is more participatory than a lecture.

Media as the content of other media   When using a new medium, McLuhan argued, humans take an older form of communication and make it the content of the new form. Many of the first writings, for example, were of poetry and dialogues – that is, of *spoken* forms. Similarly, many of the first printed books were typeset versions of manuscripts – that is, of *writing*. Many early movies were filmed versions of vaudeville acts or plays – that is, of the *stage*. Later, the form of the novel became the content of movies, even when no corresponding novel existed prior to a movie's filming. Thus, McLuhan saw media as existing in pairs, with one form of communication being the content of another. Implicit in this argument is the view that cultures rarely see the full potential of a new medium, and often use it at first to extend the use of an old form of communicating.

Rear-view mirror   Another key McLuhan theme is that people tend to drive through the present and into the future looking in the rear-view mirror. That is, new media and other phenomena are perceived through old frameworks. Thus, in the USA of the 1950s – a period that encouraged cultural conformity, ideological purity, oaths of loyalty to government, and employee identification with the corporate employer – television was dominated by programs mythologizing the rugged individualism of the nineteenth-century "wild west." Similarly, television's early impact was judged on the quality of its "theater" and "news." In the electronic era, McLuhan claimed, we live "mythically and integrally" in a world where action and reaction occur almost simultaneously; yet "we continue to think in the old, fragmented space and time patterns of the pre-electric age" (p. 4). McLuhan argued that while most members of a society see the present through the filter of the past, artists are able to see and understand the present and future more clearly.

Understanding Media contains many other arguments. It also offers the raw elements of principles that McLuhan would develop further in other writings and lectures, including his analysis of the difference between "light on" media (such as painting and movies) and "light through" media (such as stained glass windows and television, where the viewer is in a sense the screen) and his double dialectic "tetrad" of media evolution: extension, obsolescence, retrieval, and reversal (McLuhan and McLuhan, 1988). Moreover, the careful reader is rewarded with scores of examples of the complex interplay among media and the interaction between media and different cultural patterns, all of which belie the claims of critics that McLuhan espoused a simple, linear technological determinism.

McLuhan's rise and fall

After the publication of *Understanding Media*, McLuhan's provocative arguments and unconventional style drew the attention of corporations interested in predicting the future of their businesses and bottom lines, of media institutions that were no doubt relieved that he was not simply repeating familiar attacks on their choice of content, and of a select group of literati, including Tom Wolfe, whose 1965 magazine article helped make McLuhan famous. Of McLuhan, Wolfe wrote, "Suppose he is what he sounds like, the most important thinker since Newton, Darwin, Freud, Einstein and Pavlov – what if he is right?" (1967, p. 31). Within a short period, McLuhan became the subject or author of articles in numerous magazines, including *Vogue, Life, Look, Harper's,* and *Newsweek.* He was featured in television network programs, interviewed by *Playboy,* and mentioned in *New Yorker* cartoons, and was variously dubbed "the oracle of an electronic age," the "sage of Aquarius," and the "Dr. Spock of Pop Culture." A few of McLuhan's slogans and terminology (particularly, "The medium is the message," "hot" and "cool" media, "global village") became well known, though they were often misunderstood. The debates over whether anyone really grasped his non-linear, punny prose served as the basis for a sight-gag in Woody Allen's 1977 movie *Annie Hall,* where Allen silences a long-winded "explicator" of McLuhan's theories by pulling the real McLuhan into the scene to declare, "You know nothing of my work."

Yet, to the extent that the literary and scholarly worlds responded to McLuhan, it was generally with attacks on the content and form of his arguments. After all, when *Understanding Media* appeared, the TV quiz show scandals were still a fresh societal memory, and many intellectuals were echoing FCC Chairman Newton Minow's famous 1961 attack on television as a "vast wasteland." In intellectual circles, McLuhan's serious approach to television and pop culture (with its explicit *disregard* for differences in quality and types of programming) was seen as a sin that needed to be exorcised. McLuhan himself predicted this reaction to his analysis of the impact of electronic media on the values fostered by the written word: "Highly literate people in our time find it difficult to examine this question without getting into a moral panic" (p. 82). There were exceptions to the attacks. A handful of authors presented very positive assessments (e.g. Kostelanetz, 1968; Culkin, 1968). Some offered balanced analyses (e.g. Boulding, 1967; Weiss, 1968; Nairn, 1968). And even many hostile reviews were tempered with at least one passing positive remark about McLuhan's creativity or daring. But the majority of reactions fulfilled McLuhan's prediction of "moral panic."

Most of the literary essays about McLuhan's work were sarcastic and contemptuous, sneering at his popular success and referring to his admirers as cult members or disciples of a new feel-good religion. Raymond Rosenthal (1968), who edited *McLuhan: Pro & Con*, set the mostly "con" tone of the anthology in his introductory attack on McLuhan for advocating the "barbarism of sensation" over reason and for praising "ecstatic systems that would destroy the humanness we know" (pp. 4–5). Dwight Macdonald (1968) wrote that *Understanding Media* is "impure nonsense, nonsense adulterated by sense" (p. 31). John Simon (1968) noted that "McLuhan plays the history-of-ideas game . . . none too well" (p. 97). Geoffrey Wagner (1968) attacked McLuhan's "antiprint mania" and suggested that even the alliteration in the catch phrase "The medium is the message" ought to make it suspicious, because it exhibits the dominance of sound over sense (p. 153). Benjamin DeMott (1967) dismissed the work as "McLuhanacy" that encourages "abdication from all responsibility of mind" (p. 248). Anthony Burgess (1968) accused McLuhan of "heresy" for "refusing to accept that ideas are stronger than media" and that "the influence of media is . . . marginal" (p. 233). And Burgess questioned whether McLuhan's conversion to Catholicism contributed to his forsaking his responsibility to "speculate about the purpose of life" (p. 230). Theodore Roszak portrayed McLuhan as using "pretentious nonsense" to ingratiate himself with the "publicity makers" (p. 258). He also commented that "Of all the single-factor explanations of human and social behavior I have ever come across, McLuhan's exaltation of 'media' is, I fear, the most inane" (p. 268).

Among Marxists, critical theorists, and cultural studies scholars, McLuhan was typically attacked for being an apologist for – even an agent of – the ruling classes, because his work encouraged a defocusing on issues of economics, power, and the class struggle. Raymond Williams (1975), for example, characterized McLuhan's work as a "determinism . . . which ratifies the society and culture we now have, and especially its most powerful internal directions" (p. 127). Similarly, Stuart Hall dismissed McLuhan's *Gutenberg Galaxy* and *Understanding Media* as mere "celebrations" of modern media, in which McLuhan was "just lying back and letting the media roll over him" (Grossberg, 1996, p. 132). Without considering the questions McLuhan asked (about differences among media), Hall simply grouped him with those "postmodernist ideologues" who declared an end to history (Grossberg, 1996, p. 134). Though revealing much more understanding of McLuhan's claims, James Carey (1968) argued that McLuhan had distorted the significant arguments of Harold Adams Innis into a utopian mythology, a "secular prayer to technology . . . designed to quell one's fears" about where society is heading (p. 303). For its part, the social-scientific community mostly rejected (or ignored) McLuhan because of his lack of operational definitions, recognizable methodology, or systematic data gathering through descriptive or experimental techniques.

McLuhan's poor reception among scholars may be related to a paradox he presented them in their evaluation of his work. He suggested that traditional scholarly analyses are based on a false assumption that linear thinking is the *only* way to reason – an assumption spawned by the linearity of writing and print. In a sense, McLuhan argued, print "wrote over" and obscured the value of oral forms of reasoning, in the same way that electronic forms of experience were sweeping over print ways of knowing and bringing back oral forms of consciousness and logic. Most scholars and cultural commentators who approached McLuhan's arguments for evaluation called on traditional critical (print-based) skills to evaluate work that questioned the necessity and universal value of those very skills. Ironically, but predictably, the response of many critics was emotional, hostile, and, at times, *ir*rational.

Jonathan Miller (1971), a physician, writer, performer, and director, made rather stringent demands on McLuhan's frameworks before he would entertain them. Attacking McLuhan's notion that the spread of phonetic writing and reading altered the prior ratio of the senses, for example, Miller wrote that McLuhan "makes no effort to specify the units [the 'natural ratio' of the senses] comprises, and unless such a specification can be made the notion of 'ratio' has no meaning" (p. 86). Miller concluded that McLuhan's work was a "gigantic system of lies" (p. 124). Kenneth Burke (1968) challenged McLuhan's argument that we have been moving from a machine culture to an electronic culture, triumphantly reporting that when he looked up "electric dynamo" in the dictionary, he discovered that it is a *machine* where something rotates to produce an electric current (p. 169). Thus, in Burke's view, no technological transformation had taken place. Burke was seemingly unaware of McLuhan's notion that, when pushed to an extreme, a technology flips into a new form (pp. 33–40). And he completely ignored the very different quality of human interactions with mechanical devices and with electronic media.

In reviewing the early criticisms of McLuhan against what he actually said and wrote, one can see that many of the critics simply misstated what he was arguing and then dismissed their own versions of his observations. When McLuhan argued that print was "obsolescent," for example, many critics countered that he was crazy to think that print would disappear, and evil to endorse its demise. Critics also argued that McLuhan disproved his thesis by writing books that became popular.

Yet McLuhan's argument was that the *cultural patterns* he attributed to print culture would diminish in significance in the face of patterns fostered by electronic media; he freely acknowledged that more books were being printed than ever before (p. 82). This distinction was lost on Lewis Mumford (1970), who accused McLuhan of outdoing the Nazis in the destruction of book culture. The public bonfires of the Nazis were "relatively innocent manifestations" of the book-burning process, Mumford reasoned, since they "disposed of only a token number of the world's store of books." McLuhan, however, was embracing and promoting "total illiteracy, with no permanent record except that officially committed to the computer, and open only to those permitted access to this facility" (p. 294).

Similarly, Sidney Finkelstein (1968) completely missed McLuhan's point when he wrote that McLuhan was wrong about writing giving tribal peoples "an eye for an ear," because literate people continue to speak and listen. This is like arguing that the field of sociology was based on a false premise of the impact of industrialization because people continued to grow food and make many products by hand. Finkelstein also missed McLuhan's point about the *form* of an older medium becoming the *content* of a new medium. Ignoring the distinction between the two, Finkelstein argued that McLuhan was wrong because, while some novels are made into movies, others are not, and the best movies are those that have original content. (Dwight Macdonald, 1968, offered the same off-base critique.)

When McLuhan argued that we were living in a global village, critics attacked him for making a utopian argument about global harmony. Yet he was describing a dissolution of boundaries, not a change in degree of harmony, and he explicitly described this global village as a place filled with new and intense forms of tensions, malice, and violence. (See, for example, his comments to Gerald Stearn, in Stearn, 1967, p. 272.) When McLuhan proposed that schools had to change their teaching styles to adjust to the electronic era, critics charged that he wanted to replace teachers with TV sets. Yet he was arguing for a much more involved, participatory, and individualized form of learning (Meyrowitz, 1996).

Even McLuhan's most famous aphorism, "The medium is the message," confused many conventional scholars. Wilbur Schramm, for example, said that this claim made no logical sense, since, clearly, the message is the message and the medium is the medium. To demonstrate what he saw as the inanity of McLuhan's claim, Schramm (1973, p. 128) pointed out that Americans reacted with similar horror to the news of President Kennedy's assassination regardless of whether they heard the message in conversation, over the radio, on TV, or in a newspaper. Schramm's example, however, missed the McLuhanesque point that the mourning was so intense because of the preexisting, *TV-induced* intimacy with JFK and his family. This intimacy began in the famous debates with Richard Nixon, where the same content was perceived quite differently by those who heard the debates on radio, where Nixon seemed to dominate, and those who watched them on TV, where Kennedy seemed much more appealing. The medium of television was clearly a key component of the Kennedy message.

Some critics simply invented out of whole cloth what they saw as "McLuhanism" and then dismissed it. James Morrow (1980), for example, asserted that "McLuhanism contends that as kids glue themselves to their TV sets they absorb subliminally a full working knowledge of film grammar," and therefore, if McLuhan were correct, these children should be able to make excellent movies (p. 2). But McLuhan never made such a claim. Although knowledge of film production variables is not the same as media "content," it is also not the same as what McLuhan analyzes as a medium's environment. (For an analysis of three distinct aspects of media – "content" versus "grammar" versus "medium" – see Meyrowitz, 1998). To say that youth resonate with the environment fostered by a new medium they have experienced since birth is not to say that they are professional producers within that medium.

One of the oddest aspects of McLuhan criticism is the tendency of authors to cite examples that support McLuhan's argument as if they were demolishing his claims. To attack McLuhan's theories about literacy, Miller (1971) argued that people still speak face to face and that literature has "created an unprecedented interest in the minute variations of individual temperament" that are experienced in such encounters (p. 104). Yet this focus on individuality and individual variation is a key component of McLuhan's claims about print's impact. McLuhan also argued that electronic media make it difficult to contain minorities and foster a rejection of narrow "jobs" in favor of more inclusive "roles." Women's rejection of the job of housewife in favor of broader social roles is consistent with this claim. Yet Morrow (1980) almost seemed to gloat as he wrote, "History has not been kind to McLuhan's prophecies. . . . [C]ontrary to the TV chapter in *Understanding Media*, the alleged 'role involvement' mandate of the video image has hardly caused women to crave fulfillment as wives and mothers. (Witness the women's movement!)" (p. 1). More recently, the ad copy for Jeffrey Scheuer's 1999 book, *The Sound-Bite Society*, says "McLuhan was wrong: the medium *slants* the message" – thus restating McLuhan's basic argument as though it disproves his view. (The book itself mentions McLuhan only in passing.)

Such misunderstandings have severely affected McLuhan's reputation. In his first rise to prominence, McLuhan's star burned as briefly as it did brightly. The attention given to his theories on television and radio, in books, newspapers, and magazines, served as a double-edged sword. On the positive side, it brought the idea of non-content media analysis to the consciousness of wide segments of the population in the late 1960s and early 1970s. Yet the association of the study of each medium's effects with McLuhan's unconventional style of argument turned many scholars away from serious attention to the subject. By the time of McLuhan's death at age 69 on the last day of 1980, he had largely lost on both cultural fronts. Many of his terms still echoed in popular arenas, yet few who used them seemed to grasp their meaning or implications. And in scholarly arenas, his ideas were virtually banished. By the end of the 1980s, *Understanding Media* and most of his other books were out of print. Moreover, scholars who tried to publish works about, or built on, McLuhan's frameworks often ran into resistance from peer-reviewers.

Resurrection

By the 1990s, however, McLuhan was enjoying a revival. Appreciation for McLuhan has grown dramatically as his writings have come to be seen as predicting events and processes that did not occur until decades after his description of them. McLuhan wrote about the "retribalization" of youth years before Woodstock and decades before MTV. Twenty-five years before the fall of the Berlin Wall and the end of the Cold War stunned the "experts," McLuhan described the types of boundary crumblings and systemic shifts that could foster such changes. He wrote about "discarnate" electric experiences 30 years or more before most people could even imagine spending hours a day at keyboards communicating with disembodied others, and he spoke about the "global village" long before there was a CNN or a World Wide Web.

The first page of *Understanding Media* offers a prescient image of satellite TV and the Internet, as McLuhan describes electric technology extending our nervous system "in a global embrace, abolishing both time and space as far as our planet is concerned" (p. 3). Again, the absolutist expression ("abolishing") hurt his acceptance by scholars, but it allowed him to capture the essence of what we now call "globalization," a change to which virtually all his critics were oblivious. It is not surprising, then, that when *Wired* magazine was founded in 1993, McLuhan was named as its "patron saint." And McLuhan's books began to appear in print once again. As Lewis Lapham wrote in his introduction to the thirtieth-anniversary edition of *Understanding Media*, "Much of what McLuhan had to say makes a good deal more sense in 1994 than it did in 1964" (p. xi). Indeed, the recent focus on cyber*space* redeems McLuhan's basic argument. The perceived impact of the Internet is not derived from the sum of e-mail messages or web-site content. Instead, the Net is generally understood as a new type of social setting or environment – which is precisely the perspective on communication technologies that McLuhan put forward.

As debates swirl over whether and how to stop the transfer of music, text, graphics, and other material from any computer user in the world to any other computer user in the world, McLuhan's global village no longer seems like a fanciful notion. As students do their homework while IM-ing (instant messaging) with friends, putting in requests for songs from online radio programs, downloading text and graphics for a school report via links that can almost instantly bridge any content on the web with any other, their experience matches McLuhan's world view much better than it matches the stodgy descriptions of his critics. The term "World Wide Web" itself has a McLuhanesque ring to it.

As even McLuhan's critics would have to acknowledge, *Understanding Media* gave us our current conceptions about, and awareness of, "media" and the "information age." It is difficult to believe now, but when McLuhan wrote the first draft in 1959 (as a high school media curriculum for the US National Association of Educational Broadcasting), a generally enthusiastic reviewer cautioned that the term "media" was not in the average teacher's vocabulary and would need to be explained clearly (Gordon, 1997, p. 181). Similarly, some early critics of McLuhan put the words "media" and "medium" in quotes to distance themselves from what they saw as McLuhan's odd usage. (See, for example, Wagner, 1968; Burke, 1968; Roszak, 1968.) Hugh Kenner (1968), generally critical of McLuhan, acknowledged McLuhan's "discovery" and naming of the topic "media" (p. 24). And in one of the few positive comments in Jonathan Miller's book on McLuhan (1971), he acknowledges on the final pages that reading McLuhan made him consider print, photography, radio, and TV as things in themselves to be analyzed (pp. 123–4).

Fittingly, the changes that McLuhan heralded have now naturalized his text; that is, social transformations along the very lines he predicted have made his initially "odd" writing style seem more normal. In 1967 *Newsweek* found McLuhan's writing "repetitious, confused and dogmatic." Thirty years later, Paul Levinson (1999) noted that "the aphoristic bursts of his writing that still so vex his critics seem ideally suited to the Internet and the online milieu" (p. 30). Levinson adds:

One can start anywhere in the book . . . and find a set of themes and referents that will serve as ready passport to almost any other part of the book. Each chapter, in other words, contains a blueprint of the entire book, much like the DNA in each of our cells contains a recipe for our entire organism, or the pieces of a holographic plate contain information sufficient to reproduce the entire three-dimensional image recorded on the original, intact plate. (p. 31)

Similarly, James Morrison (2000) notes that "McLuhan thought and wrote in a manner akin to hypertext: in multilinear webs of association that stress connections among multifaceted phenomena." Print-oriented minds would grapple with the same phenomena "only by disassociating, categorizing, and reeling out in homogeneously linear sequence" (pp. 4–5). In both the content and form of his arguments, McLuhan described and embodied what we now call post-modern thought (Grosswiler, 1998, pp. 155–81).

In the 1960s, McLuhan's critics seemed to have the upper hand in exposing the ways in which his claims leaped far beyond the technologies he was analyzing. (Levinson does a good job of outlining these limits.) By the start of the twenty-first century, however, the technologies seemed to have leaped into McLuhan's frameworks, leaving his critics in the silicon dust. In *Digital McLuhan*, Levinson (1999) outlines in impressive detail how McLuhan's theories are an even better match for the era of cyberspace than they were for the media world of McLuhan's day.

One of the more surprising sources of reconsideration of McLuhan is found among a new generation of critical theorists. Critical theory and its offshoot, cultural studies, have provided some of the more potent criticism of McLuhan over the years, noting correctly that he (unlike Harold Adams Innis) paid almost no attention to the role played by powerful political and economic interests in the development of communication technologies and in the way media are employed. In this serious omission, of course, McLuhan merely mirrored the typical weaknesses of the political and economic critiques, which have tended to ignore the different characteristics and influences of different media forms.

Donna Flayhan (1997) has called for a fusing of these two incomplete perspectives, those of Marxism and the "medium theory" of McLuhan and others, into a coherent theory of media influences that also recognizes the pressures from the larger capitalist system and highlights the need for social activism. She argues that the materialist base of medium theory makes it quite compatible with the Marxist view of history. And although she is very critical of McLuhan's lack of attention to economics and human agency, she acknowledges that his *Understanding Media* was a better predictor of the social changes that followed its publication than was a critical theory work published in the same year, Herbert Marcuse's (1964) *One-Dimensional Man*. She also notes that, ironically, the medium-theory perspective, in general, is more dialectical (at least implicitly) than much critical theory that explicitly espouses a dialectical approach. Thus, critical theory, she argues, is often reduced to a "dismal distress over ideological domination" that "leads only to cynicism, pessimism, and criticism" (p. 222), while medium theory is more optimistic and more compatible with hopeful human activity for progressive social change.

Working on a related mission, Paul Grosswiler (1998) has argued that McLuhan's theory of media and social change is less deterministic than Marxists and neo-Marxists have claimed, and that McLuhan's method resembles Marx's early humanist dialectics. Grosswiler writes in the hope that the fields of cultural studies and post-modernism will "reappraise and reclaim" both McLuhan's and Marx's dialectical methods and their theories of technology and society. Grosswiler notes how the works of John B. Thompson (1994) and Nick Stevenson (1995) have already made advances in this direction.

Consistent with the appeals of Flayhan and Grosswiler, American cultural studies scholar James Carey (1998) has recently revised his assessment of McLuhan, noting how the passage of time has made visible McLuhan's multifaceted intellectual contributions. Similarly, Durham and Kellner's *Media and Cultural Studies: Key Works* (2001) includes McLuhan's "The Medium is the Message" chapter. As the editors explain, "McLuhan was a prophet of both the media and computer age, noting . . . how more and more forms of culture and consciousness are being rendered into 'the form of information'" (pp. 112–13).

One reason for this general reassessment of McLuhan among those concerned with issues of power may be that the fear of top-down control over information and thought does not seem to fit the rise of the personal computer, Internet, camcorder, mobile phone, and other new technologies as well as it fit (and still fits) radio and television. Indeed, these new technologies have been used, at least by sizable minorities, to organize resistance to dominant corporate and government power, thereby supporting McLuhan's notions of electronic media fostering participation, decentralization, and a flattening of hierarchies.

Conclusion: essential anti-text

In summary, McLuhan's *Understanding Media* has earned its place among essential texts in media studies. Despite their unconventional style, his probes and mosaics offer insights into general patterns of social change that are often invisible within more traditional schemata. Although incomplete and sometimes baffling, McLuhan's writing stand out from that of almost all his contemporaries as pointing clearly to dramatic structural changes in society and world affairs: changes in our experience of time and space, in borders and boundaries, in sensibilities concerning public and private, in categories of media content.

It is true that at least a few of McLuhan's more specific (and "testable") predictions – such as his argument that television spelled doom for baseball (pp. 239, 326) – have turned out to be wrong. (A dedicated McLuhanite, however, might counter that baseball had to transform itself into a different spectacle with close-ups, slow motion, instant replays, and so forth, to compete with other television sports.) Yet, more often than not, McLuhan's predictions were accurate. He correctly saw that advances in technologies would lead executives to do work once done by servants and secretaries (p. 36), that it was becoming impossible to isolate minorities and youth from the larger culture (p. 5), that boundaries between disciplines would begin to disappear (pp. 35–6), that distinctions between high and low culture would blur (p. 282), that computers would allow rapid translation from one language to another (p. 80), that pressure from the TV experience would transform the motion picture into a portable book-size cartridge (what we know as the video cassette) that could be viewed at home (pp. 291–2), and that there would be an unprecedented sense of "involvement" spanning old boundaries within and across nations (discussed throughout his work).

Perhaps more than any particular prediction, however, McLuhan's work in all its dimensions – clear or foggy, predictively accurate or misguided – called for us to pay attention to the ways in which the tools we shape work to reshape us. McLuhan's work stands out as authoritative less on his analysis of particular changes than on his focus on second-order change – that is, his call for us to look at changes in the nature of change: change in the rate of change, in the type of change, in the criteria used to judge change, in the narratives used to describe change. Such issues have taken up the attention of McLuhan's followers. But his ideas have also permeated the thinking of those who criticize him, and even those who are unaware of his arguments. As I have described in an essay on McLuhan's theories and the evolution of education (Meyrowitz, 1996), educational theorists and practitioners have enacted many of the reforms that McLuhan called for, even though they seem unaware of his contribution to the field. Some of these reforms include open classrooms, cooperative learning, less strict age-grading, shared decision making, minimized gender distinctions, critical and post-modern pedagogies, expanded conceptions of multiple literacies and multiple intelligences – *and* the abandonment of traditional canons.

If McLuhan is right in all details, then we should abandon the notion of canonic texts. Yet, if he is wrong enough for us to ignore him on this issue and maintain a canon, I think he is right enough on other things to be included in it.[2]

Notes

1   Unless another McLuhan source is indicated, all page references are to the thirtieth-anniversary edition of *Understanding Media* (1994).
2   The author would like to thank Renée Carpenter and the editors of this volume for their comments and suggestions regarding this chapter.

References

Arlen, M. J. (1968) Marshall McLuhan and the Technological Embrace. In R. Rosenthal (ed.), *McLuhan: Pro & Con*, New York: Funk & Wagnalls, 82–7.

Boulding, K. (1967) It is Perhaps Typical of Very Creative Minds . . . In G. Stearn (ed.), *McLuhan: Hot & Cool*, New York: Signet Books, 68–75.

Burgess, A. (1968) The Modicum is the Message. In R. Rosenthal (ed.), *McLuhan: Pro & Con*, New York: Funk & Wagnalls, 229–33.

Burke, K. (1968) Medium as "Message." In R. Rosenthal (ed.), *McLuhan: Pro & Con*, New York: Funk & Wagnalls, 165–77.

Carey, J. (1968) Harold Adams Innis and Marshall McLuhan. In R. Rosenthal (ed.), *McLuhan: Pro & Con*, New York: Funk & Wagnalls, 270–308.

Carey, J. (1998) Marshall McLuhan: Genealogy and Legacy. *Canadian Journal of Communication*, 23 (3), 293–306.

Culkin, J. (1968) A Schoolman's Guide to Marshall McLuhan. In R. Rosenthal (ed.), *McLuhan: Pro & Con*, New York: Funk & Wagnalls, 242–56.

DeMott, B. (1967) A Literary Self . . . In G. Stearn (ed.), *McLuhan: Hot & Cool*, New York: Signet Books, 240–8.

Durham, M. G. and Kellner, D. M. (2001) *Media and Cultural Studies: Key Works*. Malden, MA: Blackwell.

Finkelstein, S. (1968) *Sense and Nonsense of McLuhan*. New York: International Publishers.

Flayhan, D. P. (1997) Marxism, Medium Theory, and American Cultural Studies: The Question of Determination. Unpublished Ph.D. dissertation, University of Iowa (UMI #9731793).

Gordon, W. T. (1997) *Marshall McLuhan: Escape into Understanding*. New York: Basic Books.

Grossberg, L. (ed.) (1996) On Postmodernism and Articulation: An Interview with Stuart Hall. In D. Morley and K-Y. Chen (eds), *Stuart Hall: Critical Dialogues in Cultural Studies*, London: Routledge, 131–50.

Grosswiler, P. (1998) *The Method is the Message: Rethinking McLuhan through Critical Theory*. Montreal: Black Rose.

Kenner, H. (1968) Understanding McLuhan. In R. Rosenthal (ed.), *McLuhan: Pro & Con*, New York, Funk & Wagnalls, 23–8.

Kostelanetz, R. (1968) A Hot Apostle in a Cool Culture. In R. Rosenthal (ed.), *McLuhan: Pro & Con*, New York: Funk & Wagnalls, 207–28.

Lapham, L. (1994) The Eternal Now. Introduction to the MIT Press edition of Marshall McLuhan, *Understanding Media*, pp. ix–xxiii.

Levinson, P. (1999) *Digital McLuhan: A Guide to the Information Millennium*. New York: Routledge.

Macdonald, D. (1968) Running it Up the Totem Pole. In R. Rosenthal (ed.), *McLuhan: Pro & Con*, New York: Funk & Wagnalls, 29–37.

Marcuse, H. (1964) *One-Dimensional Man*. Boston: Beacon Press.

McLuhan, M. (1962) *The Gutenberg Galaxy: The Making of Typographic Man*. Toronto: University of Toronto Press.

McLuhan, M. (1994) *Understanding Media: The Extensions of Man*. Cambridge, MA: MIT Press. (Originally published in 1964.)

McLuhan, M. and McLuhan, E. (1988) *Laws of the Media: The New Science*. Toronto: University of Toronto Press.

Meyrowitz, J. (1985) *No Sense of Place: The Impact of Electronic Media on Social Behavior*. New York: Oxford University Press.

Meyrowitz, J. (1996) Taking McLuhan and "Medium Theory" Seriously: Technological Change and the Evolution of Education. In S. T. Kerr (ed.), *Technology and the Future of Schooling*, 95th Yearbook, National Society for the Study of Education, Chicago: University of Chicago Press, 73–110.

Meyrowitz, J. (1998) Multiple Media Literacies. *Journal of Communication*, 48 (1), 96–108.

Miller, J. (1971) *Marshall McLuhan*. New York: Viking.

Morrison, J. (2000) No Prophet without Honor. In *New Dimensions in Communication*, vol. 13, Proceedings of the 57th Annual Conference of the New York State Communication Association, Monticello, New York, 1–28.

Morrow, J. (1980) Recovering from McLuhan. *AFI Education*, 3 (5), (May–June), 1–2.

Mumford, L. (1970) *The Pentagon of Power*. New York: Harcourt Brace Jovanovich.

Nairn, T. (1968) McLuhanism: The Myth of Our Time. In R. Rosenthal (ed.), *McLuhan: Pro & Con*, New York: Funk & Wagnalls, 140–52.

Playboy ([1969] 1995) Interview: Marshall McLuhan. In E. McLuhan and F. Zingrone (eds), *Essential McLuhan*, New York: Basic Books, 233–69.

Popper, K. (1959) *The Logic of Scientific Discovery*. London: Routledge. (Originally published in 1935.)

Rosenthal, R. (ed.) (1968) *McLuhan: Pro & Con.* New York: Funk & Wagnalls.

Roszak, T. (1968) The Summa Popologia of Marshall McLuhan. In R. Rosenthal (ed.), *McLuhan: Pro and Con,* New York: Funk & Wagnalls, 257–69.

Scheuer, J. (1999) *The Sound Bite Society: Television and the American Mind.* New York: Four Walls Eight Windows.

Schramm, W. (1973) *Men, Messages, and Media: A Look at Human Communication.* New York: Harper & Row.

Simon, J. (1968) Pilgrim of the Audile-Tactile. In R. Rosenthal (ed.), *McLuhan: Pro & Con,* New York: Funk & Wagnalls, 93–9.

Stearn, G. E. (1967) *McLuhan: Hot & Cool.* New York: Dial Press.

Stevenson, N. (1995) *Understanding Media Cultures: Social Theory and Mass Communication.* London: Sage.

Thompson, J. B. (1994) Social Theory and the Media. In D. Crowley and D. Mitchell (eds), *Communication Theory Today,* Cambridge: Polity, 27–49.

Wagner, G. (1968): Misunderstanding Media: Obscurity as Authority. In R. Rosenthal (ed.), *McLuhan: Pro & Con,* New York: Funk & Wagnalls, 153–64.

Weiss, I. J. (1968) Sensual Reality in the Mass Media. In R. Rosenthal (ed.), *McLuhan: Pro & Con,* New York: Funk & Wagnalls, 38–57.

Williams, R. (1975) *Television: Technology and Cultural Form.* New York: Schocken Books.

Wolfe, T. (1967) Suppose He Is What He Sounds Like . . . In G. Stearn (ed.), *McLuhan: Hot & Cool,* New York: Signet Books, 31–48.

PART V
British Cultural Studies

———

Introduction

Inspired by scholars trained in literary criticism, social history, and linguistics – notably Richard Hoggart, Raymond Williams, and Stuart Hall – the "cultural studies" project was conceived at the Centre for Contemporary Cultural Studies at the University of Birmingham in the late 1960s, where it flourished throughout the 1970s. Unlike the Frankfurt, Columbia, or Chicago schools, however, cultural studies is not labeled "the Birmingham school" in the collective memory of media research. This is perhaps due in part to its meteoric expansion into other fields besides communication, such as English literature, art, music, and history. Also, although it has become an object of historical study, cultural studies is still very much at the center of contemporary debates over future directions.

Nevertheless, we must return to Birmingham to pinpoint some of the concerns, motivations, and key ideas of the forefathers. First, there is the redefinition of "culture." Before Birmingham, cultural critics in the USA (Adorno and Horkheimer) and in Britain (Q. D. and F. R. Leavis) evaluated (or rather, condemned) "industrial" culture by applying aesthetic and moral criteria that juxtaposed elite culture (good, "ours") and "organic" or "folk" culture (good, "theirs") with "mass" culture (bad, "theirs"). Hoggart and Williams transformed the terms of the debate by dropping the reference to "intrinsic or eternal values (how good?)" in favor of "reference to the overall map of social relations (in whose interest?)" (O'Sullivan et al., 1994). To fit the revolutionized definition, a new methodology for the study of culture was required: an anthropological approach that incorporated historical and autobiographical elements and focused on the ways in which cultural practices and products become "the very material of our daily lives . . . what we wear, hear, watch, and how we see ourselves in relation to others" (Willis, in Turner, 1979, p. 2).

At the same time, the anthropological gaze shifted from distant tribes to the lives of disadvantaged groups at home, starting with working-class people and moving on to include ethnic, gender, and sexual minorities. With this move, the relationship between researcher and subjects switched from talking about "them" to talking about "us." Also, in an effort to avoid romanticizing the culture of working people in Britain (for Hoggart and Williams, the culture of their own families), British cultural studies adopted a neo-Marxist Gramscian approach, according to which taken-for-granted practices are not "natural" but constructed and, as such, serve the interests of the ruling elite. Finally, the mass media were demoted from the primary determinants of the formation of minds to just one source among many, and audiences were deemed capable of resisting – even subverting – media messages (Hall, 1980; Morley, 1980).

The dilemma inherent in the wish to accord recognition and value to a lived culture while at the same time exposing it as repressive is exemplified by *Coronation Street*, the longest-running British soap. The program paints a nostalgic picture of a working-class community, portraying "the full and rich life" of a warm, tightly knit neighborhood in which public culture (the pub, the local newspaper, the choir) is organically interconnected with family roles, gender relations, language styles, and community "common sense." But this self-conscious effort to promote the culture of ordinary folk may also be seen as a paternalistic reenactment of "culture as the sphere in which class, gender, race and other inequalities are naturalized and represented in forms which sever the connection between these and economic and political inequalities" (O'Sullivan, 1994, p. 71). Indeed, the series "naturalize[s]" inequality by equating the boundaries of the street with those of the world of the soap, thus sealing off the characters from any options of upward mobility (Liebes and Livingstone, 1992).

A critique of cultural studies could point to the same ambiguity of togetherness versus hegemony in the writings of British cultural studies scholars. Nevertheless, while cultural studies offers the illusion of coziness and security at the cost of abandoning the struggle for equality and opportunity, it also creates informal loci for debating community issues and trying out solutions, in the spirit of its view of culture as "the means by and through which various subordinate groups live and resist their subordination" (O'Sullivan et al., 1994, p. 42).

British cultural studies forced media research to face the question of audience interpretation. Thus, Williams argues that ideas and feelings are still molded by patterns of social and family life; Hall claims that the same text can produce different readings by the invocation of different codes; while Mulvey, though dealing with an implied spectator rather than empirical audience, sees the interaction between text and audience as the site of the male gaze. All of these scholars have inspired subsequent ethnographic work within various communities, traditional and diasporic, real and virtual, torn by axes (race, ethnicity, sexuality) not interrogated in the 1960s and 1970s.

The real proof of the overriding success of British cultural studies is that the "British" has been dropped (though keeping its historical relevance), positioning "cultural studies" as the latest dominant paradigm in the field, open to embrace the ever-growing flow of new communities as soon as they discover their group identity.

References

Hall, S. (1980) Encoding/Decoding. In Hall et al. (eds), *Culture, Media, Language*, London: Hutchinson, 128–38.

Liebes, T. and Livingstone, S. (1992) Mothers and Lovers: How American and British Soap Operas Cope with Women's Dilemma. In J. G. Blumler, J. M. McLeod and K. E. Rosengren (eds), *Comparatively Speaking*, London: Sage, 94–120.

Morley, D. (1980) *The "Nationwide" Audience*. London: British Film Institute.

O'Sullivan, T. et al. (1994) *Key Concepts in Communication and Cultural Studies*. London and New York: Routledge.

Turner, G. (1996) *British Cultural Studies*, 2nd edn. London and New York: Routledge.

11

Retroactive Enrichment: Raymond Williams's *Culture and Society*

John Durham Peters

In no obvious sense is *Culture and Society* a text in or about media research. Of all the texts nominated in this book, it is perhaps the most remote from the recognizable tradition of English-language academic study of media and society. And yet it synthesizes the key intellectual positions of what may be the richest and most foundational period of intellectual flourishing in communication theory after the 1920s: the 1950s. It is one of several texts to define an intellectual framework for analysis of the social, cultural, and political setting of media that would not only become the heirloom of British cultural studies, but also shows striking and rarely noted affinities with both German critical theory and mainstream American media sociology. Together with the other founding works of leftist analysis of culture and society in Britain, Richard Hoggart's *The Uses of Literacy* (1957) and E. P. Thompson's *The Making of the English Working Class* (1963), as well as Williams's own sequel *The Long Revolution* (1961), *Culture and Society* is made more richly and diversely intelligible by the work that emerged in its wake, much of it directly on media texts, audiences, and institutions, most famously at Birmingham but with branches in Leicester, Milton Keynes, London, Chapel Hill, Sydney, Taipei, and elsewhere.

Culture and Society exemplifies the hermeneutic principle of retroactive enrichment. Descendants can give life to their ancestors. Sentences in Williams now resonate to frequencies unheard when it was written. What were small streams in 1958 can be reread in 2002 as the sources of mighty intellectual rivers. Subsequent history can be kind or cruel to human works, and *Culture and Society* has enjoyed a rather blessed afterlife. It would be much less resonant without what has emerged in its wake. As a source (or at least a carrier) of much of the intellectual DNA still reproducing in media studies, *Culture and Society* deserves its place in the canon.

Intellectual history as social theory

Culture and Society is an extended study of intellectual life in Britain from the late eighteenth century to the mid-twentieth century. No potted history of ideas, it is rather an engagement with – even invention of – a tradition of reflection on, and criticism of, the social and cultural trans-formations of modern British life. Williams's coverage of such figures as Edmund Burke, the Romantic poets, J. S. Mill and Thomas Carlyle, Matthew Arnold, D. H. Lawrence, T. S. Eliot, and George Orwell may look now like a standard syllabus, but as Williams notes (1990, pp. v–vi), there was no self-conscious category in British intellectual life as a culture-and-society tradition when he wrote it. *Culture and Society* is remarkably willing to recruit thinkers with conservative credentials – Burke, Coleridge, Carlyle, Lawrence, Eliot – to the cause of a common culture and as indigenous resources for cultural criticism, a reclamation project shared by other 1950s British intellectuals on the left (Mulhern, 2000, p. 67). The intelligence, subtlety, and often productive ambival-ence of his readings of diverse figures make *Culture and Society* still a useful primer on the history of social thought in Britain, as well as on Williams's own thought.

Williams's history of the idea of culture is itself a cultural and political project. The title of the German edition of *Culture and Society* translates as *Intellectual History as Social Theory*, a title that concisely captures the book's aim and method. "*Culture and Society* is a work which, in the very act of 'placing' a tradition, places itself within it" (Eagleton, 1976, p. 26). Williams was doing a title search for his own practice as a cultural critic, especially in the book's splendid conclusion. Here Williams writes as a socialist concerned for democracy, a humanist concerned for the quality of expression, and a moralist concerned with the adultera-tion of human possibilities. The conclusion's "effort at total qualitative assessment" recalls Arnold and Mill, Burke and Cobbett, Eliot and Leavis – indeed, the group of thinkers the book comments on. The conclusion serves as Williams's own assimilation of, and installment in, the culture-and-society tradition; in it he appears "as the latest figure in the lineage he traces, a character within his own drama" (Eagleton, 1976, p. 23). Here he speaks as voice, not as commentator, with diverse echoes from the authors treated, both topically and tonally.

Theorizing mass communication in the 1950s

It might be a surprise from the description thus far to discover that the conclusion is in large part a wrestle with the meaning of mass communication. *Culture and Society* is one of several works in an international moment (or "conjuncture," as Williams would later say) rethinking the political, social, and cultural meaning of the mass media. In the United States, 1950s media sociology can be symbolized by Paul Lazarsfeld and C. Wright Mills studiously ignoring each other at the water cooler in the Columbia Department of Sociology. Lazarsfeld's work was empirical, quantitative, externally funded, and politically mainstream. It fit with the view of democracy as a functioning system which did not require active participation of citizens, but rather a consensual balance among various interest groups, a position explicit in the conclusion to Berelson, Lazarsfeld, and McPhee's *Voting* (1954). Lazarsfeld largely neglected the industrial and technological context of media in his work, though not in his thinking, as can be seen in essays with Robert K. Merton (Lazarsfeld and Merton, 1948) and in Lazarsfeld (1948). By showing psychological and sociological barriers to mass media influence, Lazarsfeld's Bureau of Applied Social Research offered a kind of defense of the capacity of ordinary people to think, talk, and associate for themselves. By showing how people interpret, filter, ignore, or even resist media influence, Elihu Katz and Paul Lazarsfeld's *Personal Influence* (1955) serves, as Simonson (1996) notes, as a democratic apologetic. Katz and Lazarsfeld argued that people still talk and have social relations; that selectivity and interpersonal relations dampened both the threat of the big bad media (Frankfurt school) and the hope of big good media (Chicago school). In a brilliant piece of data reduction Katz and Lazarsfeld show that these two outlooks, however opposed they may seem, in fact agree that media have major effects; both are in thrall to visions of mass society.

In contrast, Mills, ultimately drawing on both Chicago and Frankfurt sources, painted a much gloomier picture. In his draft analyses of the fieldwork in Decatur, Illinois, which he directed in 1944 and which would later become the basis of *Personal Influence*, Mills wrote of power as well as influence, social structures as well as group ties. More pointedly, in chapter 13 of *The Power Elite* (1956), Mills unfurled a theory of mass society which is a clear intramural skirmish with Lazarsfeld and, specifically with *Personal Influence*, a battle that would continue with his attack on Lazarsfeld's "methodological inhibitionism" in *The Sociological Imagination* (1959). In *The Power Elite*, Mills argued that media do not simply shape people's voting, fashion, movies, or shopping choices, but provide ordinary people with their aspirations, identities, and even experiences. Clearly, for Mills, media effects (not a term that he used) were pervasive, not rare. To be sure, Mills's views of media were embedded within a much broader historical account of the structural transformation of the modern public, an account that owes something to both Walter Lippmann and John Dewey: media fill the historical gaps left open by modern personal alienation, social uprooting, and the retreat of educational and other institutions. Mills called for a critical – and empirical – sociology that would draw on biography and history as its chief sources, and have as its object the growth of reason and the emancipation of humanity. The task of sociology, he believed (like Raymond Williams), was historically continuous with that of the novel: to bring modern social order to an imaginative self-clarification, resulting in a heightened responsibility to fact and experience.

Mills versus Lazarsfeld in the 1950s, like Adorno versus Lazarsfeld in the 1940s, became cemented in the historical self-consciousness of mass communication research in the late 1970s (Gitlin (1978) taking the Adorno–Mills side, Morrison (1978) taking the Lazarsfeld side) as the divide between critical and empirical research, a division that Lazarsfeld himself first named. These debates offered dualisms that are unfortunately still with us as historical and political categories for describing media studies and its history, even if the best work of the past two (and maybe six) decades has skirted them: minimal versus strong effects; optimism versus despair about popular consciousness; quantitative versus qualitative methods; affirmative versus radical politics. For too long it was assumed that choosing one side of the dichotomies was a package deal: if you believed in the wisdom of ordinary people, then you must also take an affirmative stance to the culture industry and engage in survey research. But while the terms on each side do have an elective affinity, there is nothing naturally given about them.

Between critical and empirical

This is one lesson of Williams's conclusion. Its position on mass communication is a stunning arbitration of positions that in the 1950s and after were largely polarized in the United States. Again, it belongs to an international moment that is clearer retrospectively than it was at the time. In the same year as *Culture and Society* appeared, Hannah Arendt's *The Human Condition* (1958) and Aldous Huxley's *Brave New World Revisited* (1958) also came out. A year after Williams's *Long Revolution* (1961) came Jürgen Habermas's *Structural Transformation of the Public Sphere* and also the founding manifesto of the New Left in the United States, the Port Huron Statement (1962). Among Marxists, independent radicals like Mills, and humanist centrists like Arendt and Huxley, there was a concern for communication as cure and disease of modern life, with the mass media playing a particular role in each text, sometimes as villain. These works all deal with the threat of mass society, of lonely crowds, and seek ways to rebuild a more vital democracy. They were all composed in the light of the rise of the New Left: the effort to build a program of humane, progressive, coalition-based social justice. To twist Gitlin's title (1995), these texts reflect the dawn of common dreams. Habermas's public sphere, Arendt's realm of speech and action, and Williams's common culture all point to a vibrant, democratically engaged politics, however much these thinkers differ on details, histories, politics, and even principles.

Though attempts at canonization are always partly acts of will or imagination, it requires no leap to read Williams's conclusion as being about mass communication theory. The terms and questions are plain for all to see, as in the section titled "Mass-communication" on pp. 300–5 and the one titled "Communication and Community" on pp. 313–19. Williams both mediates late 1950s debates (with the salutary effect of forcing a rethinking of the critical–empirical divide) and offers an original vision of his own. He is perhaps best known in media studies for his 1970s work on television and Marxist cultural theory, but a reading of *Culture and Society* also places him, appropriately, among a different generation: one of the sanest voices speaking amid the din and loathing of the mass culture debates of the late 1950s.

In Williams, Arendt, and Habermas alike, there is a strong working conviction that words serve as secret records of social transformations. Words like *culture*, *public*, or *mass* end up, in their works, revealing entire histories of human struggles and societal changes. Indeed, one of the many genres of writing that Williams worked in – along with history, criticism, novel, theory, and essay – was the dictionary, and his *Keywords* (1985) grew out of the project begun in *Culture and Society*. For Williams, the history of words can serve as a record of changed structures of feeling. Like Habermas and Arendt, Williams sees intellectual history not as a leap from mountaintop to mountaintop, but as a tracing of social struggles. For all three, lexicography serves as social and cultural history, with words offering privileged access to seismic changes in human experience. Ways of seeing are regarded as being socially conditioned in a strong way; in Williams's famous phrase, "there are no masses, only ways of seeing people as masses" (1990, p. 300). Our modes of vision are saturated with social experience, but also help, in turn, to shape possible relationships with others. Whether literature, journalism, and drama, or social science, history, and statistics, stories are ways of both imagining and enacting social worlds.

Hence Williams's positive evaluation of entertainment, at least as a potential form of social connection. Though most of what is on offer is cheap, silly, or escapist, the sheer abundance of drama available to people in the twenty-first century enriches our possible modes of mutual connection, a claim finding its greatest statement in Williams's 1974 inaugural lecture at Cambridge, "Drama in a Dramatised Society" (O'Connor, 1989). As "any real theory of communication is a theory of community" (Williams, 1990, p. 313), scholarship, as one of many imaginative labors, has a privileged role in social description and criticism: "To take a meaning from experience, and to try to make it active, is in fact our process of growth" (p. 338). "In every problem we need hard, detailed inquiry and negotiation" (p. 338). "Inquiry plus negotiation" defines Williams's method well, both political and intellectual, one he shares with Mills, Arendt, and Habermas. He belongs to a moment in which the best scholars blended methods of social science and humanities – a call that Katz (1959) was also making at the same time.

Williams's account of mass communication takes pains to avoid technological determinism or contempt for audiences. Williams is decidedly not a medium theorist. "The techniques, in my view, are at worst neutral" (p. 301). At best, new technologies alter the emphases of extant social activities and relations; they never revolutionize them. Technologies themselves are shaped by the context of use and social decisions about their deployment, a point that anticipates his *Television: Technology and Cultural Form* (1974), which includes a blistering attack on McLuhan. To take technology as a determinant, Williams believes, is to risk freezing a particular social practice into something natural rather than historical. The mere fact that many of the media of mass communication are impersonal and involve one-way flows does not imply that the audience is anesthetized: "Reception and response, which complete communication, depend on other factors than the techniques" (1990, p. 302). Mass communication, Williams argues, is really multiple transmission, a means of distributing symbols that emerged first with the printing press and grew into broadcasting. The social meaning of multiple transmission is also at least ambiguous. Williams finds it ironic that historical developments that gave millions unprecedented access to cultural materials are largely interpreted as harming those people. For him, the very notion of mass communication participates in the depreciation of audiences by painting them disparagingly as *masses*. The key question is not the forms in the abstract, but the intentions underlying communication practices and the social relationships they sustain.

Like *Personal Influence* (Katz and Lazarsfeld, 1955), but with a much clearer political program, Williams is opposed to the mass society notion of audiences as dupes or dopes. His claim that "Communication is not only transmission; it is also reception and response" (1990, p. 313) could be the motto of 40 years of British cultural studies, with its interest in how people receive and reply to, appropriate and abuse, media matters. Like the Columbia tradition, he opposes the notion of powerful media, though his formulation again has a sharper critical twist – the danger is a "dominative" habit in thinking about communication (p. 313). The media are only one among many influences on the formation of minds: "ideas and feelings are, to a large extent, still moulded by a wider and more complex pattern of social and family life" (p. 308). The effort to register an impact on the mass mind "has failed, and will continue to fail, when its transmissions encounter, not a confused uncertainty, but a considered and formulated experience" (p. 313). The mass media cannot manufacture conviction out of thin air. While it would clearly be a mistake to exaggerate the affinity of the overall visions and programs of Williams and Lazarsfeld, the structure of their arguments about audience resources for resisting media influence is quite similar. Where the Columbia school refers to psychological selectivity, canalization, and primary groups, Williams talks about experience, practice, and social relations. Williams's vocabulary is politically and culturally richer, as Lazarsfeld's is scientifically more replicable. The common enemy for both is mass society theory (something that rarely existed as a positive program; more often it was used as a construct in the hands of its detractors). *Culture and Society* and *Personal Influence* both distrust cultural pessimism – the vision of people as "hollow men" without souls – as an artifact of a bad set of spectacles, not as the real nature of social experience.

Williams's account of the rise of mass culture undercuts the historical decline narratives that underlie mass society theory without substituting a happy account of progress as an alternative. Belief in an earlier golden age – for instance, the eighteenth century as the high point of the English novel – depends in large part, Williams suggests, on the selective preservation of the historical record. Novels from the eighteenth century that are still read today tend to be good ones, while many poorer ones have been forgotten. Today, by contrast, we live in a historical mix in which a consensus on taste has not yet been reached and in which lots of hackwork is available. Williams is no cultural Darwinist who thinks works compete and survive on the sole strength of their aesthetic virtues: his point, rather, concerns the problem of historical framing. To describe modern culture as being in decline, one has to choose a beginning point, and this choice always has specific consequences. One can start in 1870 or 1740 – or, as he notes in chapter 2 of *The Country and the City* (1973), one can trace the ever-receding horizon of a whole and happy rural life back to Eden. Williams is highly sophisticated about historiographical deck loading: to say that modern life involves a decline in taste is a proposition that must first account for the differential survival of texts, the choice of starting points, and, above all, the obvious fact that modern life has seen an expanding, not a contracting, culture. Like Lazarsfeld and Merton (1948), Williams takes care to distinguish relative from absolute changes: "In every case, certainly, the proportions [of serious culture] are less than we could desire, but they are not negligible" (Williams, 1990, p. 308). Perhaps even more heretically for a thinker of critical sympathies, Williams's common sense does not wilt before the lure of the commodity. About the charge that consumerism has wholly bought off political radicalism, he replies: "It is wholly reasonable to want the means of life in such abundance as is possible" (p. 324). People who acquire refrigerators and radios are not necessarily becoming spoiled; they are gaining "objects of utility" (p. 323). Again, Williams is not a happy capitalist, a proponent of progress, or an anti-green celebrant of consumerism, but someone who treats modernity with a differentiated gaze.

His refusal of despair, nostalgia, and celebration – the usual emotional palette for media critics – is reflected in his criticism of both "old democrats," who have a touchingly virginal faith in the goodness and intelligence of the people, and "the new sceptics," who are so aware of the constraints and conditions of modern democracy that they abandon hope in it. Williams believes that both these attitudes – which strikingly resemble those of Dewey and Lippmann, respectively, or in more recent terms, communitarians and realists – leave the door open for con artists and cultural hucksters. In contrast to Berelson, Lazarsfeld, and McPhee's *Voting* (1954) and Lippmann's *The Phantom Public* (1925), Williams takes the deficiencies in public interest and information themselves to be political and historical, not natural, facts: interest and inertia derive from the organization of society (1990, p. 310); sullenness is a social product, not bovine inertia in human nature or the masses (p. 316). Yet, as much as the Columbia scholars, Williams despises cynicism: "there is a huge area of general suspicious disbelief, which, while on particular occasions it may be prophylactic, is as a general habit enfeebling" (p. 316). Williams warns us against the dangers of both realism (cynicism) and blind faith (folly) in democratic attitudes. The standoff between innocence and experience only leaves the political field open for exploitation by hard-headed opportunists.

The grounded sociological sense shared by Williams and the Columbia tradition also shows up in his account of audience interpretation of media texts. In *Culture and Society* he has not yet developed the more complex scheme of "Base and Superstructure in Marxist Cultural Theory" (1980a, originally published in 1973), a piece that not only sees interpretation of artifacts as a kind of productive labor, but also allows for a variety of interpretive strategies; but there are seeds of an interest in subculture: "Active reception, and living response, depend in their turn on an effective community of experience" (1990, p. 316). Williams's defense of working-class culture as an elaborated, rather than a restricted, code suggests the importance of communities of interpretation in decoding. Working-class culture, he argues, does not lack ideals – it has a different ideal: that of solidarity, instead of the middle-class ones of individualism or service. Working people do not lack creativity or intelligence – they express them in alternative ways.

Williams wants to pluralize modes of knowing so that literate and educated modes do not steal all the prizes. Gardening, carpentry, and organizing can also be modes of intelligent human activity. For Williams, as for Richard Hoggart in *The Uses of Literacy* (1957), the defense of working-class culture (indeed, the very notion of working-class *culture*) is shaped by his warm, extended family background; both are defending their aunts and uncles, not crusading for bloodless abstractions. The defense of subculture, the notion of collective interpretation, the defense of intelligence as something exercised in response or practice as much as in literate utterance, are all principles that resonate in work that followed in Williams's broad wake: that of Hall, Hebdige, Brunsdon, Morley, McRobbie, Ang, Fiske, and many others.

Indeed, as James Curran pointed out (1990), the celebration of active audiences in cultural studies was in many ways an unwitting re-creation of the central finding of the Columbia tradition. British cultural studies, like the Columbia school, has long prided itself on offering a more subtle take on popular capacities than the Frankfurt school. For the latter, at least in its worst moments, the culture industry was an apparatus that had its terminus in the head of every person. Horkheimer and Adorno could write sentences portraying the petit-bourgeois shmucks at the movies as incipient Fascists or infantilized sadists. By contrast, Williams manages a clear criticism of the concentrated power to communicate without also flirting with the suggestibility of the people. He thinks of his family and himself in the audience, not as others. Indeed, in one of his famous lines, reflecting Sartre's famous remark that "hell is other people," he says: "Masses are other people" (1990, p. 300). His point is to criticize the alienating abstraction of an observer's, rather than a participant's, role. The Columbia tradition, in turn, rarely concerns itself directly with culture industries as such; but it does offer a defense of the dignity of audiences, who, it claims, still talk and still read despite the coming of radio and television. Effects research reveals the intermediate steps between the media's messages and the audience's attitudes. Williams stands between these two options, offering a critical theory with a heart, a theory of the culture industry that is not also a theory of the consciousness industry.

The Columbia school rarely offered normative solutions. Prior to Habermas, the Frankfurt school thought explicit norms vain (and Habermas's life's work has been to correct this lack). But Williams has a positive program for reorganizing channels of communication. Needed is "a different attitude to transmission, one which will ensure that its origins are genuinely multiple, that all the sources have access to the common channels" (1990, p. 316). Here are all the key leftist principles of a transformed media system: diversity of channels, alternate sources, popular access. Like Mills (1956, p. 301), Williams laments the disjunction between distribution and contribution – that is, the gap between the ability to hear (possessed by many) and the ability to be heard (possessed by few). Williams of course has a critique of mass culture, but it is more thoroughgoing than that of many in the late 1950s, who predictably blasted away at degraded taste; his critique extends to the concept of the mass itself. Williams denies the Olympian view of the critic, showing the politics of ready-made categories of cultural critique, and allows more resources of hope than Adorno's vision of mass deception. Williams does not see the cultural industry as a totally closed system like vertically integrated Hollywood, but as a reformable set of arrangements. His analysis of media industries, however, is perhaps too dismissive of organizational culture or structural constraints – he seems to believe that new management and popular control would be sufficient (a replacement of the "cheapjacks"), a view he would later complicate in "Means of Communication as Means of Production" (1980b).

Williams's attack on low cultural quality is insistently ethical and political: that is, it is a defense of the intelligence of the receiver, and a critique of cultural machinery that is so frankly elitist and exclusive. His attacks on media are never solely aesthetic. He is not reluctant to condemn most of what is on offer, but the condemnation turns not only on poor quality, but on organizational exclusion and governance, a lack of popular access to the "training" (1990, p. 310) to interpret culture, a point reminiscent of Bourdieu's cultural capital. Indeed, Williams is both an ethical and a political critic, whereas most of his followers drop the ethical dimension. Stuart Hall, for instance, has a politics, but not an ethics. I do not mean the person, who is one of the splendid human beings of our times, but rather a developed program of intellectual analysis and a center of gravity. In this Williams learned a great deal from the authors he criticized, such as Burke, Coleridge, Mill, Arnold, Lawrence, Orwell, and of course, Leavis.

National complications

Nations, like canons, are modes of organizing disparate materials: the task of both is to establish relations between the living and the dead. And new relations with the dead enable new relations among the living. Much of my interest in Williams concerns the way in which he enriches and resolves debates that came to an apparent impasse in the United States in the late 1950s and have continued since. A widened canon provides resources for escaping from false dichotomies that come down from the past. In the USA it is striking to find a leftist thinker in the formative postwar era who takes a nuanced look at the social consequences of the mass media, while most intellectuals were lamenting the spurning of their leadership by the industries of popular culture (as Lazarsfeld and Merton (1948) also note). Just as the 1989 translation of Habermas's *Structural Transformation of the Public Sphere* gave a blast of fresh air to Anglophone media studies by showing that a critically minded scholar was already, in 1962, engaging in historical and empirical mass communication research at the highest level, so Williams's conclusion, if read as a partner in a transatlantic conversation on the meaning of mass communication, is astonishingly relevant for our debates today. Williams reads smartly if placed in dialogue with his fellow late-1950s worriers about modernity. His historical method resembles those of Arendt, Mills, and Habermas; his view that media audiences are insulated by social relationships from media influence and insulted by elitist intellectuals resembles that of Katz and Lazarsfeld; and his analysis of the economics, class basis, and concentration of media power resembles those of Mills and Adorno. Among the immortals, dialogues can be arranged that never took place in life. One point of canons is to orchestrate the concourse of the spirit world. *Culture and Society* should become a site for dialogue among Chicago, Columbia, Frankfurt, Toronto, and British cultural traditions.

Both nations and canons offer frames for interpretation, and I want to conclude by suggesting that Williams may be a richer text today abroad in the USA than at "home" in the UK. This may reflect a difference in the intellectual place of media in the USA and Britain, one of many curious differences in the intellectual life of the two countries, as Corner (1995, pp. 159–60) points out. In the late 1950s, most intellectuals abandoned the relatively new medium of television after the quiz show scandals, a desertion that might also reflect the transformation of television from a regional, New York City-based medium carrying "quality" dramatic programming for an elite audience to a national, Los Angeles-based system. FCC Commissioner Newton Minow gave television its sealing malediction in 1961 as a "vast wasteland," coolly deploying one of the great pessimistic tropes from modernist literature, T. S. Eliot's *The Waste Land*. The TV field was abandoned to a new breed of pop thinkers like Marshall McLuhan. In Britain, the story was different: many intellectuals maintained a constructive engagement with the medium as critics, consultants, and script-writers, Williams himself being a good example of all three; and the BBC retained a commitment, however paternalistically executed in practice, to the troubled category of "quality" programming. In England, the long-standing basis of mass-cultural criticism from Leavis to Hoggart was print culture, not television: in *Culture and Society*, as in *The Uses of Literacy*, television hardly rates a mention. In the USA, one way to sell lots of books is to blame television for some social ill and praise print as the cure; the television jeremiad is a well-recognized and well-remunerated genre. In contrast, pioneering studies touching on television written in the UK, such as the 1960s writings compiled by O'Connor in *Raymond Williams on Television* (1989) or Stuart Hall and Paddy Whannel's *The Popular Arts* (1964), are written discriminatingly, always seeing the possibility of genuine experience of art together with the dangers of stupefaction and exploitation.

If, in an American setting, *Culture and Society* gains contemporaneity as the rearranger of the entire historical legacy of media research by combining the best of what hitherto seemed embattled traditions, in Britain today the text has a certain obvious lack: its monocultural vision of the nation. In its status as official predecessor to British cultural studies, *Culture and Society* neglects gender, race, and sexuality, though there is class and nation and even a brief mention of imperialism. Subculture is implicit, though built on class lines rather than on other sorts of affiliation. Resistance, too, is implicit in the notion of experience as the first court of appeal when facing a media text. But there is no close engagement with media artifacts, though that shouldn't be surprising for a programmatic statement; certainly, as a television and theater critic, Williams did enough of that elsewhere (O'Connor, 1989). To some recent critics – for example, Paul Gilroy (1991, pp. 49–51), Williams's Achilles' heel is his vision of race and nation: calling himself a "Welsh European," Williams's vision of the political and intellectual dissident is a white male British working-class hero. By today's conventional wisdom, it is remarkable that *Culture and Society* claims to be a history of British thought in the nineteenth century while barely noticing the colonial and imperial context in which ideas of culture were applied, with the British Empire covering over one-fifth of the earth's surface in the same period. Problems of culture and society from 1780 to 1950 were not insularly British, but global in their elaborations and effects. To be fair, Williams later explicitly acknowledged these absences (1979, pp. 113ff), and regarded *Culture and Society* with the alienation that serious authors have for their previous work. At a time in which Britain is rethinking itself as a multicultural, multiracial nation, in which the empire strikes back in curry, language, fashion, people, and music, the island-based, white-guy character of *Culture and Society* is perhaps the part that requires the most interpretive generosity today. When past and present meet, they cast light on each other's potentials as well as each other's lacks.

Culture and Society, in sum, mediates the best of the critical and the empirical takes on media effects, offering a synthesis, before the fact, of British cultural studies, critical theory, and effects studies that can steer us around unhelpful false dichotomies, especially that of the critical and the empirical. Williams shows us how we might rethink the past, and hence the present and future, of work on media, culture, and society.

References

Arendt, H. (1958) *The Human Condition*. Chicago: University of Chicago Press.

Berelson, B., Lazarsfeld, P. F. and McPhee, W. (1954) *Voting*. Chicago: University of Chicago Press.

Corner, J. (1995) *Television Form and Public Address*. New York: Edward Arnold.

Curran, J. (1990) The New Revisionism in Mass Communication Research: A Reappraisal. *European Journal of Communication*, 5 (2–3), 135–64.

Eagleton, T. (1976) *Criticism and Ideology*. London: New Left Books.

Gilroy, P. (1991) *There Ain't No Black in the Union Jack*. Chicago: University of Chicago Press. (Originally published in 1987.)

Gitlin, T. (1978) Media Sociology: The Dominant Paradigm. *Theory and Society*, 6 (2), 205–53.

Gitlin, T. (1995) *The Twilight of Common Dreams*. New York: Metropolitan.
Habermas, J. (1989) *Structural Transformation of the Public Sphere*. Cambridge, MA: MIT Press; Cambridge: Polity. (Originally published in 1962.)
Hall, S. and Whannel, P. (1964) *The Popular Arts*. New York: Pantheon.
Hoggart, R. (1992) *The Uses of Literacy*. New Brunswick, NJ: Transaction. (Originally published in 1957.)
Huxley, A. (1958) *Brave New World Revisited*. New York: Harper.
Katz, E. (1959) Mass Communications Research and the Study of Popular Culture. *Studies in Public Communication*, 2, 1–6.
Katz, E. and Lazarsfeld, P. F. (1955) *Personal Influence*. Glencoe, IL: Free Press.
Lazarsfeld, P. F. (1948) Communication Research and the Social Psychologist. In W. Dennis (ed.), *Current Trends in Social Psychology*, Pittsburgh: University of Pittsburgh Press, 218–73.
Lazarsfeld, P. F. and Merton, R. K. (1948) Mass Communication, Popular Taste, and Organized Social Action. In L. Bryson (ed.), *The Communication of Ideas*, New York: Cooper Square, 95–118.
Lippmann, W. (1925) *The Phantom Public*. New York: Macmillan.
Mills, C. W. (1956) *The Power Elite*. New York: Oxford University Press.
Mills, C. W. (1959) *The Sociological Imagination*. New York: Oxford University Press.
Morrison, D. E. (1978) *Kultur* and Culture: The Case of Theodor Adorno and Paul F. Lazarsfeld. *Social Research*, 45, 331–55.
Mulhern, F. (2000) *Culture/Metaculture*. London: Routledge.
O'Connor, A. (1989) *Raymond Williams on Television*. New York: Routledge.
Simonson, P. D. (1996) Dreams of Democratic Togetherness: Communication Hope from Cooley to Katz. *Critical Studies in Mass Communication*, 13, 324–42.
Thompson, E. P. (1963) *The Making of the English Working Class*. New York: Pantheon.
Williams, R. (1961) *The Long Revolution*. New York: Columbia University Press.
Williams, R. (1974) *Television: Technology and Cultural Form*. New York: Schocken.
Williams, R. (1979) *Politics and Letters: Interviews with New Left Review*. London: New Left Books.
Williams, R. (1980a) Base and Superstructure in Marxist Cultural Theory. In *Problems of Materialism and Culture*, London: Verso, 31–49. (Originally published in 1973.)
Williams, R. (1980b) Means of Communication as Means of Production. In *Problems of Materialism and Culture*, London: Verso, 50–63.
Williams, R. (1985) *Keywords: A Vocabulary of Culture and Society*. New York: Oxford University Press.
Williams, R. (1990) *Culture and Society*. London: Chatto & Windus. (Originally published in 1958.)
Williams, R. (1993) *The Country and the City*. London: Hogarth Press. (Originally published in 1973.)

12

Canonization Achieved? Stuart Hall's "Encoding/Decoding"

Michael Gurevitch and Paddy Scannell

The centrality of Stuart Hall's "Encoding/Decoding" essay in the cultural studies literature has long been recognized. This paper does not purport to offer yet another analysis of the "encoding/decoding" model, a vein that has been mined extensively and has produced a rich literature. Rather, it considers briefly the issue of the canonization of scholarly texts, provides a "biography" of Hall's essay, and concludes with some thoughts on the assumed canonic status of that essay.

A number of questions emerge when we consider the canonic status of any text in the mass communication literature. The first has to do with identifying the boundaries of the field. Defining the field of mass communication scholarship narrowly – that is, as a self-contained and bounded field – the pool of works from which "canonic" texts are to be selected will necessarily be fairly limited, and the works chosen will have to be assessed as meriting such status within that small pool – as the bigger fish in a fairly small pond. If, however, we locate mass communication research within the broader context of the social sciences, or as a sub-area within the more general study of the sociology of knowledge and culture, then the formerly big fish may be dwarfed by even bigger fish. Canonic status is thus clearly relative.

A second question has to do with whether canonic status inheres in the text itself – in its power, its revelatory insights – or whether it depends in larger measure on the work it spawns. In other words, is canonization achieved? Or is it bestowed by virtue of its progeny, its impact on future work? If the latter, then perhaps it is more appropriate to describe an influential work as *seminal*, rather than canonic. Thus, the impact of a given work is revealed in the works that follow it, are inspired by it, or carry its ideas further. A search for the DNA of scholarly works could reveal their parenthood, their longevity, their short- and long-term impact.

More generally, however, canonization depends on death, for sainthood can be authenticated only when life has ended. Perhaps it is the same with texts: their canonization is at once their sanctification and their mortification. The canonized text no longer lives within a set of concerns and commitments. It is no longer something to be thought with or about, engaged with and argued over, confronted or challenged. It becomes something to be ritually invoked, like the auxiliary saints summoned from the dead to give aid to the living. Such a fate, we argue, has befallen the text known today as the "encoding/decoding model," the ur-text of media studies as it developed within the larger project of cultural studies at the Centre for Contemporary Cultural Studies (CCCS) under Stuart Hall's direction at the University of Birmingham in the 1970s.

Biography of an essay

"Encoding/Decoding" was published in *Culture, Media, Language* in 1980. It appeared in the third subsection of the book, called "Media Studies." A footnote at the start of the article tells us that, as published, it is an edited extract from a longer piece called "Encoding and Decoding in the Television Discourse," CCCS Stencilled Paper no. 7, produced at the center in 1973. The paper was originally presented by Stuart Hall to a colloquium at the Centre for Mass Communication Research at the University of Leicester in 1973; for the benefit of CCCS students, some notes on its reception at the colloquium and points for further consideration were subsequently added at the end. The paper received another airing a year later, when it was presented as "Encoding and Decoding" in a symposium on Broadcasters and the Audience held in Venice as part of the Prix Italia. Throughout the 1970s CCCS produced and published, along with its stencilled papers, a series called *Working Papers in Cultural Studies* (*WPCS*). At the end of the decade Hutchinson contracted to publish the material hitherto produced and disseminated by the center, along with unpublished work in progress and future projects. *Culture, Media, Language* is subtitled *Working Papers in Cultural Studies, 1972–1979*. Thus the appearance of "Encoding/Decoding" in a published book marks both an end and a beginning – the end of a samizdat culture of dissemination and circulation, and the entry into mainstream academic literature.

At first sight, the published version of "Encoding/Decoding" (hereafter E/D) is a slight piece. It is only ten pages long, and is not overburdened with scholarly footnotes and references. It has a provisional, unfinished air about it. It is a "work in progress" that might be further reworked. Its title proposes a topic that needs no further elaboration than two words separated by a slash. It has by now contracted to an internal shorthand reference that all concerned (the members of CCCS) understand. At the same time it indicates an external reference point, *S/Z* (Barthes, 1975), which elaborated a model for analyzing the various codes that constitute the (literary) text. In itself E/D makes no claims whatever to canonical status. It is a text without aspirations to an afterlife.

Thus, the significance of E/D might be understood as running counter to the Derridean proposition that "Il n'y a pas de hors texte." The importance of this particular text lies not just in its immanent properties, but also in what lies outside it: the issues, concerns, and commitments that called it into existence and that prompted its changes of direction and revisions. These concerns were not static, but evolved over the eight or so years that preceded its emergence in published form. To clarify those concerns is not to furnish a historical backdrop to the text (its "context"). It is to begin to account for the textual features of the published article itself in its provisional and unfinished character. If the text-as-published does not seem to propose itself as something that was conceived in the first place as written-to-be-published, we might reasonably seek its *raison d'être* as residing elsewhere. To illuminate the text in this way, then, is to recover the concerns to which it was a crucial contribution. That means invoking the working life of the center in the 1970s and its samizdat culture of writing as work-in-progress, working papers that contribute to the unfolding project of cultural studies, the study of contemporary culture.

Even "insiders" – those who were part of CCCS's work in the 1970s – may find it hard now to recover the excitement that permeated the center at that time; how eagerly, for instance, one awaited the next issue of *WPCS*. When "On Ideology" (*WPCS* 10) appeared in 1977, it was as if in answer to prayer: now at last the rest of us might catch up and find out what on earth it really meant. We knew we were getting it direct from the source, from where the action was. Today, media, communication, and cultural studies are all recognized as cognate areas in higher education, and undergraduate, graduate, and postgraduate programs in them are ten a penny. They are furnished with their appropriate fields of inquiry, established bodies of research, and theoretical literatures. But 30 years ago none of this existed. To a very considerable extent, a new academic field emerged from the work of the CCCS in the 1970s. It was not clear at the time that that was what, in fact, was happening. Rather, in a brief, ten-year span, something extraordinary crystallized at CCCS, inspired by the charismatic brilliance of Stuart Hall, who enthused and energized a generation of students. They would become his disciples, going forth to spread the word and establish the academic credentials of something that was yet to be recognized as "cultural studies."

The period between the first presentation of E/D (1973) and its publication (1980) was one of astonishing productivity for Hall himself. The aptly named "working bibliography" of his writings at the end of a book produced in his honor by David Morley and Kuan-Hsing Chen (1996) reveals a continuing flow, in these years, of written contributions to an extraordinarily wide range of issues (pp. 504–14). For all the tensions generated by the center – and doubtless, in part, because of them – the 1970s was the high point of Hall's work in terms of teaching and writing, and the encoding/decoding model was at the center of both. Colin Sparks (1996) describes it as "one of Hall's major intellectual achievements during [this] period" (p. 86).

By the time *Culture, Media, Language* was published in 1980, Hall had left Birmingham to take up a chair in sociology at the Open University. He had been at CCCS since 1964, and its director since 1968. After fifteen years, he was exhausted:

> I felt I'd been through the internal crises of each cultural studies year once too often. . . . Then the question of feminism was very difficult to take . . . if I'd been opposed to feminism, that would have been a different thing, but I was for it. So, being targeted as "the enemy", as the senior patriarchal figure, placed me in an impossible position. . . . In the early days of the Centre we were like the Alternative University. There was little separation between staff and students. What I saw emerging was that separation between generations, between statuses – students and teachers – and I didn't want that. . . . So I wanted to leave, because of all these reasons. (Morley and Chen, 1996, p. 500)

Now none of this – the life of the center in the 1970s, its "lived reality" – is necessarily relevant to its written output. There is no necessary correspondence between life and works, in the case of either individuals or institutions. However, the rows, the banging doors, the angry silences, the bruised egos were provoked not, as in soap operas, by the grittiness of interpersonal life and family relations, but by passionate commitments to particular political and theoretical positions (Brunsdon, 1996). To hear in the texts produced and published by the center the echoes of "the noise of theory," of things hotly and loudly contested, is to begin to see how they once mattered and what they meant at a time which, though only 20 or 30 years ago, now seems infinitely remote. But why should that matter now? It matters not at all if texts are proposed as autonomous objects of inquiry, uncoupled from their historical conditions of production, palimpsests upon which later readers inscribe their own concerns. That, however, is not the position that E/D argues for.

A model in opposition

"Encoding/Decoding" can be seen as a response to what was regarded as the dominant paradigm in media scholarship at the time, associated primarily with the American tradition of media effects research. The mainstream of American work until the late 1960s still carried the hallmarks of a positivist, quantitative, empirically oriented study of mass media roles in society and their effects on audiences. Interestingly, however, Hall's critique is aimed not at American scholars, but rather at a target closer at hand, British media scholarship, which he viewed as belonging in that positivist, empirical tradition. When asked about the origins of the essay in an interview conducted in the early 1990s, Hall said:

> The piece has a number of different contexts. . . . The first, in a sense, is a kind of methodological/theoretical context, because the paper was delivered to a colloquium, which was organised by the Centre for Mass Communication Research at the University of Leicester. Now the Centre for Mass Communication Research was a traditional centre, using traditional empirical positivistic models of content analysis, audience-effects survey research, etc. So the paper . . . has a slightly polemical thrust. It's positioned against some of those positions and it's positioned, therefore, against a particular notion of content as a performed and fixed meaning or message. (Cruz and Lewis, 1994, p. 253)

And, a little later: "The encoding/decoding model was not a grand model. I had in my sights the Centre for Mass Communication Research – that was who I was trying to blow out of the water" (p. 255).

Some time later Hall was invited to participate in a Council of Europe colloquy on "Training in the Critical Reading of Television Language" organized by James Halloran, then director of the Centre for Mass Communication Research in Leicester. Hall acknowledges Halloran's contribution to the proceedings as properly raising the question of studying "the whole mass communication process," from the structure of the production message at one end to audience perception and use at the other. However, the key difference between Hall and Halloran (and, more generally, between Birmingham and Leicester) is that the former came out of literary studies (initially concerned with texts, language, and meaning), whereas the latter came out of sociology, more particularly American mass communication sociology. Furthermore, the concerns of Hall and of the CCCS were beginning to be situated within a specifically Marxist framework, whereas Leicester had no such clear theoretical/ political agenda.

The key point of difference, for Hall, is that the communication process, through all its various stages, is not neutral. Mass communication sociology regards communicative failures as kinks in the system, "technical faults in transmission" (1973, p. 19). Through the interventions of professionals in sociology and education, cultural policies might be directed towards "helping the audiences to receive the television communication better, more effectively" (p. 1). As Hall saw it, such a position does not begin to address – does not even see – what the problem really is: namely, that "in societies like ours, communication between the production elites in broadcasting and their audiences is necessarily a form of 'systematically distorted communication'" (p. 19). The presumed neutrality of both the communicative process and the interventions of academics contributes to that systemic distortion and is, albeit unconsciously, a political choice, even if not seen as such:

> To "misread" a political choice as a technical one represents a type of unconscious collusion to which social science researchers are all too prone. Though the sources of such mystification are both social and structural, the actual process is greatly facilitated by the operation of discrepant codes. It would not be the first time that scientific researchers had "unconsciously" played a part in the reproduction of hegemony, not only by openly submitting to it, but by simply operating the "professional bracket". (p. 19)

These are the concluding sentences to Hall's 1973 paper, which clearly fire a broadside at a rival research center in the same field. They were excised in the 1980 published version, however, for the focus of attention had changed by then.

A text in transition

Let us consider, then, which parts of the earlier draft disappeared in the later, revised version that got into print. The focal topic of the Leicester colloquium – television as discourse – in part determined the paper's address, while its location in part determined the "take" on the topic: what the paper was setting itself against, as much as what it was for. What it was arguing for was a semiotic decoding of elements of popular culture, which are variously treated as texts, messages, and practices of signification. To decode the text is not simply to produce a "reading" of the message, as if it were in any way transparent. Rather, it invokes a "hermeneutics of suspicion" that regards the forms of popular culture (cinema and television in particular) as "systematically distorted forms of communication."

This phrase, introduced in quotes in the first paragraph of the paper but not attributed until much later (Hall, 1973, p. 16, n. 23), is from an essay of that title by Jürgen Habermas (1970), which treats Freudian psychoanalysis as a "scientific" resource for unraveling the systematic distortions of the unconscious as manifested in the discourses of patients in the therapeutic situation. If the texts of popular culture are like dreams "that express in 'disguised' form the repressed content of a culture" (Hall, 1973, p. 11), then the critical analytical task is akin to Freudian decodings of the "condensation and displacement [that take place] in the encoding of latent materials and meanings through manifest symbolizations" (p. 10). If "depth analysis" gets through to the latent meanings concealed by the "phenomenal forms" of popular culture, then decoding is the means of cracking open what is hidden (disguised) in their codes. The emerging field of semiotics, most closely associated in the essay with the work of Umberto Eco and Roland Barthes, is used to move between the surface structures of popular texts and their deep, mythic structures. These ideas are developed in a lengthy discussion of the western as a genre in cinema and, later, television (pp. 5–11), no traces of which remain in the published version of the paper.

David Morley and Charlotte Brunsdon (1999), in their engaging account of the working life of the center in those years, note that "[t]here were many boxes of something labelled 'The Western' in Birmingham in the 1970s, the uncompleted labour of yet another CCCS project" (p. 3). This was doubtless the trace of a much earlier engagement with cinema on Hall's part. In 1961 he began teaching media, film, and popular culture at Chelsea College, University of London. Through the education department of the British Film Institute, he worked on film and television with Paddy Whannel between 1962 and 1964, which resulted in their joint publication, *The Popular Arts* (1967). But the concern with cinema (a key popular art) and television fiction genres, which was the substantive heart of E/D in 1973, had vanished seven years later.

E/D is thus a text in transition. Present in the first version, but on its way out, is the residual trace of a complex of concerns with the textual analysis of the forms of popular culture. There, but not yet central to the model, is the break into a complex Marxism that would become the defining characteristic of Hall's work through the 1970s. For this, the concept of ideology would be central. Althusser's essay on "Ideological State Apparatuses" and Gramsci's more historical concept of hegemony drawn from *The Prison Notebooks* both take a bow towards the end of the paper. Each had become available in English only a year or so earlier. But neither had yet been fully assimilated into a reworked Marxist analysis of culture, which would become Hall's most significant contribution to a field of study that he, more than any other individual, helped to establish.

The 1980 text

The main difference between the stencilled paper and the text as published is the excision of the semiotics of the western, which reduces the overall length by a third. The paper has, moreover, been topped and tailed. Gone are the references to the topic of the colloquium to which it contributed, and the overt polemics against the sociology of mass communication and behaviorist psychology have been much toned down. Whereas the earlier paper read like a contribution to the deconstruction of texts via semiotics, the published version reads like a contribution to the interpretation of texts by audiences within a Marxist/class-based problematic, with the "dominant ideology" as the master concept underpinning the piece. The emphasis in the model and its theoretical base has shifted.

For those reared in the American tradition of mass communication research, an initial reading of the essay may first trigger a sense of *déjà vu*. The terms "encoding" and "decoding" have been familiar since Claude Shannon's 1949 essay, "The Mathematical Theory of Communication," in which Shannon, an electrical engineer, sought to enhance the integrity of the communication process by protecting messages from being garbled and distorted by "noise." His model of communication and information processing consisted of

source → encoder → message → decoder → destination

This outline was picked up by Wilbur Schramm (1964), who elaborated the model of the communication process between two people as

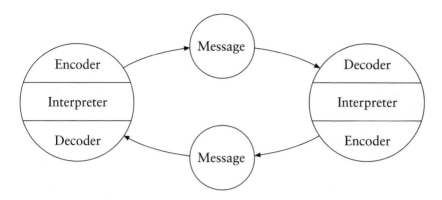

Source: © Mary Schramm Coberly, Boulder, Colorado.

Schramm thus introduced notions of feedback into the model, and then further contextualized it within the general framework of social relationship and a socio-cultural environment.

Hall's use of the terminology of encoding and decoding looks superficially like a throwback to the Shannon and Schramm models. But that impression is misleading. Hall begins his essay by referring to the "traditional" model of sender–message–receiver. He then criticizes the linearity of this model with its focus on message exchanges, and offers an alternative based on Marx's model of commodity production, comprising the stages of production, circulation, distribution/consumption, and reproduction. Thus, Hall incorporates the notion of production, essential to an analysis of the mass media as content-producing entities, into the encoding/decoding framework.

Hall then highlights the institutional structures of the production of media messages, in terms analogous to Marx's "labour process," and uses the encoding/decoding labels to identify what he calls "meaning structure 1," referring to the encoding side of the equation, and "meaning structure 2," referring to the decoding side. The two meaning structures are not necessarily symmetrical. In fact, Hall assumes that they rarely, if ever, overlap. Unlike Shannon, however, Hall is not concerned about this absence of symmetry. On the contrary, he views it as essential to the argument that the decoding process may be independent of the encoded meaning, with a life and power of its own. Thus, while his theoretical framework draws on the basic principles of structuralism and semiology, it also challenges the semiological claim about the power of the encoded text and the notion that meanings are firmly embedded in the text. The receivers of messages are not obliged, on this view, to accept or decode messages as encoded, and can resist the ideological power and influence of the text by invoking divergent or oppositional readings.

The model can therefore be applied in at least two ways, depending on whether the emphasis is placed on the moment of encoding or that of decoding. More exactly, what is obscured in titling the piece "Encoding/ Decoding" is the crucial question of what is encoded in the first moment and decoded in the second: namely, "the television discourse." To flesh it out more fully: the first moment is "encoding → program (text)-as-discourse," and the second moment is "program (text)-as-discourse → decoding." While the stencilled paper focuses more on the moment of encoding, the published version moved towards the moment of decoding.

This leads to another significant contribution of the essay: namely, the introduction of the notion of different modes of decoding. This discussion is adapted from a typology of value systems proposed by Parkin in *Class Inequality and Political Order* (1971). Parkin proposes a threefold typology: a dominant value system, which results in deferential or aspirational orientation among people in a class system; a subordinate value system, leading to accommodative response; and a radical value system, which promotes oppositional interpretation of class inequalities. Hall's typology is, by and large, similar. He labels the first the "dominant-hegemonic position," in which the message is decoded "in terms of the reference code in which it has been encoded." Located within this position is the professional code, "which the professional broadcasters assume when encoding a message which has already been signified in a hegemonic manner." The second he labels the "negotiated code," which "contains a mixture of adaptive and oppositional elements." Finally, the "oppositional code" refers to decoding in a "globally contrary way" (Hall, 1980, pp. 136–8).

Despite the similarities between Parkin's and Hall's typologies, however, there is a basic and significant difference between them. Whereas Parkin's typology of value systems is essentially a *sociological* one, relating different value systems to class differences, Hall's typology is *semiological*, deploying the typology to identify different modes of decoding and meaning making. This shift from the sociological to the semiological provided the theoretical grounding for the first major study informed by the encoding/decoding model: namely, Morley's *The Nationwide Audience*.

The Nationwide Audience: an empirical application

Hall's 1973 text had a largely internal reference point, having been produced for the students at CCCS, and the Media Studies Group in particular, as a kind of diagnostic model and tool kit for their work in progress. This largely accounts for the provisional feel of the text and its "incompleteness." What completes the piece, what validates it (or not), is its application in concrete instances. This is a text whose autonomy is indeed relative – relative, that is, to the work it inspired and supported. In his note on responses to the paper as presented at Leicester, written as an addendum "for Centre Members Only" (note the strong sense of an exclusive in-group), Hall (1973) remarked, "The paper was quite well received, many of the questions being directed to discover whether the centre had begun to make the schema outlined at the end of the paper [i.e. the different ways in which the television message might be decoded] 'empirical and operational'!" (p. 21). Hall's exclamation mark signals that center members already knew the answer to that question. The whole point of the schema was precisely to make it operational – that is, to apply it to television programs and to test empirically whether "real" viewers decode the programs in the ways predicted by the model.

The work of two students in the group, Charlotte Brunsdon and David Morley, was developed precisely to test aspects of the model: namely, the codes of television as inscribed in a particular program, *Nationwide*, and in a separate exercise, how actual viewers made sense of the program's encoded "ideological problematic" as they had analyzed it. Did viewers "buy" its message unproblematically? Did they adopt a more nuanced ("negotiated") interpretation of it? Or did they refuse to buy the program's (ideological) world view and possibly come up with an oppositional decoding that "saw through" and unmasked the program's ideological discourse (a highly specific framing of the meaning of "nationhood")?

Morley and Brunsdon hoped to run a full check on the model – the moment of encoding, the program as encoded, and the program as decoded by selected viewers – but succeeded in dealing only with the last two. They wanted to study the production process, the internal operational practices, the professional culture of broadcasting, and the "moment of encoding" that yielded the program-as-broadcast (David Morley, personal communication). But that was virtually impossible, for, with a few exceptions, access to the BBC was very hard to come by for academics in the 1970s. The model had proposed a tripartite structure whose three "moments" were integrally connected, so that the "proof" of the schema lay in examining all three aspects of it. But it was the model's subsequent fate to be read with such an emphasis on the moment of decoding that the other two moments were gradually effaced.

Through the 1980s and into the 1990s, E/D was ritually invoked as the ur-text of a reincarnated audience studies, kick-started by Morley's work on *Nationwide*. What was lost was the full heuristic value of the model for research into the culture of television. To recover something of the ways in which it was put to use at the center, we must flesh out the key theoretical problems it attempted to resolve within the given Marxist take on culture (itself a contentious issue), and to note something of the trajectory of the Media Studies Group across the decade. To address the latter point first is to elaborate further the attempts at the time to implement the model at both the encoding and the decoding ends of the process in relation to the professional culture and practice of broadcasting.

Largely overlooked now, but very important at the time, was the Media Group's detailed study of one *Panorama* program (Hall et al., 1976), the third and final of three programs broadcast during the run-up to the election. It was transmitted on Monday, October 7, 1974, three days prior to polling day, and was called "What Kind of Unity?" – a title that questioned the theme of national unity against a background of resurgent nationalisms in Wales, Scotland, and Northern Ireland and pressures for political devolution. The paper is a careful analysis of the operations of ideology, understood as the struggle over meanings within an accepted, unquestioned consensus (the legitimacy of parliamentary politics). It is a brilliant exploration of the ways in which preferred meanings are inflected through television discourse, which, in this program, was controlled partly by the BBC and partly by representatives of the political parties. What is programmatically sketched in E/D is thus put to work here in a detailed case study of the moment of encoding: "In relation to the messages available through Television we shall suggest that they never deliver one meaning: they are, rather, the site of a plurality of meanings, in which one is preferred and offered to viewers, over the others, as the most appropriate" (Hall et al., 1976, p. 53).

> The broadcasters' encoding practices . . . aim at establishing a transparency between the presentation of the topic, as embodied in the program, and the view which the audiences "take" of it. The broadcaster tries, by all the technical and communicative competences at his command, to bring the encoding and decoding moments into alignment: it is an attempt to realise a certain kind of ideological closure, and thereby to establish a preferred reading of the topic. . . . However, it is in the nature of all linguistic systems which employ codes, that more than one reading can potentially be produced. . . . It follows, in our view, that different audiences . . . can make more than one reading of what has been encoded. (Hall et al., 1976, p. 67)

The article is much longer and more closely argued than E/D, as published. Reading both pieces together makes clear the essentially programmatic and diagnostic function of E/D itself, whose subsequent fate was largely to serve as a mandate for the study of how audiences decoded the messages of television. What did not carry forward was the commitment to a careful, detailed analysis of the discourses of television, as exemplified in the *Panorama* and *Nationwide* studies. The focus on the moment of decoding at the expense of the moment of encoding uncoupled whatever audiences made of television programs from the study of the ideological labor that went into their making. Thus, the two halves of an integral model were torn asunder. The unity of E/D itself, at the moment of its publication in 1980, was not retained, since the "moment" of CCCS itself had already passed into history.

The beginnings of canonization

It could be argued that by shifting the attention of critical researchers toward the audience, *The Nationwide Audience* unintentionally launched the process of E/D's canonization. In a historical narrative describing the contexts in which the work of CCCS's Media Group took place, Morley identifies the study's two different histories, one external and the other internal. The external context was the political and economic convulsions in Britain in the early 1970s: notably the miners' strike and the eventual ascendance of Margaret Thatcher to 10 Downing Street. The internal one had to do with the

> imported mixture of "continental Marxism" (Althusser, Benjamin and Gramsci) and semiology (Barthes, Eco and Gauthier) which provided what seemed like powerful new theoretical tools with which to address both the general question of the role of ideology in the maintenance and reproduction of the social order and, more particularly, the role of the media in the dissemination of ideology. (Morley and Brunsdon, 1999, p. 5)

Within that broader framework, a more specific trajectory emerged, albeit in a minor key, that focused on the need to develop a better model of the media audience than was offered at the time by either the media effects or uses and gratifications approach. Morley refers here to the "hypodermic needle" approach, on the one hand – an early (and quickly discredited) paradigm of media effects – and the "liberal models of the sovereignty of the media consumer and their relative imperviousness to media influence," on the other (p. 6). The latter seems to lump together two profoundly different approaches: the "limited effects" school of thought and the uses and gratifications tradition, which holds a wholly different view of audiences as media consumers. While one might object to the easy dismissal of such different approaches to the study of media effects, it is nevertheless correct that absent from these approaches was any theorized discussion of the notion of meanings in media contents, and of audience members making sense of media messages – that is, their role as decoders. E/D provided a model in which the role of audiences as decoders was reinstated.

The publication of E/D not only facilitated a return to the audience in cultural studies, but also gave a new inflection to the role of media organizations as ideological agencies – that is, as encoders. Audiences had been assumed to be passive recipients of media messages, subject to the ideology carried therein. As Morley (Morley and Brunsdon, 1999) notes, "the 'common sense' of cultural studies as we have it today, with its taken-for-granted prioritisation of matters of consumption and its recognition of the importance of 'active audiences' simply did not exist at the time of *The Nationwide Audience* in 1980." E/D opened the door for the notion of audience resistance to media messages, inspired by Gramsci's notion of hegemony, as well as by the evidence of ordinary viewers' consumption of television. Clearly, if securing hegemony required ongoing ideological work, it was due to possible audience resistance. And if media consumption required audience activity in decoding media content, the possibility of resistance was built into the process.

How is canonization achieved?

E/D's contribution to media studies would alone have secured its position as a seminal text. It is useful, however, to consider as well the conditions under which *any* scholarly work achieves a position of influence. First is the importance of timing. Although clearly unanticipated at the time, it can be argued with hindsight that the significance of any single piece of scholarship depends on its appearance at the right, and ripe, time. E/D challenged the dominance of positivist social science at a time when this tradition was increasingly under attack. By the time it appeared, the barrenness of social-scientific approaches to the study of audiences had become quite apparent. Even the uses and gratifications approach, despite its interesting insights into audience behavior, could not respond adequately to attacks by critical scholars (see, e.g., Elliott, 1974). At the same time, the preoccupation of cultural studies with textual analysis showed a different, and no less damaging, form of myopia with regard to the audience. E/D offered a corrective to both.

Second, E/D offered new, radically different wine in what at first appeared to be old bottles. As suggested earlier, the terminology of encoding and decoding was introduced into the study of communication generally, and mass communication research specifically, almost from the moment of its birth. It was thus well entrenched. While E/D spoke a new language, it may not have struck non-Marxist media scholars as alarmingly revolutionary. Thus, the terminology may have suggested continuity, even as it subverted the older conceptual frameworks.

But the test of seminality inheres primarily in a text's capacity to open new doors and trigger new questions. The emergence of reception analysis as a new approach to audience study attests to E/D's influence. Within that framework, interest in audience decodings coincided with an awakening to the possible consequences of media globalization. The encoding/decoding framework facilitated new approaches to questions about how audiences in different societies and of different cultures made sense of imported texts crafted in a different cultural environment (see, e.g., Ang, 1985; Liebes and Katz, 1990). This, in turn, highlighted the significance of comparative audience studies. Growing interest in the globalization of television news could now be addressed not only to the institutional dimensions of the process, but also to different national audiences' decodings of television news stories.

A final (skeptical) note

No one is a prophet in his own town. Since the publication of "Encoding/Decoding," questions have been raised about various aspects of the model, not least from inside the critical/Marxist school. Political economists, especially, have been critical of the possibility of audiences negotiating media messages and even resisting their meanings. In a different vein, the notion that a preferred reading is built into the text may be attractive analytically, but is not easy to test empirically. Likewise, assumptions about the dominant mode of encoding raise questions about the intentionality of those who craft the message. More generally, in a polysemic world, any hard-and-fast classification of modes of encoding and decoding becomes slippery.

The doubts do not stop there. According to Sparks (1996), "Hall appears to have abandoned the attempt to develop [the encoding/decoding] model at the start of the 1980s." By then, he had turned his attention elsewhere. In a wide-ranging interview about E/D, Hall reflected on the model and its problems: "the encoding/decoding model wasn't a grand model . . . I didn't think of it as generating a model which would last for the next twenty-five years for research. I don't think it has the theoretical rigor, the internal logical and conceptual consistency for that." Later, on the problems of testing the model, he said:

> Morley's work is not quite the encoding/decoding model . . . it wasn't a model which was specifically designed to be the reference of a long period of empirical work. It's only once I have written it that I saw that if you were going to contest an old model of audience research and open a new one, then somebody's going to try and put it into effect. And then, with Dave Morley, we had the real problem: how the hell do you actually test it with some actual folks?

But never mind. As we argued at the opening of this essay, despite the problems, the difficulties, the doubts, and the self-doubts, the canonic status of a text often inheres not in the text itself, but in what it brings about. Some texts are born canonic, some achieve canonization, and some (at their peril?) have canonization thrust upon them.

References

Ang, I. (1985) *Watching* Dallas: *Soap Opera and the Melodramatic Imagination.* London: Methuen.

Barthes, R. (1975) *S/Z.* London: Jonathan Cape.

Brunsdon, C. (1996) A Thief in the Night: Stories of Feminism in the 1970s at CCCS. In D. Morley and K-H Chen (eds), *Stuart Hall: Critical Dialogues,* London: Routledge, 276–86.

Cruz, J. and Lewis, J. (1994) *Viewing, Reading, Listening: Audiences and Cultural Reception.* Boulder, CO: Westview Press.

Elliott, P. (1974) Uses and Gratifications Research: A Critique and a Sociological Alternative. In J. Blumler and E. Katz (eds), *The Uses of Mass Communication,* London: Sage, 249–68.

Habermas, J. (1970) Systematically Distorted Communication. In H. P. Dretzel (ed.), *Recent Sociology,* vol. 2, London: Collier-Macmillan, 57–74.

Hall, S. (1973) Encoding and Decoding in the Television Discourse. Stencilled Paper 7. University of Birmingham: CCCS.

Hall, S. (1977) On Ideology. Working Papers in Cultural Studies, Centre for Contemporary Cultural Studies, University of Birmingham. (Stencil.)

Hall, S. (1980) Encoding/Decoding. In *Culture, Media, Language: Working Papers in Cultural Studies, 1972–1979,* London: Hutchinson, 128–38.

Hall, S. and Whannel, P. (1967) *The Popular Arts.* Boston: Beacon Press.

Hall, S., Connell, I. and Curti, L. (1976) The "Unity" of Current Affairs Television. In *Working Papers in Cultural Studies,* vol. 9, Birmingham University: CCCS, 51–94.

Liebes, T. and Katz, E. (1990) *The Export of Meaning: Cross-cultural Readings of* Dallas. New York: Oxford University Press.

Morley, D. (1980) *The Nationwide Audience*. London: British Film Institute.

Morley, D. and Brunsdon, C. (1999) Introduction: The Nationwide Project: Long Ago and Far Away. . . . In *The Nationwide Television Studies*, London: Routledge, 1–17.

Morley, D. and Chen, K-H. (eds) (1996) *Stuart Hall: Critical Dialogues*. London: Routledge.

Parkin, F. (1971) *Class Inequality and Political Order*. New York: Praeger.

Schramm, W. (1964) *The Process and Effects of Mass Communication*. Urbana, IL: University of Illinois Press.

Shannon, C. (1949) *The Mathematical Theory of Communication*. Urbana, IL: University of Illinois Press.

Sparks, C. (1996) Stuart Hall, Cultural Studies and Marxism. In D. Morley and H-K. Chen (eds), *Stuart Hall: Critical Dialogues*, London: Routledge, 71–101.

13

Afterthoughts on Mulvey's "Visual Pleasure" in the Age of Cultural Studies

Yosefa Loshitzky

Laura Mulvey's classic essay, "Visual Pleasure and Narrative Cinema," published in 1975 in *Screen*,[1] was canonized as the foundational text of feminist film theory "inspired" by psychoanalysis. Taking Freud's conceptualization of sexuality and the unconscious as a point of departure from which to launch a feminist critique of the place women occupy in a phallocentric order, Mulvey asks how the unconscious of patriarchal society has been integrated into narrative cinema. According to her articulation of the structuring of the gaze in mainstream cinema, the power of the look is male, and the female is positioned as the object rather than the subject of fetishistic and voyeuristic desire, channeled through the male gaze.

In 1981, in reaction to criticism leveled at her breakthrough article by many feminist film theorists who claimed that her essay ignored and, even worse, "masculinized" the position of the female spectator, Mulvey published another article entitled "Afterthoughts on 'Visual Pleasure and Narrative Cinema' Inspired by King Vidor's *Duel in the Sun* (46)" (1981). In this article Mulvey reformulated some of the theoretical premises underpinning her original essay and elaborated a revised theory of female spectatorship based on her reading of Freud's (1979) lecture, "Femininity."[2] Her analysis included an attempt to answer the question of whether women spectators are positioned differently from men. Relying on Freud's description of women's early sexuality as a process of oscillation between boyish activity and "properly" passive femininity, Mulvey maintains that the female spectatorial position reproduces this libidinal experience, thus turning the female viewer into a temporary "masculinized" spectator. To illustrate her thesis, Mulvey provided an interpretation of King Vidor's western, *Duel in the Sun* (1946). Her reading of the film suggests that the sexuality of Pearl (the film's female protagonist) oscillates between a regressive phallic narcissism and a passive femininity, an oscillation that expresses the girl's passage from active, preadolescent masculinity to passive, mature femininity (presented by Freud as the normative path of female development). Mulvey further claims that this passage is reproduced through the woman spectator's experience which positions her as a "masculinized" viewer.

Mulvey's revisionism constituted part of a lively, and sometimes stormy, debate in the 1980s among feminist film theorists (e.g., Kuhn, 1982; Silverman, 1983; de Lauretis, 1985; Doane, 1987; Studlar, 1988; Penley, 1989) over issues pertaining to spectatorial positioning and pleasure and gender-based subject construction in and by the filmic text. Since the publication of Mulvey's first essay, film theory in general – and feminist film theory in particular – has become almost exclusively not only inspired, but dominated, by the Lacanian (1979) psychoanalytic paradigm, which remains one of the most influential bodies of work in film theory. This, despite the fact that, as Christine Gledhill points out, "The theoretical convergence of psychoanalysis and cinema has been problematic for feminism in that it has been theorized largely from the perspective of masculinity and its constructions" (1992, p. 193). Conceiving of women as both objects and spectators produced and generated by the cinematic apparatus has proved to be one of the most contentious and politically laden aspects of feminist film theory since the 1970s, because Mulvey's (1975) seminal essay, assisted by psychoanalysis, called for the "destruction of pleasure as a radical weapon" (p. 7). Subsequently, fantasy, understood both as a psychical process of the spectator and as film itself, became the focus of investigations of the representation of woman in cinema.

Muriel Dimen suggests that just as "psychoanalysis synthesizes and articulates in one convenient place the ruling ideas of patriarchy, thereby constituting both an attack on women and a means for feminism to deconstruct sexist ideology, so feminism exerts a pressure on psychoanalytic thought" (1998, p. 211). In film theory additional forces have begun to erode the privileged position of the psychoanalytic paradigm, creating ruptures in what, until the mid-1980s, looked like a united theoretical front. These forces include the emergence of the cognitive paradigm, as well as the more traditional formalist approach to film best represented by the film scholar David Bordwell (1985, 1989).

Another, more significant, challenge to the prevalence of psychoanalysis in film theory has been posed by the growing invasion of cultural studies into the field of cinema studies. This fast-growing discipline, with its emphasis on ideological analysis of structures of power and domination as manifested in a variety of social, political, and cultural practices and discourses, as well as its persistent focus on historical specificity, community-based negotiations of particular texts, local narratives, and political agency, has greatly eroded the explanatory power of the psychoanalytic paradigm in film theory and its claim to universal validity. New methodologies and sensibilities developed and articulated in cultural studies have provided a critical challenge to Mulvey's two canonic texts by showing, implicitly or explicitly, the limitations of the psychoanalytic paradigm and demonstrating how it fails to do justice to the complexity of its object of study due to its overemphasis on spectatorial subjectivity and insufficient attention to the location of the filmic text in time, place, history, and culture.

Despite this critique, it should be pointed out that some of the cultural studies-oriented research done in film studies, particularly as related to films made by directors who are heavily influenced by psychoanalysis such as Bernardo Bertolucci (Kolker, 1985; Kline, 1987; Loshitzky, 1995), or to the popular genre of science fiction (Sobchack, 1987; Kuhn, 1990; Penley et al., 1991; Bukatman, 1993) aims to put psychoanalysis and cultural studies in dialogue with each other.[3] Inspiring models for such a dialogue exist already in the tradition of the grand syntheses of Freud and Marx as elaborated by the Frankfurt school, Herbert Marcuse (1966), Louis Althusser (1969, 1971), and others. As Dimen suggests, feminist theory itself mediates social theory and psychoanalysis, thus completing a historical process and continuing a project, the "Marx–Freud synthesis, begun and then suspended in the 1920s and 1930s" (1998, p. 213). The feminist project, according to Dimen, uses psychoanalytic insights into interior life to understand, in order to alter, the internalization and persistence of some of the most oppressive social norms.

To a certain extent, we can claim that Mulvey's ground-breaking articles opened a new chapter in contemporary intellectual history, particularly in what feminists define as cultural politics. Mulvey's articles are responsible for creating a consensus about what feminist film theory should entail. Her theoretical premises pushed feminist film theory to address such topics as cinematic representations of women, the cinematic construction of femininity, the nature of spectatorship, and narcissistic fantasy and identification processes. It ignored, however, more culturally oriented topics such as consumption and value issues related to film genres about, and marketed to, women, and in particular, the plurality of the female spectator with regard to her various affiliation communities such as class, race, ethnicity, nationality, religion, and sexual orientation.

This lacuna is most noticeable in Mulvey's second seminal essay "Afterthoughts on 'Visual Pleasure.'" Nowhere in this essay, as Monica Hulsbus (1996) points out, does Mulvey acknowledge race. The fact that Pearl's future in the film is shaped by her family background, where race and gender are conflicting categories, is never addressed in Mulvey's essay. Pearl is portrayed as a "wildcat." She is a half-breed, or hybrid, and her father is the town judge who murdered his adulterous Native-American wife, Pearl's mother. Pearl's figure thus "becomes the site of contention where race and desire are conflated yet not allowed any dignity" (Hulsbus, 1996, p. 84). The narrative presents the conflation of sexuality and race as a classical double bind. Marriage and a place within the community are not available to Pearl "because of her sexuality – which is in turn a result of her racial impurity" (p. 84). In Hulsbus's view, Mulvey fails to produce a more accurate reading of the film because she does not contextualize it within the historical moment of the difficult reinsertion of the African-American soldier into domestic society after World War II. Mulvey's reading, according to Hulsbus, does not suggest an understanding of the relationship between race and sexuality as interrelated categories, and their function in the stabilization and homogenization of maleness and whiteness. The failure to elucidate these points, she argues, "could exacerbate the double bind both postwar women and African American soldiers were caught in due to governmental and institutional policies" (p. 85).[4]

The historiographical approach to *Duel in the Sun* provided by Hulsbus is the kind of reading advanced by cultural studies. It situates the film at the intersection of the popular discourses of the time, allowing us to better understand (and reconstruct) the conflation of ideology, class, race, and gender in the process of cultural production. Relying on psychoanalysis alone, Mulvey reads *Duel in the Sun* as an enactment of the drama of universal femininity, ignoring historical specificity related to issues of race and ethnicity as they play out in the film. A more accurate reading of the film, like the one suggested by Hulsbus, would conceptualize it as an allegory on racism, colonialism, cultural hybridity, miscegenation, and forbidden love.

As many feminist theorists argue, the problem is power. *Duel in the Sun* is the story of an attempt to cultivate the wild Pearl into a cultured Pearl, as well as a symbolic story on the failure of the "civilizing mission" of white male colonialism. It is a story of the power relationship between "native" and colonizer, master and slave, white male and hybrid woman. Feminist theorist Elizabeth Cowie (1997) argues that cinema as

a public space for playing with, and playing out, fantasies is an important political realm. After all, as Jose Brunner argues, what makes "a
theory of social relations political is not its reference to the public realm,
parties, or governments but rather its concern with the structures and
dynamics of power and authority . . . including those of the family" (1998,
p. 85). Freud's understanding of social relations within the family was
fundamentally political, according to Brunner, "since he conceived of
the family not only as a social institution that gives rise to emotional
ambivalence but also as an arena of power struggles" (p. 85). The social
construction of desire is also political, an aspect that, according to Dimen,
psychoanalysis resolutely denies, since it is "a threat to its own institutional power" (1998, p. 216).

The Frankfurt school, however, and Herbert Marcuse in particular,
placed the juncture between the erotic and the political dimensions at
the heart of their radical thinking. In *Eros and Civilization*, Marcuse
(1966) advanced the thesis that the liberation of instinctual needs is a
precondition for liberation from repressive affluence,[5] challenging Freud's
identification of civilization and progress with a necessary libidinal and
instinctual repression. To replace Freud's thesis (or rather, to extrapolate
the hypothesis of a non-repressive civilization from Freud's theory of
instincts), Marcuse proposed that erotic sublimation based upon an emancipation of the libido and re-eroticization of man's relations to man and
nature might become the basis of an entirely new non-repressive civilization based on the pleasure principle.

The union between psychoanalysis and politics was later adapted by
the French Marxist philosopher Louis Althusser (1969, 1971), whose
conception of ideology was influenced by Jacques Lacan's psychoanalytic theory of the "imaginary" and the "symbolic," which explains
the constitution of individual human beings as subjects. For Althusser,
"ideology in general" is "profoundly unconscious" (1969, p. 233). It acts
through images, representations, and structures, not via consciousness.
The work of ideology, he proposed, escapes men, because men "live"
their ideologies. Ideology "is a matter of the lived relation between men
and their world." This relation appears as "conscious" but is, in fact,
"imaginary" in the Lacanian sense. In a later, influential article, "Ideology and Ideological State Apparatus," Althusser elaborated and refined
his definition of ideology in general, and compared it to Freud's hypothesis about the unconscious: "I shall adopt Freud's expression word for
word, and write ideology is eternal, exactly like the unconscious. And I
add that I find this comparison theoretically justified by the fact that the
eternity of the unconscious is not unrelated to the ideology in general"
(1971, p. 161). After incorporating Lacan's theory into his own, Althusser

emerged with the definition, "Ideology is a 'Representation' of the Imaginary Relationship of Individuals to their Real Conditions of Existence" (p. 162).

Freud's oedipal paradigm provides, on the one hand, critical insights into social relations. On the other hand, it constitutes "a reductionist theoretical construct, which turns masculine development into the norm, is strongly phallocentric and authoritarian, and slides into mythical universalization" (Brunner, 1998, p. 92). This is especially true of Freud's lecture on "Femininity," which Mulvey used as the theoretical base for her second canonic essay. Yet, what some feminist critics view as psychoanalysis's weakness is viewed as its strength by other cultural critics, notably Peter Gay, the cultural historian, graduate of the Western New England Institute for Psychoanalysis, and author of *Freud: A Life for Our Time* (1989), an internationally acclaimed intellectual biography of Freud. Gay states, "It is precisely the ambitiousness of [Freud's] thought, a thought that by its very nature professes universal validity, that makes it relevant to the tough-minded questions historians ask and to the tough-minded answers they attempt to supply" (1998, p. 119).

Ann Kaplan, who, unlike Gay, comes from a post-modernist and anti-universalist position, reminds us that the discussion of the invention of cinema and Freudian psychoanalysis

> has assumed that the male and female spectators are white. . . . Sophisticated 1970s and 1980s feminist analyses mainly explored ways in which the figure of the "white" woman was dominated to accommodate specific unconscious (white) male desires, fears, and fantasies. Even now, little has been done in relation to psychoanalysis, cinema and race, although research on ethnic images in Hollywood has advanced. (1998, pp. 158–9)

Drawing our attention to this phenomenon, Kaplan warns feminist theorists of the dangers inherent in the uncritical adoption of psychoanalysis and its view of the white male as a universal model for all humanity.

Freud's descriptive explanation in "Femininity" of woman as a "dark continent" has stood the test of time in the rubrics of film theory's exploration of the symbolic space that females occupy in the representational practices of cinema. It is significant, therefore, that Freud himself, referring to his lack of direct knowledge about female sexuality, labeled it the "dark continent" of psychology, thereby "binding the term into infelicitous contemporary colonialism" (Hulsbus, 1996, p. 86).

In a failure of nerve, Freud's anatomical map "inscribes things female in a metaphor that buries in femininity the underproblematized racism of psychoanalysis" (Dimen, 1998, p. 207). This racism, according to Kaplan, is embedded in the discipline's institutional founding, which,

"like that of cinema itself, took place in the era of European imperialism." It would be too much, she argues, "to expect nineteenth-century
psychoanalysis to avoid some of the racialized discourses that prevailed
and were embedded in language, such as the 'savage/civilized' linguistic
duality that had become linked to a black/white dichotomy" (1998,
pp. 159–60). As Ann Pellegrini observes, "Psychoanalysis, after all, dates
to a historical period when the medical and natural sciences were deeply
concerned with and, to some degree, even determined by biological theories of 'race'" (1997, p. 110). Ironically, Freud himself, as a Jew, as well
as the new "Jewish" field he established, was subject to racist attacks. As
Sander Gilman observes, "Freud could not have expected his colleagues
or his culture to treat him invisibly – his very practice was built of the
cornerstone of the Jewish mind and body (his own), however much he
universalized his research on that body" (1991, p. 243). This is precisely
the reason why Pellegrini claims that "In the historical context of psychoanalysis, 'race' means 'Jewishness'" and "'Black' Africa was one
region to which the 'racial' difference of the Jew was frequently traced
back" (1997, pp. 110, 111). This more favorable view of psychoanalysis, which redeems it from charges of racism by showing that it was in
fact a theory *in flight from racism*, is also held by Julia Kristeva, who
argues that psychoanalysis can be experienced "as a journey to the strange-
ness of the other and of oneself, towards an ethics of respect for the
irreconcilable" (1991, p. 182).

Within the framework of feminist film theory, the point where race
and the unconscious meet has been little explored. For example, as Kaplan
(1998) points out, few have studied what unconscious fears and fantasies may have been calmed for white spectators through the circulation
of Hollywood images of ethnic "others" in lowly, ridiculed, or depraved
roles, as are the images of African-Americans, Native-Americans, His-
panic, and Chinese in the film *Duel in the Sun*. Nor has the psychoanalytic impact of such images on black or other ethnic spectators been
much researched. The question, then, is, how can psychoanalysis and
cultural studies meet in order to provide a more comprehensive explanation of the relationship between race and ethnicity with the unconscious?

The first task, when confronted with this question, is to challenge the
universalist claim of psychoanalysis, so that psychoanalysis will be more
adjustable and sensitive to different cultures. Indeed, as Kaplan argues,
"psychoanalysis is precisely the tool needed to understand racial as well
as gendered thought, whether conscious or unconscious" (1998, p. 160).
As an example of psychoanalysis's adaptability to different cultural contexts, she considers Frantz Fanon's (1967) ground-breaking work, which
includes "readings that evacuate race and gender as the 'cause' for illness

and personal neurosis and readings that account for black neurosis in social terms" (Kaplan, 1998, p. 161). In contrast to Fanon's conceptions, Kaplan argues, "Hollywood and popular culture generally have had a role in displacing the cause for mental disorder from the social order to the individual in the case of women and blacks. Many Hollywood movies [as is evident in *Duel in the Sun*] try to account for neurosis as simply an individual's defect not linked to larger social matters" (p. 161).

A film's meaning is produced in a context, and every film is historical and political in the way it situates the spectator in relation to its context of production and reception. Despite the fact that the nexus of psychoanalysis and feminism enriched the debate in film studies over the unconscious work of the spectator and the gendered structure of spectatorship, it neglected the ideological effects of spectatorship and considerations of class, ethnicity, nationality, and gender in the process of cultural production and reception. As many critics have observed (e.g. Stam et al., 1992), the psychoanalytic conception of the cinema spectator is a very particular kind of viewer, drastically different from the one conceptualized by cultural studies-influenced media studies. The audiences discussed by the latter consist of "real people" acting in the "real world." These people, who, in accordance with the researcher's ideological positioning, are clustered under rubrics of class, gender, ethnicity, cultural background, and the like, are perceived as active, even critical viewers, in control of the meanings they produce out of the screened texts. They are not atomized and isolated empty spaces to be randomly filled by anybody, but rather, historically, politically, and culturally constituted subjects existing in a specific public sphere. And the cinematic apparatus is not only a hypnotizing machine aimed at stimulating and fascinating the unconscious, helpless spectator (a conception favored by psychoanalytically oriented film theory), but also a money machine operated by big industries and global corporations.

It is interesting to note that the emergence and relative dominance of the psychoanalytic-feminist approach in film studies also accelerated the shift in cinema studies from the study of canonic films and *auteurs* to the study of a new set of canonic texts. During its early radical phase, feminist film theoreticians – Mulvey in particular – favored radical political avant-garde films, especially those by Jean-Luc Godard, that consciously struggled against Hollywood's ideology of spectacle by advocating a new politics of representation based on dialectical and epic principles, in the spirit of Bertolt Brecht. Paradoxically, although the valorization of radical avant-garde cinema was based on the negation of Hollywood cinema, pioneering feminist film theoreticians favored American classical films – melodramas and the so-called woman's film in particular – as objects of inquiry.[6] These were later redeemed from their traditional "lowly" status and elevated to that of privileged texts for representing female subjectivity in films. This paradigm shift affected the curriculum of cinema studies, which has since shown less interest in "national cinema" and the great *auteurs* associated with it.

Paradoxically, this transition from world cinema to American cinema coincided with broader processes of globalization which, according to many critics of post-modernity, are a euphemism for processes that have further perpetuated the hegemony of American products, including Hollywood films, in the world market. The decline of world cinema, particularly the European film industry (Hollywood's main rival), as a consequence of Hollywood's hegemony, was followed by the gradual disappearance of cinephile culture, the last bastion of world cinema buffs. This decline, in turn, coincided with the transition in cinema studies from the study of canonic films and filmmakers (both American and non-American), organized, in many cases, around the axis of state and nation, to a discipline occupied (if not obsessed) with theoretical concerns articulated by the psychoanalytic approach. With the invasion of cultural studies into film studies, the emphasis has latterly shifted towards issues pertaining to race, gender, class, ethnicity, nationality, and the like, and films as objects of inquiry have acquired the status of socio-cultural and historical documents from which one can learn about political life and social practices. This theoretical and methodological shift in film studies indicates that only a productive dialogue between the psychoanalytic paradigm and the cultural studies approach will ensure that the complexity of the objects of study will not be reduced by theoretical dogmatism. The entire social order has to be taken into account when analyzing a film, something that psychoanalytic theory alone cannot do.

Notes

1   Throughout the 1970s in Britain, the most important consistent attempts to discuss and analyze the relations between culture and meaning took place in the pages of *Screen*. The *Screen* of the 1970s was itself a product of the radical political movements of the late 1960s in Europe. Psychoanalysis, which dominated the theoretical position of *Screen*, became a battleground for political and institutional disagreements in the British cultural scene of the late 1970s. For an account of these struggles, see MacCabe (1985).
2   For a major feminist critique of this article's assumptions see Irigaray ([1974] 1985).

3   A major contemporary theoretician who has devoted himself to synthesizing Lacan's psychoanalytic thought with radical theory is Slavoj Žižek (1992, 1993, 2001), who has also published several influential books on cinema.

4   Elihu Katz notes that the media events literature offers several case studies of the way this double bind operated in the cases of O. J. Simpson and *Anita Hill versus Clarence Thomas*, where African-American women prioritized race over gender (private communication).

5   For Marcuse, liberation from repressive affluence meant the liberation of what he called "one-dimensional man" from a surplus repression imposed on him by the oppression of alienating late post-industrial capitalism. Marcuse's utopianism was based on a synthesis of Marx's economic terms (the notion of surplus value) with psychoanalytical terms, particularly those related to Freud's theory of sexual oppression. Marcuse's radical critique saw consumerism as one of the most oppressive and repressive forces operating in post-industrial, affluent societies. In a capitalist consumer society, Marcuse (1966) argued, "scientific management of instinctual needs has long since become a vital factor in the reproduction of the system: merchandise which has to be bought and used is made into objects of the libido" (p. xii).

6   1980s and 1990s feminist film theory tended to favor the science fiction and horror film genres, both associated with American popular culture and cult status. These genres have been approached critically as bearing, producing, and at times transgressing patriarchal ideology, and establishing (or criticizing) the myth of masculine mastery of nature. See, among others, Sobchack, 1987; Kuhn, 1990; Penley et al., 1991; Bukatman, 1993.

References

Althusser, L. (1969) *For Marx*, tr. B. Brewester. New York: Pantheon Books.

Althusser, L. (1971) *Lenin and Philosophy and Other Essays*. New York and London: Monthly Review Press.

Bordwell, D. (1985) *Narrative in the Fiction Film*. Madison: University of Wisconsin Press.

Bordwell, D. (1989) *Making Meaning: Inference and Rhetoric in the Interpretation of Cinema*. Cambridge, MA: Harvard University Press.

Brunner, J. (1998) Oedipus Politicus: Freud's Paradigm of Social Relations. In M. S. Roth (ed.), *Freud: Conflict and Culture*, New York: Alfred A. Knopf, 80–93.

Bukatman, S. (1993) *Terminal Identity: The Virtual Subject in Post-Modern Science Fiction*. Durham, NC, and London: Duke University Press.

Cowie, E. (1997) *Representing the Woman: Cinema and Psychoanalysis*. Minneapolis: University of Minneapolis Press.

de Lauretis, T. (1985) *Alice Doesn't: Feminism, Semiotics, Cinema*. Bloomington: Indiana University Press.

Dimen, M. (1998) Strange Hearts: On the Paradoxical Liaison between Psycho-analysis and Feminism. In M. S. Roth (ed.), *Freud: Conflict and Culture*, New York: Alfred A. Knopf, 207–20.

Doane, M. A. (1987) *The Desire to Desire*. Bloomington: Indiana University Press.

Fanon, F. (1967) *Black Skin, White Masks*. New York: Grove Press.

Freud, S. (1979) Femininity. In J. Strachey (ed. and tr.), *New Introductory Lectures on Psychoanalysis*, The Pelican Freud Library, vol. 2, London: Penguin Books, 145–69.

Gay, P. (1989) *Freud: A Life for Our Time*. New York: Anchor Books, Doubleday.

Gay, P. (1998) Psychoanalysis and the Historian. In M. S. Roth (ed.), *Freud: Conflict and Culture*, New York: Alfred A. Knopf, 117–26.

Gilman, S. (1991) *The Jew's Body*. New York and London: Routledge.

Gledhill, C. (1992) Pleasurable Negotiations. In F. Bonner et al. (eds), *Imagining Women: Cultural Representations and Women*, Cambridge: Polity, 193–209.

Hulsbus, M. (1996) The Double/Double Bind of Postwar Race and Gender in *Duel in the Sun*. *Spectator*, 17 (1), 81–7.

Irigaray, L. ([1974] 1985) The Blind Spot of an Old Dream of Symmetry. In *Speculum of the Other Woman*, tr. G. C. Gill, Ithaca, NY: Cornell University Press, 193–209.

Kaplan, E. A. (1998) Freud, Film and Culture. In M. S. Roth (ed.), *Freud: Conflict and Culture*, New York: Alfred A. Knopf, 152–64.

Kline, T. J. (1987) *Bertolucci's Dream Loom: A Psychoanalytic Study of Cinema*. Amherst: University of Massachusetts Press.

Kolker, R. P. (1985) *Bernardo Bertolucci*. New York: Oxford University Press.

Kristeva, J. (1991) *Strangers to Ourselves*. New York: Columbia University Press.

Kuhn, A. (1982) *Women's Pictures: Feminism and Cinema*. London: Routledge.

Kuhn, A. (ed.) (1990) *Alien Zone: Cultural Theory and Contemporary Science Fiction Cinema*. London: Verso.

Lacan, J. (1979) *The Four Fundamentals of Psycho-Analysis*. New York: W. W. Norton.

Loshitzky, Y. (1995) *The Radical Faces of Godard and Bertolucci*. Detroit: Wayne State University Press.

MacCabe, C. (1985) The *Screen* Dream: The Rise and Fall of Britain's Leading Theoretical Film Journal, as Told by a Co-Conspirator. *American Film*, 11 (1), 10–14.

Marcuse, H. (1966) *Eros and Civilization: A Philosophical Inquiry into Freud*. Boston: Beacon Press.

Mulvey, L. (1975) Visual Pleasure and Narrative Cinema. *Screen*, 16 (3), 6–18.

Mulvey, L. (1981) Afterthoughts on "Visual Pleasure and Narrative Cinema" Inspired by King Vidor's *Duel in the Sun* (46). *Framework*, 15–17, 12–15.

Pellegrini, A. (1997) Whiteface Performances: "Race," Gender, and Jewish Bodies. In J. Boyarin and D. Boyarin (eds), *Jews and Other Differences: The New Jewish Cultural Studies*, Minneapolis and London: University of Minnesota Press, 108–49.

Penley, C. (1989) *The Future of an Illusion: Film, Feminism and Psychoanalysis*. Minneapolis: University of Minnesota Press.

Penley, C. et al. (1991) *Close Encounters: Film, Feminism, and Science Fiction*. Minneapolis: University of Minnesota Press.

Silverman, K. (1983) *The Subject of Semiotics*. New York: Oxford University Press.

Sobchack, V. (1987) *Screening Space: The American Science Fiction Film*. New Brunswick, NJ: Rutgers University Press.

Stam, R., Burgoyne, R. and Flitterman-Lewis, S. (1992) *New Vocabularies in Film Semiotics: Structuralism, Post-Structuralism and Beyond*. London and New York: Routledge.

Studlar, G. (1988) *In the Realm of Pleasure*. Urbana: University of Illinois Press.

Žižek, S. (1992) *Everything You Always Wanted to Know about Lacan but were Afraid to Ask Hitchcock*. London: Verso.

Žižek, S. (1993) *Enjoy Your Symptoms! Jacques Lacan in Hollywood and Out*. New York: Routledge.

Žižek, S. (2001) *The Fright of Real Tears: Krzystof Kieslowski between Theory and Post-Theory*. London: British Film Institute.

Index